# STONES, FLOWERS, AND LESSONS LEARNED

ISBN: 9798998509100
Published by: Alegria Publishing
Book cover and layout by: @mckadamia

# STONES, FLOWERS, AND LESSONS LEARNED

Alejandra Acuña, PhD, LCSW

ALEGRÍA

PUBLISHING

## Dedication

To the top five on my rotation.
My securest attachment figure, my inner voice,
my everything: God.
My mom.
My daughter.
And my books and articles.

# Suicide Prevention Resources

## To Anyone Struggling,

Your life matters. Your presence matters. You matter. If you or someone you know is struggling with suicidal thoughts, please know there is help. When the world feels heavy, reach out—there is someone ready to listen.
If you want the pain to stop, there is hope.
Here are resources you can turn to for immediate support:

## International

- International Suicide Hotlines: Visit befrienders.org for a list of helplines worldwide.
- Canada: Call Talk Suicide Canada at 1-833-456-4566
- United Kingdom: Call Samaritans at 116 123 (free, 24/7)
- Mexico: Call SAPTEL at 800-472-7835 (24/7)

## United States

- National Suicide Prevention Lifeline: Dial 988 (24/7, free, and confidential) Website: 988lifeline.org
- Crisis Text Line: Text HOME to 741741 (24/7)
- Veterans Crisis Line: Dial 988, then press 1
- Trans Lifeline: Dial 877-565-8860 (peer support for transgender individuals)

## California

- California Peer-Run Warm Line:
  Dial 855-845-7415
- Emotional support for non-crisis situations
  Each Mind Matters: www.eachmindmatters.org
  (resources for mental health awareness)

## Los Angeles

- Los Angeles County Department of Mental
  Health (LACDMH): Dial 800-854-7771 (24/7)
  Access crisis counseling and mental health services.
- Didi Hirsch Suicide Prevention Center:
  Dial 1-800-273-8255 or visit www.didihirsch.org

# Foreword

Alejandra's story is a blessing. Reading it is a reminder of how important it is to share from the heart, even when it is hard. What captured me about the stories and lessons shared is that they come from a deep yearning to be who in essence we are. It's a woman's struggle, certainly, but it is everyone else's too.

I got to know Alejandra during her time on the Tia Chucha's Centro Cultural & Bookstore board. She was recommended by another board member who held her in very high esteem and was convinced that Alejandra could offer much to our organization. And she did. She could engage with complex or seemingly daunting matters, entertain the nuances, then cut straight to the chase with solutions. She did this with grace and confidence. No messing around, and finding the joy in it. Alejandra's book has given me a more complete picture of a woman I already appreciated.

Recently, I was at a ceremony with a *maestra* from Mexico skilled in the art of traditional Indigenous practices. As she created her altar, she reminded us that when you make an offering, you have to give it your all, your best – for that's what you will receive in return. Maybe not immediately, or even in the way you expect, but your offering will come back to you. This book, which is an offering too, shows that Alejandra has instinctively taken this approach with her life. She has opened her heart, revealing her trials and triumphs, and let us witness her process of making meaning and gathering clarity of purpose along the way. With her allies, books, and tools she has combed through her life's tangles, and faced them squarely, truthfully. Fear has not paralyzed her. She has not gotten stuck crossing thresholds. Not surprisingly, she tackled the hardest part of her life first– her beginning, her mother-wound–and alchemized it into her rebirthing.

What I've come to know is that other people's lessons, when shared, become our lessons if we pay attention. How beautiful that she has let us into her world of memories and let us see how she panned for the gold in them.

With her depth of curiosity and analysis, she points the way with a hefty cache of science, wisdom, and resources. Let the ones that resonate with you help you. She has shared generously so we could grow and flower too.

All of us have stories. Mine is still partially hidden. With her example, she is showing us the value of conscious vulnerability, transparency, and integration to help us see ourselves and reality more clearly and live our lives more fully. The fire in her has been tested many times. She has learned to stoke it with patience and creativity, trusting in an energy bigger than herself and tapping into that same energy inside of her.

There is a calling that I have posted at my desk, one that speaks to me about the importance of growing through the challenges we face: "*Guerreros y guerreras, quiero ver flores!*" Fighters (of all genders), I want to see flowers!

I see Alejandra as a fighter, one that has taken on the most important battle of all: the inner battle that prepares us for all other battles. She is a fighter determined to own her life and make it what it was meant to be: a life that blooms, a life that flowers. I'm thankful for the flowers that blaze with her unique imprint: her writing, her poetry, her songs. In Mexika cosmology she is now an elder. Elders are supposed to offer lessons from their lived experiences so that we may all benefit from their wisdom. This is what Alejandra has done. Alejandra, thank you for your generous offering. You gave it your all, your best. Now we get to take it in. What a blessing!

- Trini Rodriguez, Tia Chucha's Centro Cultural
& Bookstore co-founder

## A Daughter's Note
## by Paolina I Acuña-González

I don't remember when I first met Alejandra Acuña. That is mostly due to the fact that I was distracted by being freshly born out of her, an experience I bet she doesn't want to remember either. Witnesses at the scene do recall that I cried really hard but instantly stopped when she called out for me, recognizing the sound of her voice from all the times she'd talk to me while pregnant. But what I do remember is the first time I read something my mother had written (that wasn't a dense academic paper).

The fun thing about my mom is that she never talked down to me as a child. She literally once asked me as an infant to "use my words" and my one-word-at-a-time brain could only turn out "Words!" as a response. Either way, I was born a fellow peer. She brought me along to every adult event, from classy art shows to matinee screenings of The Devil Wears Prada, a movie she believed a four-year-old would definitely understand. Whether this was an earnest attempt to culture my young, impressionable mind with substantial media or merely because she couldn't be bothered to hire a babysitter, I'll never know (I could ask her right now because I'm writing this in the room right next to her, but I don't feel like getting up). Either way, her fortuitous laziness made way for her to bring me along to her (and my) first ever playwriting class.

For the longest time I thought my mom was all logic and numbers. She was the breadwinner, the one with the real adult job, who toiled for hours analyzing quantitative data at her laptop in the living room and actually liked school so much she voluntarily kept getting degrees well into her forties. She was all left brain and I must've inherited my love for creating weird art from my other ancestors. (Probably one of my slutty grandfathers. You'll see.) But seeing her in this class, bringing earnest attempts to craft narratives and plots divorced from field research and data, made me realize that she's always carried that spark of creative magic in her. There's a common pattern in families in which the children of immigrants feel the pressure to secure the unsteady environments they grew up in by pursuing careers in high yielding, financially stable fields. And then the next generation, taking that privileged stability for granted, feel able to pursue careers in whatever fields they want, free of pressure. When all the other parents bragged that their kids wanted to be lawyers and doctors, my mom proudly shared that I wanted to be on SNL. She filled my after schools and summers with art classes and instilled in me the belief that I could do whatever I wanted as long as I held the desire in my heart.

Years later, when I got into NYU Tisch's Dramatic Writing program, she told me that her childhood dream was to be a writer. I couldn't help but wonder how long she deferred that dream in order to build a stable career and creativity-filled life for me. Which is why I'm so proud to see her living out her childhood dreams today, taking all the expertise from her life and her decades of research and turning it into relatable life lessons and storytelling medicine. She's the most influential and most important person in my life; I literally wouldn't be alive without her. So I'm glad that you, the reader, have taken it upon yourself to take her advice, because Lord knows I don't and will happily continue to take it for granted for years to come.

# Preface

I have stories to tell, and in the telling, I heal. My hope is that my stories help you heal too. If they resonate with yours, may we both find comfort in knowing we are not alone in our thoughts, feelings, and experiences. It is widely recognized that storytelling is a powerful medicine—it illuminates, connects, makes us smile, and inspires. My stories weave together stone and flower moments—times of struggle and moments of beauty, each carrying its own lesson. These pages hold reflections on emotional distress, heartbreak, healing, wholeness, heart's desires, joy, and love. Within them, I also share the wisdom that has shaped my journey—science, ancient teachings, and practical tools—the foundation of my healing, growth, and the creation of a life I once only dreamed of.

By the end of *Stones, Flowers, and Lessons Learned*, I hope you will carry stories and tools to help you cultivate self-awareness, self-acceptance, and self-love. Step by step, guided by joy and the pull of your heart's deepest desires, may you move closer to a life in full bloom.

In 2020, I celebrated my 52nd birthday—a significant milestone in the Mexica (Aztec) tradition. According to Luis J. Rodriguez, an acclaimed Chicano author and poet, the Mexica calendar sees 52 years as the completion of a full century: four sacred cycles of 13 years, each representing a chapter of spiritual and personal growth. This transition into elderhood is marked by the *New Fire Ceremony*, a ritual that honors past experiences, lessons, and milestones as the foundation for a new future. This book is my personal *New Fire Ceremony*. It's my way of weaving together the lessons, growth, challenges, and milestones of my past—each stone and flower shaping the journey. And with them, I kindle a new flame, a guiding light to illuminate the path forward.

To me, becoming an elder means growing older and sharing stories, passing down traditions, and embracing the responsibility to nurture wisdom and renewal. I've wanted to write since the sixth grade, but as the daughter of immigrants, I was held back by my fear that pursuing writing might lead to financial instability. Instead, I chose a career in public service, through which meaningful work and contributions to students, families, and communities came with the security of pensions. Those pensions now allow me the freedom to write, reconnect with my roots, and offer the lessons and stories that shaped me as my flower offering to the next generation.

Books and journals have always been my companions. My mother used to say, "Books are your real mother," because I was constantly reading, learning, and being guided by them. Over the years, I've filled stacks of journals—sacred places for my thoughts, wish lists, questions, hopes, and dreams. These journals have helped me process life and reflect on my journey.

Healing, to me, is not just about identifying problems or reducing symptoms. It's about setting goals inspired by the desires of your heart, whether for well-being, social justice, or abundance. Growth is fueled by the "juicy" emotions—excitement, optimism, and electric hope—that energize us to move forward and do the work. Together, we'll embark on a journey of healing and discovery, exploring how to honor our heart's deepest desires and to live our best lives.

Do you have a dream or goal that feels just out of reach? I often tell my daughter and friends, "God doesn't put a desire in your heart to mock you." I believe these desires are glimpses of what's possible—visions of your future—if you trust and take action. Even if fear, doubt, or worry make you hesitant, those feelings can be addressed. You can bloom. It's okay to believe.

In nature, blooming means yielding flowers. In life, blooming means clearing energy blocks, addressing fears, and taking consistent steps toward your dreams. With new dreams come new strategies. Let's take the first step—guided by joy—toward a life in full bloom. With a desire in your heart and the courage to begin, let's start this journey together.

# Introduction

## Autobiographical Storytelling as Medicine

There's a proverb often attributed to Jewish folklore that asks, *What's truer than the truth?* The answer: *the story.*

Through personal communication with educator and author, Stan Beiner, I learned that the rabbis used storytelling as a way to interpret the Torah, a tradition known as *Aggadah*. These narratives helped explore questions that emerged from study and filled in textual gaps. *Aggadah* encompasses tales of biblical figures (often called *Midrash*), accounts of the sages from the Talmudic era, proverbs such as those found in *Pirkei Avot* (*Sayings of the Fathers*), and elements of folklore. A powerful example of this tradition is the Passover seder. Understanding that the most effective way to teach about the suffering of centuries of slavery was through an annual ritual, the rabbis wove stories and songs into the observance to preserve historical memory. The focus is not on whether the plagues or the parting of the Red Sea occurred exactly as described, but rather on the narrative of liberation—because it is through storytelling that history becomes truth.

Stories hold immense power—they help us make sense of our lives, find meaning amidst chaos, and connect with others on a deeper level. For me, storytelling has been a lifeline, a way to navigate the terrain of wellness. I frame my journey through the metaphor of "stones" and "flowers," inspired by Narrative Exposure Therapy (NET).[1]

NET is a research-based, trauma-informed psychotherapy initially developed to support individuals in refugee camps, where trauma and conflict are often overwhelming. In these settings, a simple yet profound method is employed: a rope or string is laid on the ground to represent an autobiographical timeline. On this timeline, "stones" symbolize traumatic experiences, while "flowers" represent moments of healing, growth, or beauty.

Through this process, participants share their life stories, piece by piece. They recount not just events but also the sensory and emotional layers of their experiences— what they saw, heard, felt, and interpreted. A counselor serves as a guide, helping process their emotions, bodily responses, and thoughts while documenting these insights along the timeline.

The results are powerful. NET has consistently been shown to reduce PTSD symptoms, anxiety, and depression.[2] It has proven so effective that lay counselors have been trained to deliver it in areas with limited access to mental health professionals.[3] Even in the most challenging environments, storytelling emerges as profoundly healing.

What makes NET remarkable is its focus on integration— on weaving a cohesive narrative from the fragments of one's life. By the final session, participants are encouraged to imagine "future flowers": moments of hope and joy yet to come. This act of naming and anticipating future joy is a declaration of resilience and agency. It reminds us that while life is undoubtedly filled with stones, there will always be flowers too—and we hold the power to plant more.

As a researcher of resilience and professional quality of life, I've studied these processes in depth. But my connection to storytelling runs deeper. I have personally walked the path of stones, flowers, and lessons learned in the journey toward wellness.

Now, let me introduce myself.

## My Location of Self

**Pronouns:** She, her, hers, *ella*
**Education:** MSW at UC Berkeley; PhD at UCLA
**Work Experience:** Professor of Social Work and School Social Worker (retired from both)
**Race/Ethnicity:** Mestiza/Chicana
**Gender:** Cisgender Woman
**National Origin & Ancestry:** U.S. Citizen with ancestors from Chihuahua and Zacatecas, Mexico
**Abilities/Disabilities:** Currently Able-Bodied
**Life Cycle:** Parent of an NYU graduate (2023)
**Spirituality:** Christianity, Indigenous Practices

In her article, *Location of Self: Opening the Door to Dialogue on Intersectionality in the Therapy Process,*[1] Dr. Watts-Jones describes an approach to initiating dialogue with clients and trainees. Her words deeply resonated with me and have inspired how I now introduce myself in my work. She writes:

*"Before going forward with therapy, I like to share a bit about myself... My personal experiences also inform my vision, what I see and don't see. And so, I like to think about how my personal identities might be helpful or a limitation in our work together and get your thoughts about this..."* [2]

Inspired by Dr. Watts-Jones, I have embraced the practice of sharing my "location of self," recognizing it as a way to invite connection, reflection, and dialogue. Beyond my education and work experiences, I now disclose aspects of my race, ethnicity, gender, and other identities to start conversations about how these shape my vision—what I see and, perhaps more importantly, what I may miss.

I am a Chicana, cisgender woman. My pronouns are she/her/hers and *ella*. I was born in East Los Angeles, on Tongva Territory, and my ancestors (tracing back seven generations) are from Chihuahua and Zacatecas, Mexico. I am currently able-bodied and the proud parent of an NYU 2023 graduate. I'm also a recovering workaholic, deeply committed to understanding and promoting wellness.

As an adoptee, my search for a deeper connection to my heritage has been lifelong. A DNA test from AncestryDNA revealed a genetic reflection of Mexico's complex history: 48% Indigenous Americas-Mexico,

28% Spanish, 9% Portuguese, 6% Basque, 5% Sephardic Jewish, 3% African (Senegal, Yorubaland, and Western Bantu Peoples), and 1% Irish. This knowledge has strengthened my connection to my ancestors, inspiring me to learn more about their histories and visit the lands they once called home.

## Indigenous Roots

The Indigenous populations of northern and central Mexico, particularly in Chihuahua and Zacatecas, have rich and diverse histories. In Chihuahua, the prominent Indigenous groups include the Rarámuri (also known as Tarahumara),[3] the Tepehuán,[4] and the Guarijío.[5]

Zacatecas was historically inhabited by several Chichimeca groups, notably the Zacatecos, Cazcanes, Tepehuanes, and Guachichiles. These groups were primarily nomadic and fiercely resisted Aztec and later Spanish conquests. The Zacatecos, in particular, played a significant role in the Chichimeca War of the late 16th century. The Guachichiles, known for their formidable defense strategies, occupied a vast territory and were among the fiercest opponents of Spanish incursion.[6]

Today, Indigenous presence in these regions varies. According to the 2020 Mexican census, approximately 10.5% of Chihuahua's population self-identifies as Indigenous, whereas in Zacatecas, this figure is about 4.9%.[7] These communities continue to preserve their languages, traditions, and cultural practices, contributing to the rich fabric of Mexico.

## Jewish Ancestry in Latin America

Many in Latin America and Spain have Jewish Ancestry. According to Jewish scholar Stan Beiner (personal communication), during the Inquisition and the Expulsion, Jews who were forced to convert (known as *Conversos* and *Marranos*) continued to practice their faith in secret. Even generations later, when their descendants had lost direct knowledge of their Jewish roots, certain traditions persisted. Some continued lighting candles on Friday nights or reciting the *Kaddish* when mourning a loved one. To this day, "secret Jewish" communities exist throughout the Southwest and Mexico, maintaining these hidden practices. One lasting legacy of this history is the recitation of *Kol Nidre* on Yom Kippur, the holiest day of the Jewish year. Originally composed by *Marranos*, this prayer served as an appeal for divine forgiveness— an acknowledgment that while they outwardly practiced Christianity for survival, their faith remained intact. It allowed them to annul the religious declarations they were forced to make under duress, preserving their spiritual integrity despite persecution.

## African Ancestry in Latino Identity

African ancestry is another integral part of Latino identity. Research indicates that, on average, Mexican Americans have about 3% African ancestry.[8] Additionally, self-identification reflects this heritage; a Pew Research Center survey found that one-quarter of all U.S. Latinos identify as Afro-Latino, Afro-Caribbean, or of African descent with roots in Latin America. This recognition highlights the deep cultural and ancestral ties that continue to shape Latino communities, weaving a history of resilience, adaptation, and enduring legacy.[9]

## The Power of Naming Our Location of Self

Watts-Jones's *Location of Self* framework offers a meaningful way to reflect on the intersections of identity as a therapist and as a human being. Naming my location of self is not merely an act of transparency; it is an invitation to dialogue. It acknowledges that our lived experiences shape our perspectives and that being mindful of those perspectives is essential to building authentic relationships.

When sharing this with others, I invite them to reflect on a few key questions:

1. How does it feel to read about someone who shares or embodies my identities? Notice what comes up.

2. Does this raise concerns related to your own identity, perspectives, or experiences?

3. In the spirit of self-reflection, consider this: How might others feel about working with someone who shares or embodies your identities, your status, and your perspectives?

This practice of reflection is especially vital because women of color, particularly in academia, often face implicit biases that affect how their work is perceived. For example, studies show that courses taught by instructors with feminine names are rated lower than identical courses taught by those with masculine names.[10] This is implicit bias at work.

We are all good students of our families, cultures, and society. Stereotypes and biases about women of color have seeped into our collective consciousness, shaping perceptions in subtle but impactful ways. Thoughtful reflection allows us to challenge these biases, to see beyond them, and to grow past them.

## Main Chapters with Stories, Science, Wisdom, and Tools

This book reflects the teaching style I honed over two decades as a college professor, blending storytelling, science, and practical tools to inspire learning and growth. This book is a mix of heart, *coraje y ganas*, story and science, knowledge and raw truth. My hope isn't just to inform you but to light a spark, to help you see yourself—and the world—through a lens of love and deeper understanding.

**Stories:** Here, I lay down pieces of my life, a collection of stories and micro-stories. I write to reflect, connect, or inspire change. My stories are offered with trepidation and purposeful vulnerability.

**Science & Research:** Then, we dive into science— because if you're ready to nerd out with me, I'm all in. Each chapter offers research findings you can use. Let's connect the dots between what we know and how we live.

**Ancient Wisdom:** I make room for the wisdom of my ancestors—it's what allows me to stand on the shoulders of giants. Their cultural traditions infuse this book, weaving timeless philosophies into modern practices, grounding today's challenges in the wisdom of those who came before us.

**Tools:** I've been called a doer—someone who likes to make things happen. But how do I practice? How do I level up? In this section, you'll find practical strategies for healing, growth, and transformation.

What's one thing you can try after reading the chapter? Let's make it real.

## Chapter 1: *¡Tan-tararán!* It's All About My Mom

**Stories:** My origin story, centered on my mother, was both the hardest and most healing to write.

**Science:** Storytelling fosters emotional integration and secure attachments, aiding mental and physical well-being by transforming chaotic memories into coherent narratives.

**Ancient Wisdom:** African and Latin American traditions highlight the communal and sacred nature of motherhood, emphasizing resilience and interdependence through practices like *Ubuntu* and *familismo*.

**Tools:** Tools like the Adverse Childhood Experiences (ACEs) Questionnaire, journaling, and therapeutic rituals guide self-reparenting, helping readers confront childhood adversity and foster resilience and self-love.

## Chapter 2: My Spirituality in the Still Small Voice

**Stories:** A collection of stories and essays about my core resilience factor, my spirituality and why it's important to me, as well as all the different ways I practice, shaped by a neighborhood church in East LA and evolving through shamanism, mindfulness, and transcendental meditation.

**Science:** Spirituality enhances mental, emotional, and physical health by offering meaning, purpose, and resilience, with practices like shamanic healing and mindfulness as transformative tools.

**Ancient Wisdom:** Ancestral teachings underscore the interconnectedness of body, soul, heart, and spirit, advocating for balance and resilience through practices that honor the vessel and its essence.

**Tools:** Reflective questions and rituals deepen spiritual connection, enhance resilience, and align actions with a sense of purpose and authenticity.

## Chapter 3: The *Tonalli* of Love

**Stories:** These lessons from love include joys, heartbreaks, the role of boundaries in meaningful relationships, and stories about parenting.

**Science:** Loving-Kindness Meditation promotes emotional healing, strengthens relationships, and improves physical health, offering a holistic approach to trauma recovery and personal growth.

**Ancient Wisdom:** Ancestral wisdom from African, *Mexica*, and Jewish traditions frames love as a sacred bond, teaching balance, reciprocity, and communal connection as central to thriving relationships.

**Tools:** Step-by-step Loving-Kindness Meditation fosters inner peace and connection.

## Chapter 4: Deep End Lessons on Work and Purpose

**Stories:** Early inspirations and career challenges informed my perspective of how work and purpose intersect.

**Science:** Positive workplace dynamics, akin to healthy marriages, enhance employee engagement and retention, emphasizing the importance of collaboration and emotional connection.

**Ancient Wisdom:** Teachings from African and Mayan traditions show how concepts like *Ubuntu* and *In Lak'ech Ala K'in* transform rivalry into kinship and competition into collaboration.

**Tools:** Strategies like reframing rivalry, setting boundaries, and practicing active listening transform workplace dynamics, fostering harmony and mutual respect.

## Chapter 5: The New Fire Ceremony

**Stories:** Exploring harmony across mind, body, heart, and spirit, integration and renewal culminate in my free-verse poem, *I Am Everything*.

**Science:** Retirement brings opportunities and challenges, with well-being shaped by workplace experiences, education, and cognitive engagement, underscoring the need for tailored support and lifelong learning.

**Ancient Wisdom:** Generational wisdom about femininity and self-expression, as explored through the lens of red lipstick, weaves lessons on courage, autonomy, and navigating societal perceptions.

**Tools:** Practical tools for financial recovery, personal wellness, and honest reflection encourage growth, balance, and sustainable life transformation.

**Steps to Blooming Workbook:** A workbook that walks with you step-by-step in realizing your heart's desires. Reflective exercises and prompts to help you apply the concepts of this book, set goals, and overcome limiting beliefs.

**References** and suggested reading for further exploration of the topics discussed.

# Chapter 1
## Tan-tararán!
## It's All About My Mom

# Family Tree

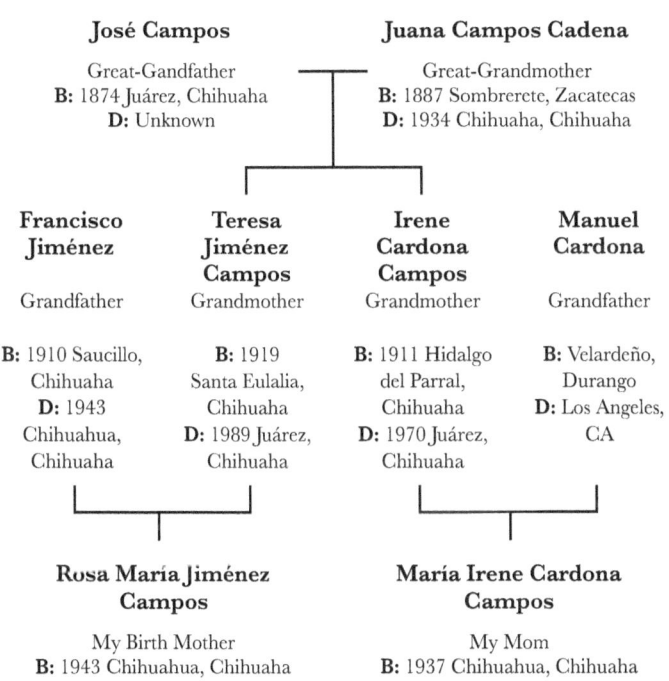

**José Campos**

Great-Gandfather
**B:** 1874 Juárez, Chihuaha
**D:** Unknown

**Juana Campos Cadena**

Great-Grandmother
**B:** 1887 Sombrerete, Zacatecas
**D:** 1934 Chihuaha, Chihuaha

**Francisco Jiménez**

Grandfather

**B:** 1910 Saucillo, Chihuaha
**D:** 1943 Chihuahua, Chihuaha

**Teresa Jiménez Campos**

Grandmother

**B:** 1919 Santa Eulalia, Chihuaha
**D:** 1989 Juárez, Chihuaha

**Irene Cardona Campos**

Grandmother

**B:** 1911 Hidalgo del Parral, Chihuaha
**D:** 1970 Juárez, Chihuaha

**Manuel Cardona**

Grandfather

**B:** Velardeño, Durango
**D:** Los Angeles, CA

**Rosa María Jiménez Campos**

My Birth Mother
**B:** 1943 Chihuahua, Chihuaha
**D:** 2008 Los Angeles, CA

**María Irene Cardona Campos**

My Mom
**B:** 1937 Chihuahua, Chihuaha
**D:** 2003 Los Angeles, CA

*"Hijo de tigre, pintito."* ("The child of a tiger is striped.") —
Mexican Proverb

My story starts with my mom, María Irene Cardona
Campos, born on April 19, 1937, in Chihuahua,
Chihuahua, Mexico. *¡Ajúa!* She would love to be the star
of this entire book, but we've made a deal: this chapter
belongs to her. Her life, her love, and her lessons are the
foundation of my origin story.

"You don't really know me."

These were her words to me in the twilight of her life, as
we sat on my blood-red IKEA couch, sunlight fading into
shadows. At the time, her statement felt like a reproach.
But now, I think it was a confession. My mom was a force
of nature who lived life on her own terms. She lived for
the spotlight, and her personal anthem, Frank Sinatra's
*My Way*, blasted from our home stereo whenever she
needed some inspiration. To love her was to stand in the
eye of her storm.

This chapter is my attempt to truly know her—to explore
the stones and flowers of our relationship—her love, her
lessons, and the complexities that shaped who I am. She
taught me to move through the world with her boldness,
even as loving her was overwhelming.

She is the most important of all my ancestors, and I
carry her in my mannerisms, my humor, my capacity to
love, and the way I view the world. This is a love letter,
an excavation, and an offering to anyone trying to make
sense of the chaotic, beautiful people who shaped them.

## How I Met My Mom

I've always known I was adopted. My mom never kept it a secret. There was no betrayal, no dramatic revelation— just love and an innate understanding that this was part of my story. I grew up calling my birth mother *Tía Rosa*.

Open adoption wouldn't be widely recognized as a best practice until the 1990s, yet back in 1968, my mom— with a *secundaria* education from *Colegio Palmore*, a private boarding school in Chihuahua—intuitively knew it was the right thing to do. I credit her instincts, shaped by the frank and direct culture of Chihuahua ("*no tengo pelos en la lengua*" - "I speak my mind without sugarcoating"), and I'm grateful.

In high school, I asked my mom to tell me the story of how I became her daughter, craving the details to piece together my identity. Meaning making helps turn pain into a coherent narrative, lightening its emotional burden.[1] Research shows that reframing emotional distress through expressive writing can ease distress and foster growth,[2] and hearing this story from my mom was that first step toward writing it here.

Her answer went something like this: My *Tía Rosa*, living in Chihuahua, was trapped in an unhappy marriage and already raising a toddler when she became pregnant with me. Overwhelmed by depression, she avoided prenatal care and threw herself into heavy chores, seemingly willing the pregnancy to end. My grandmother, also named Irene (Sr.), was deeply worried, fearing for both Rosa's health and the baby's life.

At the time, my mom, Irene (Jr.), lived in East Los Angeles with her husband and three children. When she heard from her mother about Rosa's condition, she sent for Rosa, bringing her to Los Angeles to ensure she received care. Rosa arrived frail and despondent. Doctors at Los Angeles County General Hospital warned that either Rosa or the baby, or both, might not survive. Fearing the worst, my mom filled out my birth certificate with her name listed as my mother, *por si acaso*—just in case. And then, against all odds, we both survived. By sending for Rosa, my mom had saved my life.

I was born on September 16, 1968—the day Mexico shouts its freedom to the world, fireworks painting the sky.

Mexico celebrated its independence, but freedom was not whole. That same year, the Tlatelolco Massacre stained the *Plaza de las Tres Culturas* in Mexico City with the blood of hundreds of students demanding justice for their right to democracy, their voices rising against oppression, only to be met with the gunfire of a government determined to silence dissent.[3] A few weeks later, Tommie Smith and John Carlos raised their fists on the Olympic podium, their silent protest cutting through the noise of a national anthem that did not speak for everyone.[4] I was born into a world on fire—with blood in the plaza and defiant fists in the air—a lesson that freedom is never given, always fought for.

When I was six months old, Rosa decided she was going back to Mexico and asked my mom if she could take me with her. My mom, her heart breaking, said, "Of course. The baby is yours." Soon after, grief swallowed her whole. She fell into a deep depression that landed her in the hospital. Hearing this, Rosa made an extraordinary offer: "If I give you back the baby, will you get better?" Without a pause, my mom said yes and brought me home again.

Even now, at 56, I'm still making sense of my origin story. When I first learned about the pact between my mothers, I couldn't believe it. *There has to be more! What aren't you telling me?* I asked again and again, hoping for a missing piece to make it all make sense. But it's only now, as I gather their memories and piece together their stories - their joys, sorrows, and choices - that the puzzle starts to take shape. Slowly, the picture becomes clearer. Slowly, I'm learning to see.

As an adult, I often pressed my mom to share stories from her childhood. She'd smile and indulge me, though some memories made her cry. Beautiful and extremely vain, she hated crying - hated how it made her eyes puffy and her nose red. In those moments, I found stories that connected the dots, traces of her past that shed light on who she was. And through those stories, I began to understand how my own story came to be.

My mom told me that when she was five, a baby in her neighborhood would cry alone for hours, so she would sit by the window, singing lullabies to soothe the child: *Ru ru cama de león, Tu mamá la vaca, Tu papá el ratón.* My mom pleaded with her own mother to ask the baby's mother if they could care for the child while she worked. Babies had always been her magnet.

When my daughter Paolina was born in May 2001, my mom moved in with us part-time to help care for her. She stayed Sunday through Wednesday, then returned home for the rest of the week. When she was in her kitchen, staring at Paolina's picture on the refrigerator, she'd cry, *"Paolina, me haces falta!"* She often told me, *"Siento que es mía."*

These memories help me imagine what my mom must have been like when I came home as a newborn. In my mind's eye, I can see her pouring her love into me while my *Tía Rosa* recovered—feeding me, bathing me, and filling the house with her laughter and endless chatter. I can picture her bonding with me, claiming me as her own, as she seemed to do with babies.

### *Tía Rosa's* Backstory

Discovering more about my *Tía Rosa's* life has given me a deeper understanding of the forces that shaped her and, ultimately, the story behind my mothers' pact.

Born in Chihuahua on November 10, 1943, Rosa lost her father just a month later to an epileptic seizure, at home on Christmas day. Her mother, Teresa, took a teaching job in the cold, rugged, and remote hills near Casas Grandes to support her three children. Teresa, feeling pressured by her older sister, Irene (Sr.), decided to leave baby Rosa in her care.

By all accounts, Irene (Sr.) was *canija*. The word is layered—equal part cunning, part tough, part harsh, even unfair. No one—whether children, grandchildren, nieces, or nephews—would describe her as warm or nurturing. My mom told me her mother's motto was:

*"Todo tiene su derecho y su revés"*—everything has its right side and its wrong side. It was a testament to her rigid worldview and the authority she wielded as the family matriarch.

I can't help but picture six-year-old Irene (Jr.)—my mom—showering Rosa with affection, treating her like a living doll. A child's love, tender and unfiltered, wrapped around Rosa like a balm. That early bond, forged in the tangled threads of loss and love, planted the seeds of a connection so deep it would one day shape the story that brought me into their lives.

Recently, I learned from one of Rosa's close relatives that Irene (Sr.) had Rosa do most of the family's chores and cooking. When Irene (Sr.) lashed out at Rosa with physical beatings, my mom stepped in to shield her. But protection was fleeting. At just 12 years old—still a child, not yet even menstruating—Irene (Sr.) married Rosa off to a much older man named Carlos. My mind races, trying to piece together the circumstances of that decision. The injustice of it burns—a life altered, a childhood stolen.

### Rosa & Macario

According to family stories, Carlos was abusive, and by the time Rosa was 23 and working at a bank, she was desperate for an escape. That's when my biological father, Macario, entered her life—tall, dark, and impossibly charming. She didn't resist. His older brother played the role of wingman, delivering the line: "Macario is young and inexperienced—why don't you teach him a thing or two?" Their affair unfolded in secrecy, a whirlwind of stolen moments and hotel rendezvous, fueled by the longing to feel wanted, to feel free, even if only for a little while.

Macario, with his polished boots and expensive clothes, swept Rosa off her feet, spinning tales of wealth and prestige, of a family rooted in cattle ranching and prosperity. Rosa believed him, desperate to cling to the promise of stability in a life that had already taken so much from her.

Then she became pregnant. Macario promised to marry her—but only on one condition: she had to leave her husband and child behind. His family, he claimed, would never accept her otherwise. Rosa refused. Her dignity wouldn't let her trade one injustice for another. She never heard from him again.

No wonder Rosa was heartbroken and despondent. No wonder she threw herself into grueling chores as if willing her body to reject the pregnancy. And yet I managed to grow inside her, defying her despair. I imagine my own tiny fist pumping in the air like Tommy Smith and John Carlos.

Knowing now how little love Rosa received, I understand why she entrusted me to my mom. Rosa must have recognized the bond forming between Irene (Jr.) and me and believed I belonged with her. Though technically first cousins—*primas hermanas*—she and my mom were soul sisters, connected in this life and beyond.

A few years ago, I uncovered the truth about Macario. He wasn't the son of wealthy ranchers he claimed to be but a self-made entrepreneur, building water pumps across Mexico. Tall and dark-skinned, with a preference for light-skinned Mexican women, he had a history of abandoning the children of his lovers. He was married with six children when he met Rosa and she died never knowing.

Though I never met him, he passed away in 1990, I suspect that part of my ambition comes from his DNA. A medium once told me he explained his absence by claiming he lacked a paternal instinct. I told him, through the medium, that I didn't claim him. He told me to claim myself. And I do now. Strange as it sounds, I've made my peace with it. It's a part of the story, but not the whole of it.

## Reunited With My Mom

As an adult, my mom shared another detail about my origin story. She told me that when she went to Mexico to bring me home, Rosa quietly laid me on the bed and walked away. No words passed between them. My mom picked me up and carried me back to Los Angeles. That silent goodbye marked the beginning of my life with Irene (Jr.). I try to imagine it: Rosa's conflicted heart, my mom's excitement at our reunion, and the weight of everything left unsaid, heavy in the room. Last month, a relative shared that Rosa sometimes expressed feeling as though my mom had stolen her baby. *Stolen.* Was it true? I wonder if this was grief speaking and the way she processed an incredibly difficult decision.

I had never thought deeply about what that moment meant for Rosa, but the more I learn about her early life, the more I imagine her inner turmoil:

*How can I give up my baby? But how can I let my sister, Irene, suffer and die?*
*This is my baby.*
*But how will I raise two children and leave my abusive husband?*
*My sister loves this baby. She cares for her in a way I don't know how to.*
*She raised me. She defended me. How can I say no to her?*
*How dare she ask this of me? Is this even my choice?*

I've always believed my mom and I were meant to find each other, soulmates destined to be mother and daughter. And I'm grateful—so deeply grateful—that Rosa understood that bond.

"If I give you back the baby, will you get better?" Rosa asked. And without hesitation, my mom went to Mexico to bring me home.

The pieces of my story keep surfacing, one by one, reshaping how I see identity, sacrifice, and love. Both gave me a piece of themselves, and so my life began with two mothers: one who gave me life, and one who became my soulmate.

**Her Way**
My mom moved through the world like anything was possible, like everything could be negotiated. Signs that declared "No refunds" were, to her, mere suggestions. With limited English and unshakeable confidence, she'd argue with cashiers and, if necessary, escalate to the manager. I was mortified, my wide eyes silently screaming, *Mom, can't you read? The sign says no refunds!* But of course she could read—she just didn't care. And somehow, she always got her refunds.

When I was ten, she took my little brother, then two, and me to Rosarito Beach. We sat at a sidewalk café where she ordered for us. My brother, still clinging to his bottle now and then, drank a special blend of oatmeal, milk, cinnamon, and honey. When his bottle was empty, my mom casually pulled it from her bag and asked the waiter to refill it with the same concoction. *¡Mírala!* I thought, bracing for a reaction. But the waiter didn't even blink. Without missing a beat, he nodded as if it were an everyday request. Being around my mom was a constant lesson in asking for what you want. "The worst they can say is no," she'd tell me. And time and again, she proved it—most people didn't say no to her.

Sometimes, her bluntness embarrassed me. I was a shy, reserved nerd, and her audacity felt loud and unpredictable. "Mom, you're being rude!" I'd scold. She'd fire back without hesitation: *"No soy ruda, soy franca."* ("I'm not rude, I'm straightforward.") Touché.

Her audacity shaped the trajectory of my life. When she enrolled me in the seventh grade at Stevenson Junior High School in East Los Angeles, we stood at the counter as the office lady handed her my class schedule. My mom scanned it, her eyes stopping at *Spanish 1A*. Without skipping a beat, she said, "My daughter already knows Spanish. What else do you have?" The office lady explained that the only other option was French, usually reserved for eighth and ninth graders. "Give her that," my mom replied. It wasn't a question; it was an expectation. And just like that, I was enrolled in French. That single decision set me on a path. I took French 3, at a local high school, while I was still in junior high. My mom drove me there every morning, picking me up after class with a grilled cheese sandwich and chocolate milk in a mason jar in hand. She only overslept and forgot me once.

On my first day of French 3, the teacher—a blonde, white woman—wasn't expecting me. She seemed skeptical, quizzing me on verb conjugations in front of the class. My heart pounded, but somehow, I answered her questions well enough. Maybe it was because my mom had raised me to defy expectations, to meet challenges head-on. Reluctantly, the teacher let me stay.

In high school, I was the only sophomore in Advanced Placement (AP) French. When I asked my Moroccan teacher what I could take next, he looked me in the eye and said, "If you pass the AP exam, I'd recommend community college classes. But I don't think you'll pass." Inside, I shook my head. Clearly, he didn't know the daughter of Irene, I passed.

Throughout my life, the pattern of being underestimated and then exceeding others' expectations has followed me. My mom taught me early on that other people's opinions aren't the final word. I didn't have her charisma or knack for charming people into a *yes*. She'd say, "*Ganate la gente.*" (Win them over.) And I'd say, "I don't know how!" Regardless, I found my own nerdy ways to make things happen.

In the spring of 2005, two years after my mom passed, I traveled to Paris for the first time. It didn't feel right to experience Paris without her. Maybe it was the guilt I carried from her subtle manipulations - how she'd guilt-trip me when I bought something for myself: "Where's my new dress?" she'd tease. My sisters and I used to hide our purchases to avoid her inevitable questions. Yet, as I walked through Paris, I felt her spirit with me. That day in the school office before I started seventh grade, she didn't accept the limits being placed on me, and she taught me to do the same for myself. Paris became a testament to her lessons: the worst they can say is no.

Through her example, I learned to use my voice. What I once saw as boldness became a guiding principle in how I approached life's challenges and opportunities. Her influence extended beyond my personal life. It informed the title and focus of my dissertation: *How We Talk About It: Stressful Life Events, Family Communication, and PTSD Among Public School Adolescents.*

Her philosophy also profoundly shaped how I raised my daughter. In our family, there's a rule my daughter knows well: *We talk about it—all of it—until we've digested it.* That rule keeps us connected, keeps us whole.

My mom's determination and audacity shaped so much of who I am, but they were only one side of her. Beneath the boldness and charm lay a complexity. She raised us with fierce love and unpredictable volatility—a paradox I still carry and wrestle to make sense of.

## Her Parenting Style

My mom was a mix of fierce love, explosive temper, and a kind of childlike impulsivity that could turn a moment into a storm. She told me a story about a family party we attended when I was maybe three or four. Apparently, one of the kids *le cayo mal*, something about the way she behaved annoyed her. She called me over and told me to fight the kid. I refused. Looking back, I think that's when she started to clock me as the straight-up square in her brood.

When I was four, my older siblings—ages ten, sixteen, and eighteen—and I were sitting in the living room watching TV when she became furious that we hadn't finished our chores and blamed our being too *embobados* on the screen. She marched over and kicked the TV. The screen shattered on impact. This was 1972, back when TVs were thick glass, vacuum-sealed, and built to last. Shattering glass or cradling a baby, the lady was fierce.

That wasn't the only time her anger was overwhelming and disproportionate. Once, I accidentally burned our maple wood dining room table by setting a hot pot on it. When she discovered it, she demanded to know who did it. Terrified of her volcanic fury, I lied. When she figured it out, her rage erupted. Her words cut deep - ("*animal, estúpida*") - and her belt cut deeper still. She made me kneel and apologize, her face twisted with fury as she screamed at me. The menacing swish of her belt as it came loose served as both a warning and a threat. I can still hear the crack of the belt against the table before it met its intended target. I cried, scared and hurt, but even then, I knew her anger wasn't really about me. It was about her - about everything she couldn't control. And then came the final blow: she wanted *me* to comfort *her*. *El colmo*. After everything, she needed me to forgive her, to soothe the guilt she couldn't carry alone. I was eight years old.

Her contradictions ran deep. On one hand, she was magnetic– charming, witty, and full of life– a natural performer with a voice and personality that could fill a room. She loved to sing, dance, and Flirt with a capital *F*. She could dazzle anyone. But beneath that brilliance was a darker side - manipulative, domineering, and unyielding - that came as sudden as a storm rolling in.

In fifth grade, she threw me to the ground and kicked me repeatedly. I don't remember what started it, only the shock and pain of the moment. Sometimes, a fiery family member would stand up to her, Sagittarius versus Aries. Occasionally, my mom would back down. I watched in awe and gratitude, as if witnessing a hero standing up to a fire-breathing dragon. Once, when I was around twelve, I tried to do the same, to protect a younger family member. It didn't go well. She could smell the fear on me, deeming me an unworthy opponent. As a teenager, she admitted to me that even if she knew she was wrong, she wouldn't admit it. She had to win. Always.

Her behavior wasn't all bad or all good—it was as layered as she was. When I was in college, I lived at home for a semester to save money. One night, I was pulling an all-nighter to finish a paper. At 2 a.m., I heard the hum of the vacuum cleaner. I found her vacuuming the living room.

"Why are you vacuuming right now?" I asked.

*"Pues, para acompañarte,"* she said. To keep me company.

It was a small thing, but it did help. I appreciated her solidarity.

But that same semester, a family member—infamous for schemes—sold my mom a life insurance policy on me. My daily commute to school involved multiple LA freeways, and if tragedy struck, it would mean a big payout for her.

I was stunned but not entirely surprised. It wasn't the first time she'd made me feel like her golden goose. From an early age, I understood that, in her eyes, part of my purpose was to provide what she seemed to value most: money.

## New Relationship Terms

I don't remember the exact moment I realized my mom often behaved like a tantruming toddler but knowing that helped me navigate our relationship. My little-old-lady soul learned how to manage her tantrums—or *ataques de nervios*, as she called them—as though she were the child and I the parent. I didn't always like her, but I always loved her. It was exhausting, and by the time I was 21, I'd had enough.

"Listen, Irene," I said during one particularly tense call, "I don't care who you are—my mother, my father, my brother, my sister—if you try to manipulate or abuse me in any way, I'm out."

Her voice trembled. "*Me asustas.*"

"*Pues* don't do it," I replied.

That was the turning point. From then on, our relationship operated on new terms. Even my siblings noticed how she was "on her best behavior" around me. It wasn't perfect, but it was healthier. She learned to respect my boundaries, and I learned how to balance my love for her with the need to protect my own peace.

Our relationship improved even more after I became a mom. In the final three years of her life, we both worked to make it better—and it was fun trying. Sunday nights became our thing: we stayed up late, talking about everything and nothing. We'd laugh until we cried, and I'd completely ignore how exhausted I'd feel at work the next morning. Eventually, I started pretending to be asleep when she showed up after her late-evening church service, hauling her overnight bags. As much as I loved our late-night, pee-your-pants laughter, and endless conversations, Sunday all-nighters just weren't sustainable.

We found other ways to connect. Tuesday, tamale brunches in East LA while we were both home with my baby Paolina. Eyebrow appointments at the cosmetology school in the mall. One time, the student assigned to me walked out looking a bit wild-eyed, and my mom immediately jumped up to take my place. She took the hit for me, and her eyebrows paid the price. Luckily, my mom was a pro with an eyebrow pencil until her eyebrows grew back, I miss her. Always.

In those final years, as she settled into her old-lady-grandmother stage, she was fun and funny, free from the scary rage and impulsivity that had marked so much of our earlier relationship. I loved those grandmother years with her. We laughed. We bonded. We found a rhythm that felt good.

Her contradictions, bold and loving yet volatile and impulsive, left a lasting mark on me, and I've spent years untangling and understanding them.

## Love & Trauma

You're not supposed to diagnose your family members, but in hindsight, I believe my mom may have struggled with Borderline Personality Disorder (BPD),[5] along with other mental health challenges. Viewing her through this lens isn't about assigning labels—it's about understanding her complexity with compassion. This perspective has brought clarity to her emotional outbursts, her fear of abandonment, and the chaos that shaped my childhood. What once felt terrifying and confusing now has a deeper context.

Reading about and understanding BPD feels like a form of family psychoeducation—an essential component of any effective treatment plan. It has been a tool for healing, turning confusion into understanding and judgment into empathy.

When my birth mother, Rosa, brought me back to Mexico as a baby, my mom must have felt abandoned. That pain spiraled into depression, hospitalization, and what I now recognize as suicidal despair. Years later, my mom confessed to driving recklessly on the freeway with me as an infant in the backseat. In her words, it was a moment when she felt overwhelmed by hopelessness. Even in her darkest times, though, there was a fierce love that bound her to me and my siblings.

People described my mom as volatile; her mood swings left everyone walking on eggshells. But in rare vulnerable moments, she'd admit, "*Siento que la vida no tiene chiste*"—I don't see the point of life. My mom often viewed relationships as all or nothing so she didn't keep many friends, saying dramatically, *"Ya cayó de mi gracia"* when she was disillusioned by someone. It felt as though she relied on us, her children, for companionship. "You had daughters so you could have friends," we'd joke. Even when it was hard, we stayed. She was our mom, and we saw the good along with the bad.

### The Science & Lived Experience

Borderline personality traits arise from a complex interplay of genetic, environmental, and social factors. However, these risks are not definitive. Environmental factors like therapy, supportive relationships, and stability can foster healing and growth.[6] My experiences with people with BPD show me there is no one-size-fits-all narrative. I've known family members and friends with BPD—some who sought treatment and managed their symptoms, and others who did not. This reflection is a love letter—to my mom and to everyone living with BPD. I see you. I feel you. You remind me that no matter how deep the struggle, healing and growth are always possible.

### Stones. Stones. Flowers. Flowers.

My mom was diagnosed with lymphoma in August, 2003. Just months before she died, we sat on the edge of my blood-red IKEA couch. The sun was fading, and the room darkened slowly around us. She looked at me and said, "You don't really know me."

Her words hit me like a punch to the gut. At the time, I thought she was blaming me for not knowing her better, for setting boundaries around her manipulative tendencies. But now, decades later, I realize it was a confession. There were stories she hadn't told me, parts of her life she had kept hidden.

I struggled to accept her cancer diagnosis, caught in a mix of denial and hope. I told her there was no way I was going to lose her—not when we were finally getting along and having so much fun together. Her response was her version of Christian comfort: her death would be a celebration, a reunion with Christ. I congratulated her and told her I'd be happy for her but sad for me. I'd miss her, and I planned to feel all my feelings about it.

And I did. I cried at her funeral and for the whole first year after her death. For the next five years, even hearing her name, sharing a story about her, or celebrating Paolina's milestones without her would bring me to tears—but I didn't mind. Those tears made me feel connected to her. Those waves of emotion kept her alive in my life. No matter your age, you're never truly prepared to lose a parent.

Even now, I carry her with me—in my laughter, in my love for my daughter, and in the stories I tell. Talking about her has been part of my healing. Turning jumbled thoughts and overwhelming feelings into words helped me make sense of the loss. By shaping those memories into coherent stories—with beginnings, middles, and ends—they no longer keep me up at night.

Every chapter of my life, every story I tell, comes back to her. She'd love that—being the center of attention in my memoir. Our relationship was complicated, yes, but it shaped me in ways that still echo today. This chapter— the first and most important—is all about her. It's about the good, the bad, and the horribly beautiful nature of our relationship.

## Her *Tonalli*

On the day she died, I cut a lock of her hair. It was my way of holding onto a piece of her essence. I brought scissors to the hospital room, knowing—even in my grief—that I'd want this connection. Quietly and tearfully, I asked her, "May I?" before cutting the lock. She had already gone, but I still sought her permission.

In *Mexica* tradition, *tonalli*—one's life force—resides in the body, particularly in the hair, nails, and blood. By keeping her hair, I was preserving a piece of her *tonalli*, a sacred connection to her vitality and spirit.[7]

As a little girl, my daughter Paolina, curious and playful, was drawn to that lock of hair without the weight of my intentions. She enjoyed its texture, scattering it throughout the house like a toy. At the time, it felt disruptive, almost like a second loss. But in *Mexica* belief, *tonalli* isn't meant to be contained—it's meant to flow.[8] Perhaps my mom's essence wasn't meant to stay in the gold box but to infuse our home, spreading her presence into the spaces where we live and love. Her hair was never meant to stay in the box. Of course, it wasn't. My mom wasn't one for confinement, for keeping things small or controlled or where they "belonged." It spilled out like water, like fire, like laughs so loud they can be heard on the street in a Mexican neighborhood.

The *Mexica* knew what they were talking about: *tonalli* isn't supposed to stay put. It's supposed to flow, to spread, to live on in the spaces it touches. And maybe that's what I've been doing all along—letting her flow through me, learning how to carry her chaos and her love in a way that doesn't burn me alive.

## Who Is She?

*The truth will set you free.*[9] That's what I kept saying when, seemingly out of nowhere, a family friend from Leon, Guanajuato, reached out to me last week. I can't help but wonder if my mom sent him. Over the course of a three-hour phone call, I listened as he shared story after story about her.

Some stories I'd never heard before and the weight of them was overwhelming. It was as if I was meeting her for the first time, finally seeing a version of her life I hadn't known existed. I felt overwhelmed, because *I didn't really know her.* So many stories are too complex and too intimate to share here. But he did tell me this:

"She used to say, 'I could do anything.' And she did. She lived large. She had it all. With her boundless capability and cunning, she bent men and women to her will. She lived fiercely, hitting life hard. A *bruja*, the devil herself, she was all about action and dominance. *Acuérdate de sus ojos* (piercing, unforgettable).

"For her, life was easy—the world was her playground. She unraveled the lives of others to suit her ambitions. "She crossed lines, borders, and boundaries without hesitation, always getting what she wanted. She convinced every one of her invincibility, navigating life forwards and backwards with ease.

She admitted that the only thing that stopped her was aging. The Tigress was no more. Life weighed her down, bending her to its will. She could no longer summon the vitality of her youth; it had slipped beyond her grasp."

I know, I know. You wish you were reading her memoir. She does too. My mom's newfound secrets don't haunt me—it's the trust they call into question. What kind of relationship did we really have? Even as an adult, what did she teach me about trust, love, and connection? What is real love? *How does it feel to be truly loved—without lies or double lives?*

For a moment, I doubted if her love for me was real. Could someone who lived with so much deception and manipulation truly love? I choose to believe my mother loved me—in the way she knew how and in the way she could. And it was enough. I survived childbirth and childhood. Her love, though imperfect and inconsistent, was real.

The evidence that my mama loved me? I felt it. I felt cherished, cared for, and protected. When I was in my skateboarding phase in junior high and fell hard on the sidewalk, she rushed me to the hospital to check for a concussion. Every sniffle, fever, or stomach ache meant a trip to the family clinic. I was well-fed—food was her love language. Homemade enchiladas, *mole*, and *pozole* were my birthday meals. I was well-dressed, vanity was her currency.

Despite moving every two years (we were renters, and she wasn't always responsible with money), she made sure I attended the same elementary, junior high, and high school, even when we lived outside the school boundaries. Consistency in my education mattered to her.

When I was ten, I told my mom I had been molested and she believed me with fire and arms wide enough to hold the truth and did her best to protect me. Research confirms that being believed helps restore a child's safety, their sense of self, their trust in the world.[10] And decades later, at 43, when I sat across from a shaman, she told me my soul was not fractured by this experience, because I spoke and because my mom believed me. My mom saved my life at birth, and she saved my soul at ten. I have a great capacity to love and be loved, and those closest to me feel it. That's the ultimate evidence of her love.

## Lessons Learned

When I became a mom, her advice to me was: *Observe and study your daughter. Really get to know her.* She lived by that philosophy with all her children. She clocked me as a square from the jump. She didn't teach me how to shoplift or about sex, as she did with my older family members. She shielded me from the details of her colorful life, even as an adult. I get it now. *A la gente decente se les miente.* I wasn't ready to know. Now I know. And I'm still digesting.

It wasn't the picture of healthy, reciprocal love, but it became the blueprint for my closest relationships—platonic and romantic (which I will get into in Chapter 3). Writing this chapter has been narrative exposure therapy for me, stringing together the stones and flower moments of my mom's stories along my autobiographical timeline. I'm piecing together the good, the bad, and the horribly beautiful into a coherent whole. Making sense of it all and laying it to rest. I feel whole and at peace.

I'm so glad I'm writing things down, because it feels like my once-elephant memory is slipping. Details that were once vivid are fading. Writing has helped me preserve these memories and explore the truths they hold. The fragmented stories I've gathered from my mom and ancestors offer glimpses of who they were, but they don't define me. They live in my DNA, but I decide how they're expressed. I take the good my mother taught me and leave the rest. I choose what to carry forward. At 56, I choose my environment, my people, and my path. I didn't get to choose my parents, but I get to choose my family. And my mom, for all her flaws and gifts, stays.

She was the spark and the burn, the contradiction of a woman who could shatter a television in rage but vacuum at two in the morning just to keep me company. She was never just one thing—never just the anger, the love, the manipulations, the hope. She was all of it, tangled and messy, like the stories I've inherited and tried to untangle, to make sense of, to fit into neat boxes. But she doesn't fit. She never did. And that's the point, isn't it?

The truth about her, about us, about all of this—it's both devastating and simple: she loved me in the only way she knew how. And I've decided that's enough. Because I know what real love feels like. I feel it in the way I love my daughter, in the way I double over when I laugh too loud, in the way I write these stories to keep her alive. It's messy and imperfect, but it's flowing through me, spilling out into the world, refusing to stay in a box. That's her legacy. And, as much as it burns sometimes, I'll carry it.

Because I can. Because I'm hers. Because I always will be. Like her, I live on my terms.

Nikki Giovanni captures this beautifully in her poem *Revolutionary Dreams*:[11]

*Then I awoke and dug*
*that if I dreamed natural*
*dreams of being a natural*
*woman doing what a woman*
*does when she's natural*
*I would have a revolution*

Loving and living authentically has become my revolution. If my mom shaped my identity, it was my spirituality that helped me find strength within myself—something I'll explore in the next chapter.

*Tan-Tan.*

# Science & Research

## Introduction

One concept I am passionate about sharing is the connection between storytelling and secure attachment. This was the focus of my dissertation, and it's a lesson so profound that I wish I could scream it from the rooftops or drive through the neighborhoods where I worked as a school social worker, blasting the message from a bullhorn. Here's what I've learned about the healing power of storytelling and why it matters.

## The Healing Power of Storytelling [1]

James Pennebaker's *Theory of Inhibition and Confrontation* reveals the toll of suppressing versus expressing emotions. Pennebaker explains that we naturally want to share our stressful experiences with those we trust. However, fear of judgment can hold us back. This 'inhibition' is exhausting because suppressing our thoughts and feelings takes constant effort. Over time, this chronic stress affects our mental and physical health—this is how secrets make us sick.

- ### Inhibition: The Toll of Suppression
  Imagine stuffing all your painful memories into boxes and cramming them into a closet. To keep them from spilling out, you'd need to guard the door day and night. The energy it takes to keep those emotions hidden drains you, leaving little room for healing or growth.

## • **Confrontation: The Path to Healing**

In contrast, 'confrontation' involves acknowledging and expressing our painful experiences. Talking or writing helps us to organize our thoughts by putting the experience into words, which helps us manage our emotions better. This also offers physiological benefits – not surprising since mind, heart, spirit, and body are connected as one.

## **Pennebaker's Groundbreaking Study** [2]

In one study, college students wrote about a traumatic experience or a trivial topic for fifteen to twenty minutes a day over four days. Those who wrote about *both the facts and feelings of their trauma* initially felt distressed, but four months later reported emotional improvements and a significant drop in health center visits. The writing helped integrate their thoughts and emotions, leading to improved immune function and better academic performance (e.g., higher grades). It's understandable to want to avoid talking about painful memories, and this study suggests that confronting difficult emotions leads to long-term healing.

The writing prompt was:

> *"For the next 4 days, I would like you to write your very deepest thoughts and feelings about the most traumatic experience of your entire life or an extremely important emotional issue that has affected you and your life. In your writing, I'd like you to really let go and explore your deepest emotions and thoughts. ... Don't worry about spelling, grammar, or sentence structure. The only rule is that once you begin writing, you continue until the time is up."*

I've given this prompt in class to graduate students and to parents in counseling groups. I provide them with the prompt and fifteen minutes of writing time once a week for four weeks. Sometimes people need a lot of reassurance. Sometimes I walk around the building praying silently for the group. Sometimes they doodle and choose not to write. Sometimes they wait until week two or three to write. It's that scary to write about the then and there in the here and now. But no one has ever regretted writing once they started.

## What Makes Writing Therapeutic? [3]

Interestingly, Pennebaker found that repetitive recounting about the same events without gaining new insights doesn't foster recovery. The most healing narratives evolve over time, transforming from chaotic on day one to coherent by the final session. Instead, Pennebaker found that the essays with the following elements predicted better health:

- Included event details and emotions
- Used positive emotion words (e.g., "happy")
- Balanced a moderate number of negative emotion words (e.g., "sad")
- Incorporated causal words (e.g., "because") and insight words (e.g., "realize") over the course of writing

Pennebaker found that writing about event details and emotions aligns brain activity between the left (logic) and right (emotion) hemispheres. In this way, both emotional and linguistic information is processed and integrated simultaneously. This is what achieving "integration" means, in brain function as well as mind, body, spirit, and heart. This "integration" helps us process and make sense of our experiences.

Integrating the peaks and valleys of life into a coherent story has profound benefits for our mental health, relationships, and physical well-being. Writing, as Pennebaker's research shows, is a powerful tool for achieving this integration and healing.

"Talking about the worst secret of one's life with an experienced person, being understood, and coming away feeling still accepted as a human being, seems to be remarkably important and beneficial, perhaps not unlike the rite of confession... Indeed, seeking understanding and acceptance is a deep and human need."[4]

## Attachment Security and Storytelling[5]

John Bowlby and Mary Main's research on attachment shows how storytelling predicts secure attachments. Main found that the way a parent narrates their childhood often mirrors the attachment style they form with their child.

### Secure Narratives and Secure Attachments

Parents of securely attached children typically recount balanced childhood memories, highlighting both joys and challenges. Even those who endured painful pasts were able to foster secure attachments if they processed these memories into coherent narratives.

### Insecure Narratives and Attachment Struggles

Conversely, parents of insecurely attached children often dwelled on unresolved issues or offered vague, overly positive accounts without depth. Main suggests that reconciling with one's own memories, even difficult ones, can create space for secure attachments.

The ability to weave a coherent narrative—acknowledging the good, the bad, and the horribly beautiful—fosters healing and promotes security in the next generation.

## Prompts for Reflection
Here are some journaling or storytelling prompts inspired by the work of Bowlby and Main on narratives and attachment:

*Self-Reflection Prompts*

• Reflect on your childhood memories. What are some joyful moments that stand out? What challenges did you face, and how did they shape you?
• Think about a story from your past that you find difficult to tell. How might you weave the joyful and painful parts together in a coherent way?

*Parenting or Caregiving Prompts*

• If you are a parent or caregiver, how do you think your own childhood experiences influence the way you connect with your child or children?
• Reflect on a moment when you felt especially proud of how you supported your child emotionally. What did you do, and how did they respond?

*Narrative Coherence Prompts*

- Write a short story about your life that includes both the highs and lows. How do these experiences connect to create a fuller picture of who you are?
- Create a timeline of your life, marking key events and their emotional significance. Then, write a brief narrative tying these events together.

# Ancestor Wisdom

## Motherhood: The Song of Many Voices

For over 50,000 years, where the roots of humanity intertwine with the soil of sacred stories, we find motherhood not as a solitary act but as a chorus of hearts, hands, and voices. African and Latin American traditions carry the heartbeat of this truth, reminding us that the act of mothering is both communal and holy—a ceremony that bridges earth and spirit.

## From Africa: The Sacred Circle of Mothering

Imagine the sacred circle, where the rhythm of the drum calls generations of mothers to gather. In this space, the philosophy of *Ubuntu* whispers: "*I am because we are.*" [1] Rituals honor connection, each prayer and gesture reaffirming that mothering is an eternal thread spun between past, present, and future. In the African tradition, as Jacob K. Olupona teaches, this thread is unbroken and strong, held sacred by the wisdom of those who came before. [2]

## From Latin America: The *Abrazo* of *Familismo*

In the lands of Latin America, the family is a sanctuary, its strength as deep as the copper canyons of Chihuahua and as enduring as ancient pyramids. Here, the spirit of *familismo* sways—a belief in the treasure of family ties, where mothering extends beyond the individual and is embraced by a network of care. Grandmothers, aunts, and elders are the guardians of resilience, weaving a blanket of love and support to ensure no child or mother walks alone. *Familismo* is a quilt stitched together with countless hands, each thread imbued with a lesson, a story, a promise of belonging. [3]

## Timeless Lessons: A Bridge Between Souls

To mother is to participate in an ancient ritual, a sacred exchange that transcends the self. It is a reminder that we are all bound together by invisible threads of care and courage. And in the midst of an increasingly fragmented world, these ancestral teachings whisper to us: *Come back to the circle. Sit by the fire with your relatives. Honor the spirits who came before, they live in your heartbeat and your DNA.*

## My *Corrido*

The *corrido* is a traditional Mexican narrative ballad deeply rooted in the oral storytelling traditions of our ancestors. Born in the nineteenth century and flourishing during the Mexican Revolution (1910–1920), *corridos* became vessels for memory, resilience, and resistance. With melodies shaped by waltz and polka rhythms, *corridos* sing tales of love, justice, and sacrifice across generations. They help us remember the values and experiences of their time.[4] In this spirit, "*La Madre y Su Hija*" sings of love and loss, sacrifice and *superando*. It is the story of a mother and daughter to remind us of our shared strength to carve paths from stone.

## "*La Madre y Su Hija*"

En un rincón de Chihuahua, la historia empezó,
Dos primas hermanas, el destino las juntó.
Una dio la vida, otra dio su calor,
En los brazos de Irene, la niña halló amor.

## *Coro:*

*¡Ay, tan-tararán! La estrella brilló,*
*Entre piedras y flores, su legado dejó.*
*Con fuerza y tormenta, su vida vivió,*
*La madre valiente que nunca se rindió.*

Rosa, con su pena, en silencio cedió,
A su hermana Irene, su hija confió.
"Si te devuelvo al bebé, ¿tu corazón sanará?"
Con lágrimas calladas, la niña regresará.

Irene era fuego, indomable al andar,
Con pasión y coraje, nada la podía frenar.
Sus risas y cantos llenaban el hogar,
Pero sus tormentas podían todo quebrar.

**Coro:**
*¡Ay, tan-tararán! La estrella brilló,*
*Entre piedras y flores, su legado dejó.*
*Con fuerza y tormenta, su vida vivió,*
*La madre valiente que nunca se rindió.*

Aunque con la correa el miedo sembró,
En su cocina, su amor nos mostró.
Pozole y mole en la mesa sirvió,
En cada platillo, su espíritu habló.

Hoy la recuerdo, con risas y con llanto,
Una madre compleja, un legado tan alto.
Sus flores me guían, sus rocas me forjan,
Soy hija de Irene, su esencia me forma.

**Coro final:**
*¡Ay, tan-tararán! En mi corazón vivió,*
*La madre valiente que la vida desafió.*
*Entre luces y sombras, su amor me dejó,*
*En mis risas y lágrimas, su espíritu quedó.*

## The Mother and Her Daughter

In a corner of Chihuahua, the story began,
Two first cousins, fate brought them hand in hand.
One gave life, the other gave care,
In Irene's arms, the child found love there.

**Chorus:**

Oh, *tan-tararán!* The star shone bright,
Among rocks and flowers, she left her light.
Through storms and strength, her life she lived,
The brave mother who never gave in.

Rosa, in sorrow, silently resigned,
Entrusting her daughter to her sister so kind.
"If I return the baby, will your heart be restored?"
With silent tears, the child was back once more.

Irene was fire, untamed in her way,
With passion and courage, none could dismay.
Her laughter and songs filled every space,
But her tempests could shatter and displace.

**Chorus:**

Oh, *tan-tararán!* The star shone bright,
Among rocks and flowers, she left her light.
Through storms and strength, her life she lived,
The brave mother who never gave in.

Though fear she instilled with the strap in her hand,
Her love shone through in meals she planned.
*Pozole* and *mole* served at her table,
In every dish, her spirit was able.

Today I remember her, with laughter and tears,
A complex mother, a legacy revered.
Her flowers still guide me, her rocks make me strong,
I am Irene's daughter; her essence lives on.

**Final Chorus:**
Oh, *tan-tararán!* In my heart, she remains,
The brave mother who challenged life's pains.
Through light and shadow, her love endures,
In my laughter and tears, her spirit endures.

# Tools

## Healing the Parent Wound: Tools for Resilience and Self-Love

This section explores pathways to healing the parent wound by acknowledging the impact of childhood adversity and embracing practices for self-reparenting. Using tools like the ACE Questionnaire, journaling, and therapeutic rituals, readers are guided to confront their past with courage and compassion. By understanding how early experiences shape our present and reclaiming the care we deserved, we open the door to healing, hope, and self-love.

## Tool #1: The ACE Questionnaire

The Adverse Childhood Experiences (ACEs) Questionnaire sheds light on how childhood adversity impacts lifelong health, relationships, and well-being. Research shows that higher ACE scores are linked to a greater risk of physical and mental health challenges, including heart disease, diabetes, depression, and substance use disorders. These early experiences also shape our ability to trust, connect, and cope with stress.[1] For example, in California, 62% of adults have experienced at least one ACE, and 17% report four or more. An ACE score of four or higher significantly raises the risk for chronic health issues. However, while ACE scores reflect challenging experiences, they are not a life sentence. Many individuals with high ACE scores thrive through meaningful relationships, therapeutic interventions, and resilience-building practices.[2]

Reflecting on my own ACE score of six, I recognize that while it represents a childhood filled with challenges, it does not define me. My healing journey has been one of seeking wholeness through practices that nurture my mind, body, spirit, and heart. I am grateful to the therapists, spiritual guides, and community healers who have supported my growth. This journey has reaffirmed my belief in the resilience of the human spirit and the transformative power of connection and care.

Taking the ACE Questionnaire is a brave step toward self-awareness, helping us understand the links between our past and present. It is not about judgment—it's about creating opportunities for healing and growth.

## The ACE Questionnaire

The original ACE Questionnaire consists of ten questions.[3] Expanded versions, such as the Philadelphia ACEs Questionnaire, include additional adversities like systemic racism or separation due to immigration.[4] Answer "yes" (1 point) or "no" (0 points) for each question.

1. Did a parent or adult often insult, humiliate, or frighten you?
2. Did a parent or adult often push, slap, or physically harm you?
3. Did anyone ever touch you sexually or force sexual contact?
4. Did you often feel unloved or unsupported by your family?
5. Did you lack basic needs like food, clean clothes, or protection?
6. Were your parents ever separated or divorced?

7. Did your mother or stepmother experience domestic violence?

8. Was a household member a problem drinker or drug user?

9. Was a household member depressed, mentally ill, or suicidal?

10. Did a household member go to prison?

Expanded ACEs questions may ask about systemic challenges, such as:

• Was a family member treated unfairly due to their race or ethnicity?

• Did you experience discrimination or bias because of your race or ethnicity?

This questionnaire is a starting point, not an endpoint. With support, you can rewrite your story, heal old wounds, and create a life grounded in resilience and hope.

## Tool #2: Journaling, Rituals, and Affirmations

Healing the parent wound begins with reclaiming the love and care you may not have received in childhood. Self-reparenting involves nurturing your inner child with the kindness and understanding you deserve. These practices empower you to rewrite your story with self-love and hope.

## Steps to Support Your Healing Journey:

• **Write a Letter to Your Younger Self:** Express what you needed to hear as a child from a loving parent figure.

- **Create Healing Art:** Draw a nurturing image, like a tree symbolizing growth, or a self-portrait adorned with affirmations.
- **Dedicate Time for Self-Care Rituals:** Engage in activities that feel like "parenting" yourself, such as preparing a comforting meal, taking a warm bath, or wrapping yourself in a soft *rebozo*.
- **Explore Therapeutic Modalities:** Consider Eye Movement Desensitization and Reprocessing (EMDR), a psychotherapy approach often used to help individuals process and heal from trauma or distressing life experiences, somatic therapy, or group healing workshops focused on childhood wounds.
- **Reflect and Affirm:** Ask yourself: What did I need most from my parents that I didn't receive? How can I give myself that care now?

## Example Reflection:

- **What did I need most from my parents?** Unconditional love and validation—not just for what I accomplished, but for who I was.
- **How can I give myself that care now?** Practice self-compassion and celebrate small wins without judgment.

## Affirmations for Healing:

- I am enough, just as I am.
- I deserve love and acceptance, no matter what.
- My worth is inherent, not tied to my achievements.
- I honor my needs and give myself the care I deserve.

- I am proud of my growth and love myself unconditionally.

Incorporate these affirmations into your daily routine—whether through journaling, meditation, or speaking them aloud. Repetition rewires the brain, helping you replace old narratives with self-love and empowerment.

## Closing Note:

Healing the parent wound is not about erasing the past but reclaiming your future. It's a courageous act of self-love that paves the way for resilience, connection, and hope. You are worthy of the care and love you give to others—and it starts with giving it to yourself.

## Poem for Healing

*I am the parent I needed: strong, fair, tender, and kind.*
*In my arms, I cradle and soothe myself.*
*Here, I am safe to be exactly who I am and shine.*

# Chapter 2
## The Still Small Voice

"When there is no enemy within, the enemies outside cannot hurt you." —African Proverb

Spirituality anchors me when everything else feels uncertain. From the familiar rituals of childhood church experiences to encounters with shamanism and meditation, spirituality has been a constant thread—woven through my identity and my healing.

## Confidence & Spirituality

My last therapist told me, "Your confidence is a solid nine out of ten—because we all have room for improvement." He added, "That can be intimidating." Without missing a beat, I asked, "Do I intimidate you?" He paused, then admitted, "Yes."

Where does my confidence come from? I have a few theories.

One possibility is genetic loading from the biological father I never met. Stories suggest he carried himself with confidence bordering on narcissism. This curiosity about him even led me to take online quizzes about narcissism. One quiz concluded I had confidence "like a celebrity" (but not pathological), while another said my confidence was low and needed improvement. So, the results were inconclusive, but I'm willing to entertain the idea that a bit of him lives in me.

Another theory is my love of personal development and self-help books. These books rewired my brain with their wisdom, reshaping my thoughts and beliefs. I've spent countless hours with authors whose words challenged and inspired me. As the saying goes, *Dime con quién andas y te diré quién eres* (Tell me who you walk with, and I'll tell you who you are). I didn't just read these books—I devoured them, underlined them, journaled in the margins, copied affirmations onto flashcards, and actively applied their lessons to most aspects of my life. For years, I reread the *Power of Positive Thinking* by Norman Vincent Peale every summer. My brain still reminds me of some of the ideas I learned from this book. For example, Peale suggests silently praying for the people you encounter throughout the day. It uplifts others and strengthens your own sense of peace and connection. Many of my flashcards are straight from this book.

Neuroplasticity shows us that our brains can change throughout life. These books helped me carve fresh neural pathways, creating space for growth, healing, and possibility.[1] My mom used to joke that books were my real mother because of how much I loved to read. To her credit, watching her navigate life was its own kind of education.

But most likely, my confidence is rooted in my secure attachment to God. The word "confidence" comes from the Latin *confidere,* meaning "to trust" or "to have faith."[2] For me, that trust comes from knowing God has my back. Even in my darkest moments, I hear a still small voice ask, "Do you trust me?" My answer is always yes.

God speaks to me through that inner whisper, and when it calls, I listen. I follow it, even when it leads me off the beaten path. Walking away from situations that compromise my peace might seem risky, but staying is the real danger. Have you ever seen those movie trailers where the hero walks away, completely unscathed, just as a building explodes behind them? That's me. I walk away when my inner voice says, "Go." With God as my foundation, I know I'm safe.

Deep down in my soul, I know my confidence is anchored in my faith. But I also believe genetic loading and books play their part. My brain is wired to believe everything is possible (thank you, books), everything is negotiable (thank you, Mom), and that God has my back (thank you, *Yesus*—which is how my mom pronounced it).

Late in life, my mom taught me a phrase to say when standing in the middle of a blessing. I've passed it on to my daughter. Whenever she shares good news, I ask her, "What do you say?" She replies with the same emphasis and accent my mom used: "Thank you, *Yesus*."

These words have become my mantra, my prayer of gratitude. They remind me to acknowledge the blessings that surround me, even during challenges. Confidence is not just about knowing your worth; it's about recognizing the forces—spiritual, personal, and communal—that support you along the way.

## Churchgoing: My Second Home

One song always brought me to tears, even as a little girl:

*"Una vez trabajando, oí una voz,*
*Esa voz me decía, no llores más,*
*Jesucristo ya viene en una nube blanca"*

Those words, promising Christ's return and a profound hope, stirred something in me. At church, we sang it slowly, in minor and melancholy notes. It reached into the depths of my little old-soul heart—even when I was little.

At the age of four, I began attending a Pentecostal church in East Los Angeles with my mom and older siblings. Nestled among the homes of immigrants from Mexico, like my parents, the three-story building became my spiritual foundation. My dad, a Catholic, attended mass with his sister. My parents were so different that it didn't seem strange to me that they attended separate churches.

By the time I was five, I had already accepted Jesus into my heart. During an altar call, I walked to the front of the church and repeated the preacher's words with deep conviction. From that moment, my connection to God became my most secure attachment.

Sunday School, Vacation Bible School, Missionettes, and youth services filled my days with community, purpose, and joy. I soaked up everything I learned, so when my Sunday School teacher didn't show up one day, I took it upon myself to lead the class. Not long after, I was officially asked to teach, leading lessons on Sunday mornings and Tuesday evenings.

The services were vibrant, alive with music that lifted our spirits. The sound of the piano, drums, and tambourines filled the sanctuary as the congregation sang with joy. We sang both short, repetitive *coritos* and longer hymns from Spanish hymnals—communal prayers set to melody. Church gave me structure and meaning. It was where I felt safe. Even when my family's attendance became inconsistent, I hitched rides with church members to ensure I didn't miss a single service.

I see how deeply the church shaped my sense of purpose, confidence, and resilience. It was where I learned leadership, teaching, and the joy of service, as well as the beauty of hope, belonging, and community. It fostered my love for reading the Bible and learning about God, which continues.

## Community of Refuge

It was the small, repeated rituals - the micro-moments - that shaped how I think and what I still do. Every church service - Tuesday night, Friday night, Sunday night, and Sunday morning - included time for *peticiones y testimonios*—public petitions and testimonies.

Church members would stand, one by one, addressing the congregation to share their hearts openly. A young Central American immigrant man would ask for communal prayers to help him find a job. An elderly Mexican immigrant woman asked for prayers as she prepared for surgery. A Mexican mother would ask the group to help her pray for her teenage son to return to church and stay away from bad influences.

Others shared their gratitude for answered prayers - stories of triumph and hope. The young man finally found work. The wayward son graduated from high school. The elderly woman, healed and grateful, celebrated her successful surgery by bringing homemade tamales to share with *los hermanos*.

Watching others model vulnerability made me bold. I wanted to be like the adults, so it felt like a rite of passage when I finally stood to share my own *testimonio* or *petición*. We were connected in hope and belief.

After some church services, the congregation gathered for food sales to raise money for youth trips or group supplies. The smell of taquitos frying on the porch steps in an electric skillet is still a vivid sensory memory—two taquitos with guacamole for a dollar. After long services, when hunger set in, everything tasted better.

The church basement, with its modest kitchen, was the heart of our fellowship. We came together because there was always something to celebrate - Pastor's Day, a wedding or *quinceañera*, dedicating a newborn baby with godparents, breaking a fast after a prayer vigil, or a special performance by a traveling Christian singer. I can still picture the low-ceiling room with fluorescent lighting and cement tile floors with a glossy finish filled with laughter, conversation, and feasting.

Supporting each other as a true community—sharing burdens and celebrating joys—church became my refuge and second family. Fellowship, potlucks, and shared prayers united generations, from deacons and elders to teens like me. My faith and spirituality were anchors, offering comfort amidst the chaos at home. In this community, no one grieved or celebrated alone. That's some good medicine right there.

**Glossolalia: Speaking in Tongues**

I was about twelve years old, attending a Missionettes summer camp, when I first spoke in tongues. One night, a preacher led the service and taught us how. During the altar call, I felt drawn to step forward with the others who wanted to learn. I don't remember the exact instructions, but I prayed with intent, fully open to the experience and the unknown. And then it happened—the words flowed out of me in a language I didn't understand but that felt sacred and soothing. From that moment, speaking in tongues became a part of my prayer life, a bridge to something greater than myself.

Sometimes it happens spontaneously, like when I walked through every room of my home after my divorce, praying, burning sage, and inviting peace into the walls, into the air, into myself. Other times, it happens during spiritual ceremonies, like the Bear Dance in Yosemite I attended with my cousin, the drum unlocking something old and familiar in my body.

And always, the same sounds find me—*Andára Shakara Ukiri Anda, U Shikiri Anda*—a language beyond language, a whisper from something deeper, older, unknowable, yet intimately mine.

Curious, I turned to AI for possible answers. I learned *Anda* means "go" or "prepare" in some Bantu languages and may connect to the verb *andar* (to walk, to move) in Spanish. *Shakara* loosely resembles a word in Nigerian Pidgin, meaning "to stand tall" or "to show off." *Ukiri* has phonetic echoes of Sanskrit, possibly tied to *Utkira*, meaning "rising" or "ascending." *U* in many Bantu languages can signify "being." *Shikiri*, resembles *shikilia* in Swahili, meaning "to hold on," "to grasp." In Japanese phonetics, *Shikiri* can mean "partition" or "to take charge." In Sanskrit, *Shikara* means "peak" or "summit."

These interpretations are not meant as linguistic or etymological facts but rather as a spiritual exploration—a poetic way of engaging with sounds that have surfaced in my life. While some words may have linguistic parallels, the connections drawn here are intuitive rather than scientific, reflecting the ways in which language, memory, and spirit intertwine beyond formal analysis.

In shamanic, meditative, or spiritual traditions, sounds like these often emerge from intuitive, subconscious, or ancestral knowledge rather than structured language. They carry a rhythmic, chant-like quality, resonating more as vibration and energy than literal translation. Perhaps they are a soul's language—a rhythm, a call, a knowing.

The Bible describes speaking in tongues as a spiritual gift, a way to communicate directly with God when words fail. Paul wrote in 1 Corinthians 14:2,*"For anyone who speaks in a tongue does not speak to people but to God. Indeed, no one understands them; they utter mysteries by the Spirit."* [3]

For me, speaking in tongues is a form of surrender—a way to let the Spirit move through me, guiding my words, my heart, my intentions. It's a sacred language between me and God that has carried me through life's hardest moments, comforting and connecting me to the divine. And when the sounds come, I no longer question them. I let them rise, let them fill the spaces that language cannot reach. Because some things are not meant to be translated. Some things are meant to be *felt.*

### Shock, Denial & Acceptance

My first crisis of faith came in high school. My mother took me to a restaurant she loved (*Siete Mares* on Whittier Blvd.) for a Saturday night dinner and broke the bad news. Two church leaders I deeply admired were having an affair. One was married and much older than the other. My mother knew me well. She knew how deeply this would shake me. So she made sure I ate first, let me feel good before feeling broken. Still, as I stared at her across the table, my heart sank, my world was crumbling.

She wanted to tell me over a special dinner because the next day, church members planned to bar the two church leaders from entering the building before Sunday morning service. Someone had seen them leaving a hotel together and tipped off the congregation.

I didn't know what to do with this. For a moment, I thought maybe I should throw out the whole thing—faith, church, God, all of it. If the people I trusted most could hurt other people and lie, what else had cracks beneath the surface? But something inside me wouldn't let go. My faith was rooted in something bigger than the imperfections of people.

So I clung to denial, wrapped it around me like a blanket, refused to believe the rumors, held onto the fragile hope they weren't true. I don't remember when I finally let go, but by then, I had grown enough to understand: It wasn't my role to judge. I still loved them, still appreciated what they had given me—their teachings, their kindness, the sense of belonging they had helped create. Denial had done its job, shielding me until I was strong enough to face the truth. And when I did, I was at peace.

At the time, I was too consumed by my own feelings to notice how my mother felt about it all. Looking back, I suspect she took it in stride. She'd seen worse. She, too, had lived a life with its own moral ambiguities and had lovers of her own. Until recently, I knew of three—two men, one woman. Now, I know there were more.

I remember hearing a preacher say once, "There is nothing you can do to make God love you more or love you less." That kind of love made my shoulders drop, made me exhale deeply. Another preacher reminded me: "God loves you and everyone else." Those words stayed with me. That kind of acceptance—a warm blanket on a cold night—gives me relief. It teaches me how to accept others too.

## Seeking a Spiritual Home

By my early twenties, however, cracks appeared in the sermons. They seemed to lack accurate information about the AIDS crisis and possessed a narrow perspective on gender roles, which didn't sit right with me. If the church I grew up in couldn't love and accept everyone equally, then it wasn't the place for me. I made the painful decision to walk away—not from God, but from a building that no longer felt like home.

When my daughter was born, I longed for her to experience the same richness I had experienced in a church community because it shaped and supported me. Over the years, I visited more than a dozen churches across Los Angeles County. Yet, time and again, I found myself walking out of sermons that didn't align with my belief in equality and justice. I wanted a church where I could proudly take my family and friends, knowing they'd be welcomed fully.

I embraced the words of Galatians 3:28: "There is neither Jew nor Gentile, neither slave nor free, nor is there male and female, for you are all one in Christ Jesus." (NIV)[4] This verse is an anthem for me, a call for unity and equality among all believers. It fueled my hope that a spiritual home could exist. Finally, I found All Saints Episcopal Church in Pasadena, California—a spiritual home that embraced inclusivity and compassion. It was the kind of place where I could bring anyone, confident they'd feel seen and loved. All Saints became a space where my spirituality could thrive alongside my commitment to social justice.

Reverend Ed Bacon, who served as the rector of All Saints, is known for his inclusive views on sexuality and religion. In January 2009, during an appearance on *The Oprah Winfrey Show*, he stated, "Being gay is a gift from God." This remark sparked widespread discussion and highlighted his commitment to inclusivity.[5] In his tenure he emphasized, "The entire New Testament is about inclusion, about bringing more and more people in and understanding that there's nothing God created which is inherently evil." [6] Amen and amen. Aho and Asé.

All Saints Church reaffirmed for me that faith and justice are not mutually exclusive but beautifully intertwined. It's a place where the teachings of Galatians 3:28 come alive, and where I finally felt at home again.

### Honoring My Mom's Tenacity

When my mom passed away, her funeral—her celebration of life—was held at the same neighborhood church where I had grown up. The sanctuary was packed; it was standing room only.

During the service, a woman shared a story about my mom that I'd never heard before. She said she had visited our church once at her sister's invitation but never returned. My mom, a church deacon, took it upon herself to pay this woman a home visit and invite her back.

The first time my mom showed up, the woman saw her through the window and told her husband to say she wasn't home. The second time, the woman gave the same instructions. But this time, my mom sat down on their porch and said she'd wait until the woman 'came home.'

The woman laughed as she recalled it, calling my mom her spiritual mother. Not only did she return to our church and become a member, but she also eventually led the women's ministries. Later, she rose to become the director of women's ministries for our entire region.

I smiled as I listened. *Mi mamá era canija*—cunning and tenacious—for better or worse. Always full of surprises.

## Meditating at Deer Park Monastery

In the early 2000s, I was working as a school social worker, stretched thin as I navigated challenging situations (child abuse reports and suicide assessments) and personalities (adults engaged in distorted thinking, denial or clouded by ego). Meanwhile at home, my daughter, then in elementary school, wrestled with anxiety and depression. One afternoon, while picking her up, I ran into a parent who mentioned her family attended an annual retreat at Deer Park Monastery where they meditated daily. My spirit immediately knew I needed to sign up.

Rooted in the teachings of Vietnamese Buddhist monk, scholar, poet, and peace activist, Thich Nhat Hanh, the monastery offered a five-day family retreat—a sanctuary of peace and mindfulness that felt like a lifeline. Each day followed a gentle rhythm of meditative practices: walking and singing meditation through chaparral-covered hills, sitting meditation and dharma talks in the Great Hall, mindful chores that grounded us in the present, and vegan meals shared in noble silence.[7]

Afternoons concluded with restorative naps on mats in the Great Hall. A Buddhist nun's ethereal voice would cradle us into a deep, healing rest. Even the occasional snores from older participants blended into the tranquil atmosphere—a testament to the communal rhythm of renewal and rest. I felt cared for like a preschooler at nap time.

When I left the retreat, every cell in my body sighed in relief and relaxation. My spirit was steadier, my parenting smoother. For years, I taught parenting classes, where I coached participants to use a "calm, computer-like voice" when making rules and setting boundaries with their children. But this was the first time I truly knew how to embody that advice. My mindfulness journey had begun years earlier in a graduate school course at UC Berkeley. Professor Ying opened each class (*Psychoanalytic Psychotherapy with Adults*) with ten minutes of breath counting—a practice that quieted my body and sharpened my mind. Later, as a school social worker, I introduced this exercise to my students: breathing in and out—one. Breathing in and out—two. For younger students, we started with one minute and worked up to five. I kept time by counting my breaths—twelve for each minute.

The seeds planted during that retreat flourished in my daily life. I began weaving progressive muscle relaxation and guided meditations into therapy sessions, workshops, classes, and even meetings. The response, both in my body and in those around me, was unmistakable: gratitude and relief. Mindfulness radiates peace inside and out.

One memory stands out as a testament to this effect. After my divorce, preparing for a date felt nerve-wracking—I hadn't been on one in years. To calm my nerves, I reached for a CD of the Buddhist nun's singing that I had purchased at Deer Park. As I lay on the couch, letting her voice wash over me, my anxiety dissolved and was replaced by a deep sense of calm and relaxation. My dog, curled up on the floor beside me, absorbed the shift in energy. Typically, quick to bark at visitors, he greeted my date with an uncharacteristic calm, a shared space of tranquility.

This journey of collecting practices and traditions that resonate with my spirit has been deeply satisfying. Each one strengthens the bridge between my inner peace and the harmony I strive to create in the world. Deer Park taught me that mindfulness is a gift we give not just to ourselves but to those we love and the communities we belong to.

## Shamanism: A Homecoming to Spirit

In my forties, I encountered shamanism for the first time. A course at UCLA—*Latin American Medicine, Shamanism, and Folk Illness*—broadened my worldview and felt, simultaneously, like a homecoming. I devoured the assigned reading: Michael Harner's *The Way of the Shaman*,[8] Barbara Meyerhoff's *The Peyote Hunt*,[9] and Mircea Eliade's seminal work on shamanic practices.[10] Each text opened a doorway into an ancient, yet strangely familiar, way of being.

In *The Peyote Hunt*, Meyerhoff describes the Huichol philosophy, in which *"there is no distinction between sacred and profane... The good life is the religious life. The good day's work is sacred... To be Huichol is to be sacred, and this applies to all behavior, objects, and ideas that make up the culture."* [11] That worldview resonated deeply with me. I just got it.

Ramón Medina Silva, a Huichol *Mara'akame* (shaman-priest), offers a striking contrast between his life in the Sierra Madre and that of city folk, a distinction that landed in my soul like a truth I already knew. He says, *"The Huichol lives freely. He lives there freely in the Sierra. Out in the wind, everywhere. We work as we wish, we go as we please. And the Spaniard? He cannot do this. The Huichol is different because he is free to come and go as he wishes..."* [12]

Those words hit me like a lightning bolt to the heart. *Yes!* That's it - that's what I'm talking about! They spoke of a way of being—of a sacredness and freedom in the everyday. I understood his words and felt understood.

A class visit to the Fowler Museum introduced me to a piece that captivated me: the *Nkisi Nkondi* power figure from the Yombe people of the Democratic Republic of Congo.[13] The figure, adorned with nails, cloth, and cowrie shells, symbolized petitions made by community members seeking healing or resolution. It immediately reminded me of the *peticiones* in my childhood church, where congregants openly shared their prayers for guidance and healing.

A pang of sadness struck me—how had I gone so long without connecting to my own Indigenous traditions? But soon, sadness gave way to gratitude. This knowledge had arrived exactly when I was ready for it. As though my ancestors had been waiting for me to rediscover them all along. At that moment, I felt surrounded by generations of my ancestors—50,000 years of wisdom and love. I was connected. I belonged.

Shamanic traditions exist worldwide, reflecting humanity's shared yearning for connection to the sacred. While the practices differ, their purposes remain universal: healing, guidance, and wholeness.[14] My DNA carries a mosaic of ancestral stories—from Indigenous Americas to Europe, Africa, and Sephardic Jewish roots. Across these diverse traditions, I've found recurring themes: reverence for nature, honoring ancestors, altered states for healing, and rituals as pathways to the divine. These shared practices remind me that the spirit world is accessible to all. Wisdom and healing transcend cultural boundaries, offering profound lessons for anyone open to receiving them. Connecting with spirit is both deeply personal and universally human.

For my first shamanic journey, I followed Michael Harner's instructions to find a spirit animal and receive power. I lay on my living room floor, wrapped in a blanket, with the steady rhythm of drum beats from a CD filling the room. Harner suggested beginning the journey at a natural location I'd visited before, so I pictured a cave with a waterfall in Eaton Canyon. I imagined myself standing there, waiting, but nothing seemed to happen. Then I imagined myself falling backward into darkness, my hair floating as though carried by a current. But I felt stuck, frustrated, worried that the twenty-minute drum recording would end before my journey even began.

Finally, it dawned on me that fear was holding me back. So, I asked Jesus to come with me and to hold my hand. And in that moment of surrender, my journey began. Suddenly, I was underwater, swimming effortlessly with my eyes wide open—something I've never been able to do in real life. Breaking through the surface, I was greeted by a clear blue sky, warm sunlight, and a massive cliff jutting into the ocean. The light was so brilliant I had to squint. High above, a bird soared—a dark silhouette against the brightness. I strained to see it more clearly, but it stayed distant.

As I sank back into the water, I was swept into a spinning vortex that held me together and broke me apart at once. At that moment, I felt her: my mom, long gone but undeniably present. Overwhelmed by grief and love, I called and reached out for her, like a lost child searching for a parent in a store. My body shook, my legs kicked, and my chest heaved. Eventually, I was expelled from the water and began to soar like the bird I had seen earlier. I flew over oceans and mountains, marveling at the beauty of the world unfurling beneath me. It was cinematic, dreamlike—light, free, and breathtaking (like the flight simulator ride *Soarin'* at Disneyland). The journey felt infinite, yet ended abruptly. I was pulled into a dark, starry expanse, as if crossing into another dimension— vast and mysterious. Here I thought, *My mom must be here,* and I wanted to connect to her. But, the steady rhythm of the drumbeats began to shift, signaling the end of the journey. Four slow, deliberate beats called me back, grounding me in the present.

## Journeying for Others

Over the years, I've encountered many spirit helpers, each with its own energy and lesson. During a workshop, a participant journeyed on my behalf and found a scorpion for me. At first, I was taken aback—scorpions had always seemed dangerous. In the context of spirit work, however, they symbolize resilience and fierce protection. It made perfect sense. I was navigating a difficult divorce, and the scorpion's energy embodied the strength I needed.

Another time, I journeyed for my friend, Maxine, and found a whale for her. Later, she told me she had vividly imagined herself riding a whale during the same drumming session. As she described it:

> *"I was in the middle of the ocean, when I realized I was supported from underneath by something vast—so vast that I couldn't see its edges. When I shifted to a bird's-eye view, I finally saw it was a whale. That perspective helped me recognize the immense support beneath me.*

> *I've always described my grief over my mother's loss as being like a ship without a port, adrift and without an anchor. But at this moment, I understood I am already supported—whether by land or by sea. I've also expressed the grief of losing my mother as losing my safety net. But the whale is so much larger and more secure than any safety net I could have imagined.*

*When I somatically experienced the whale's support, it became a part of me, something I could feel deeply in my body. It's not something I need to think about or conjure—it just is, I can feel it. It's my new reality. It's changed my experience in the world. I have a mama whale—the largest mammal on the planet. So subtle, yet so profound."*

These moments, when spirit helpers align their medicine with the lives of those they visit, remind me of the profound wisdom and synchronicity at play in this work.

## Shamanic Healing

At forty-three, I sought my first shamanic healing session. The shaman asked me to list every traumatic event I'd experienced and pay attention to my dreams. When I arrived, I declared confidently, "I'm here for the healing of my soul." She raised an eyebrow and asked, "How do you know your soul needs healing?"

I shared my story: a near-death experience at birth, multiple childhood traumas, and my first shamanic journey. She nodded. "Stay here," she said. "I'll do the journeying today."

I lay on her couch, an eye covering blocking out the world, as she guided me into meditation. She whistled and shook a rattle, a sound so familiar, so deeply Mexican, that tears welled up. In my mind, I saw a baby crawling back to center, as if reclaiming something lost.

She played a hand drum next, and I sank into a deep meditative state, the kind I'd felt before during a massage or the final pose of a yoga class, that in-between place where I'm here but not here, awake but asleep. I felt her brush my body with an eagle feather and blow a couple of strong breaths at the top of my head.

Afterward, I took notes as the shaman shared her observations. She told me that during childbirth, when I was teetering between this life and the next, a spirit animal helper appeared and told me to stay alive. I had a purpose to fulfill. She found another spirit animal helper hidden among dry brush.

She performed a clearing as well. A spirit, she said a relative, had been clinging to me, and she ushered them out. She told me to spend more time in nature; it was good medicine for me. She reminded me to be careful with what I know. "Not everyone appreciates or understands it." Just me, out here like a prophet shouting in the wilderness.

Finally, she said she'd brought back parts of my soul that had "checked out" during my trauma, including a part of me as a baby. "You don't need to do anything for them," she assured me. "In several months, you'll feel the difference, you'll feel whole."

Before the healing, my soul felt like a shattered bathroom mirror. I lived contorted, bending to see my reflection in a single shard large enough to brush my hair. For years, I walked through life like a porcelain plate with hairline cracks, fearing I might shatter with the slightest bump. When social interactions went wrong, my thoughts spiraled: *What did I do wrong? What's wrong with me?*

But four months later, the fog lifted. In the third year of my doctoral program, I felt whole for the first time. After the soul retrieval, the mirror of my soul was restored, clear and intact. Vulnerable, yes, but solid. I finally understood. There was nothing wrong with me.

While pursuing a PhD, I filed for divorce. A challenging experience that, according to research, is not uncommon among women in graduate programs.[15] Divorce can be a dark time. Have you seen the film *Beloved*, [16] based on Toni Morrison's book? [17] There's a scene in which thirty Black women sing and pray to a grieving mother to encourage her to come out of her house. I thought, *I need thirty women to sing and pray for me.* So, I grabbed my phone, scrolled through my contacts, and texted every spiritual woman I knew. Anyone who I believed would understand this *petición*: 'Going through a dark and difficult time, please pray for me.' Thank you, *Yesus*—I'm still here.

I celebrated my forty-fourth birthday with a big party. It was a celebration of two milestones, my birthday and filing for divorce. When someone asked, "Why now?" The best explanation I could offer was simple: *Because now I'm whole.* I knew leaving would hurt like a MF, but I also knew I could handle it. I was no longer fractured or bracing for a collapse. I was whole.

Trauma is pervasive in our world.[18] It splinters our souls and leaves us longing for wholeness. Shamanic practices remind us that healing is possible and that spirit helpers are always near, waiting to guide us. Our ancestors had access to healing in extended communities, now we wander almost a lifetime before we are whole again. Healing and wholeness are for everyone, and I want to ensure these ancient practices are accessible to all who seek them.

After gushing to someone about what I was learning about shamanism and how it was becoming my research interest, he asked, "Do you really want to be known as the 'shaman lady'?" My answer: *Yes! Yes, I do.*

### *La Santera* Sara

I met Sara in the summer of 2011 when a close friend referred me to her as I was seeking guidance. Until then, I had never consulted readers. It just didn't seem necessary. But that year, I had a lot of questions. My relationships felt shaky—close friends seemed like frenemies, though I felt guilty for even thinking it. My marriage was unraveling, and I was desperate for wisdom, clarity, or at least some reassurance.

Sara charged $35 per session, which lasted over an hour. I saw her every six months until she passed away in the summer of 2021. She was from Veracruz, Mexico, and her readings were in Spanish. She let me take notes during our sessions, and I've kept all of them in a notebook. When I need reassurance, I revisit those pages, they read like affirmations.

In the first session, without me saying a word, Sara told me my so-called friends weren't my friends. She described them in detail, like one was dark-skinned and married, the other single and light-skinned. My jaw dropped. Her insight validated my suspicions and gave me clarity.

It wasn't so much that Sara predicted my future, she read my mind, my heart, like my mom used to. I always left Sara's sessions feeling seen and understood. I often thanked her for her guidance, calling her the wise grandmother I never had. I meant it as a compliment, but she'd retort, *"¿Abuela? ¿Abuela, por qué?"* It wasn't about age, it was about her deep insight and the way she gave it to me straight. Her words felt like a salve for my soul. She'd say, *"Se te abrió los ojos—hay cosas que no te dabas cuenta."*

Sara advised me to mix honey, holy water, *loción Heno de Pravia*, and cinnamon into a perfume bottle and apply it to my body. She believed in the influence of *Ochún*, a Yoruba *Orisha* connected to love, beauty, and wealth.[19] *"La miel te trae dinero y amor"* (*Honey brings you money and love*), she explained.

Her readings were a thread of comfort and encouragement through my hardest times. She called out my tendencies to overgive and overtrust: *"Ni para atrás, ni para agarrar impulso,"* she'd warn. *"No confíes tanto. Limpia tu aura. Toma decisiones bien pensadas."*

In the section on ancient wisdom for this chapter, I've included bits of wisdom to return to when the world feels heavy. Whether you're navigating uncertainty or just need a reminder of your own strength, maybe these words will resonate. If you're missing your own *abuelita*, perhaps you'll find a bit of her there.

## Transcendental Meditation (TM)

During my doctorate at UCLA, I asked a psychology professor whose work I admired one of my burning clinical questions: "What intervention have you found to be the most effective?" His answer caught me off guard.

"Transcendental Meditation," he said, without hesitation.

He explained that while TM didn't solve all his problems, it gave him the clarity to navigate life's challenges with ease. I didn't know much about TM at the time, and his response lingered in the back of my mind for years.

That memory resurfaced when I met Lynn Kaplan, Regional Director of the David Lynch Foundation (DLF) for Consciousness-Based Education/Los Angeles at a conference. DLF was teaching TM to middle school students, and I had been hired by the school district to evaluate TM's impact on students' academic performance and mental health. Lynn invited me to learn TM myself, saying, "You'll understand it best by experiencing it."

I attended a group orientation to TM, during which Lynn explained TM's simplicity. It is a practice that unlocks a profound state of deep rest, deeper than sleep. Research shows, they explained, that TM reduces stress and improves mental clarity. As I heard more about TM, I recognized I had touched on this kind of rest before through the corpse pose in yoga, hypnotherapy, acupuncture, reiki, and shamanic journeys. TM offered a direct and accessible way to reach that transcendental, trance-like state.

Curious and hopeful, I committed to the four-day training, which included both personal instruction and group classes. Initially, TM felt unfamiliar, even strange, but during one of the group discussions, my TM teacher explained the practice in a way that suddenly clicked. The way TM gently cleared the past trauma my mind and body had been holding onto, the way it eased the weight of daily stress. TM made sense.

The day I learned my personal mantra (a sound-word-vibration that doesn't have a meaning), I was asked to bring two whole sweet fruits, six fresh flowers, and a white cloth. I chose tangerines and fresh flowers from Trader Joe's and for the white cloth, I used a vintage embroidered handkerchief I had bought at a rummage sale in the Bay Area. These items were going to be gifts for a traditional ceremony of gratitude to show respect to the ancient teachers before teaching and learning their knowledge.

One day that week, I sat in a quiet room at the DLF office, repeating my mantra effortlessly, as easily as thinking a thought. My body, tender with surrender, grew heavy. My head bowed, shoulders sank, and I slouched deep into gravity, craving to lie down. My mind floated like a helium balloon, and vivid, dream-like images played in my head as I remained awake. Not every session is remarkable, but TM doesn't need to be dazzling to work. The power lies in showing up consistently. TM helps me navigate life with calm and clarity, like a compass pointing me back to center. My favorite advice from Lynn Kaplan, which she got from her teacher is simple: "Just meditate and be natural."

The science is clear: TM offers numerous health and mental health benefits:

- Blood pressure drops. [20]
- Prolactin, the hormone of calm, increases. [21]
- Brain waves become coherent, a sign of mental functioning. [22]
- Anxiety softens. [23]
- Stress unravels. [24]
- Sleep improves. [25]
- Cells are happily repaired. [26]

When my TM teacher mentioned its anti-aging benefits, I laughed, "Don't bury the lede!" A girl has got to have her vanity. Still, like a toddler resisting a much-needed nap, I don't always find it easy to surrender to meditation. Whereas, some sessions hold me like velvet restful and delicious as chocolate cake. Group meditations amplify the energy and I feel swept deep.

In my professional work and research, I've seen TM help students and parents feel better. Middle school students who practiced TM show measurable improvements in mental health and academic performance. Parents reported feeling calmer and more connected with their families. Most parents developed hope—the kind that comes from believing they can shape a better future.

When my daughter struggled with anxiety, depression, and suicidal thoughts in high school, even though she had been benefitting from therapy and medication for years, I introduced her to Lynn who taught her TM. Around the same time, I signed her up for a community theater program, and she poured her heart into writing and performing. Each brought her closer to herself, making life a little more bearable, a little more worth living.

Paolina describes her first TM initiation vividly. She recalls the ceremony, being given her mantra, then sitting on the cream-colored couch and slipping into a deep meditative state almost immediately. She lay down and had an image of a futuristic living room with an aquarium and a woman in a metal fishtail skeleton. That image planted the seed for a story she later developed into a screenplay.

Her experience with TM mirrored what David Lynch described in his book *Catching the Big Fish*.[27] TM allowed her to access the depths of her mind, where the "big fish" live—creative, profound, and impactful ideas waiting to be caught.

TM reminds me of the profound healing we're capable of when we allow ourselves to rest and reset. The peace cultivated within naturally radiates outward to those we love.

### Listening to the Still Small Voice

"And after the earthquake a fire; but the Lord was not in the fire: and after the fire a still small voice..."
—1 Kings 19:12 [28]

I've always listened for the still small voice inside me—the one that feels as if it comes from my soul, from God, or perhaps from my ancestors. It's not loud or urgent like the world around me. Instead, it's calm, steady, and insistent, and often leads me down paths that others might fear to tread. I understand the hesitation of venturing into the unknown, but I've followed this voice for so long that I trust it completely.

When the voice speaks, I listen. When it told me to leave my full-time job and go back to school, even though I was responsible for a mortgage and a family, I didn't question it. I didn't know how it would work out, but I knew it was a path I was meant to take.

In 2009, at the age of forty, I was accepted into the PhD program at UCLA. The decision to go back to school was anything but simple. Yet, everything in my life seemed to align for this purpose. A mentor who believed in me wrote a strong letter of recommendation, and I was driven by burning research questions about the families and communities I worked with, questions that demanded rigorous studies to answer.

The final deadline to submit my intent to register was April 15, and on that morning, I sat at my desk, staring at my computer screen. My employer had already denied my request for a part-time leave to balance work and school. I felt unsure of what to do. I asked myself, *Does this mean I don't go? Or does this mean I trust God, my Creator, the Universe to figure out how I'm going to do this?* In that moment of uncertainty, the still small voice inside me whispered, *Vámonos. We're going.* The voice felt enthusiastic and certain, cutting through my doubt and fear. My soul seemed to leap out of my body, shouting, *Heck yes, I'm going!* With excitement and shaky hands, I clicked "submit" and watched as the confirmation screen appeared. A surge of joy and hope filled me, even though I had no idea how it would all work out.

Not even two hours later, my phone rang. It was a department leader calling to tell me my part-time leave had been approved after all. I burst into tears and laughter. Overwhelmed with gratitude, I whispered, "Thank you, *Yesus!*"

At that moment, I felt the wisdom of Rev. Dr. Martin Luther King, Jr. come alive: "You don't have to see the whole staircase, just take the first step."[29] Taking that leap of faith without a visible net beneath me marked the beginning of a journey that stretched me, challenged me, and ultimately transformed my life. It wasn't easy, but it was worth every step.

Looking back, I see how often the still small voice has guided me in moments of doubt or fear. It doesn't promise a smooth path or even guarantee success, but every time I've listened, it has led me toward something greater than I could have imagined. Whether it's the voice of God, my ancestors, or my own soul, it continues to light the way, one step at a time.

This moment in 2009 was just one of many reminders that faith is about trusting the process. I'm filled with gratitude for the courage to listen and for the unseen forces that aligned to carry me forward. Because of that leap of faith, I not only pursued my PhD but also deepened my connection to the still small voice. A voice that I trust with my whole life.

## Conclusion

Resilience is taking personal strengths and community resources to overcome adversities, whether they are inevitable natural disasters or cruelly human-made.[30]

Resilience is the alchemy of turning hardship into growth.

My connection to the divine has always been my anchor, reminding me that even in chaos and crises, I am never alone. And so, the still small voice became less of a guide and more of a tether, binding me to a version of myself that I could trust, even if I didn't entirely understand her. She's the one who stands at the crossroads, unflinching, and chooses the storm over the silence. She's the one who whispers back when God, or my ancestors, or some echo of myself, asks, *"Do you trust me?"* The answer is always: *"I don't know the details, but I'm coming anyway."*

My confidence is rooted in faith, life experiences, and the wisdom of voices both divine and earthly. It's not unshakeable, it wavers, bends, and cracks. But it's built on a life spent following that still small voice, even when the world around me is loud with doubt. Confidence is not the absence of fear; it's the choice to step forward, even when fear walks beside you.

Looking back, I see how deeply my faith, confidence, and resilience are connected. Each challenge, every storm and every accomplishment has taught me to trust that voice within, the one that has never led me astray. And when the winds die down and I stand on the other side of a storm, marked by the experience, I carry those words my mother taught me: *Thank you, Yesus.* Because I know I didn't do it alone.

# Science and Research

## Exploring the Connection Between Spirituality and Well-Being

This section examines how spirituality—a deeply personal yet universal experience—profoundly impacts mental, emotional, and physical health. Through the lens of research, we uncover its transformative potential in fostering resilience, meaning, and connection.

## What Is Spirituality?

Spirituality connects us to something greater than ourselves, offering meaning, purpose, and a moral compass.[1] It emphasizes personal growth, interconnectedness, and practices that deepen our connection to ourselves, others, and the universe.[2] Woven into the fabric of human culture, spirituality helps us navigate life's complexities with resilience and clarity.[3]

## The Role of Spirituality in Well-Being

Research demonstrates spirituality's critical role in enhancing mental, emotional, and physical health. For many, it serves as a cornerstone of existence:

- 53% of Americans consider religion a very important aspect of their lives.[4]
- A Pew Research Center survey found that 36% of Americans say religion provides "a great deal" of meaning in their lives.[5]
- A study published in the *American Journal of Public Health* notes that Christian spirituality among people of color tends to be deeply rooted in relationships and the community, serving as a vital source of support.[6]

## Scientific Insights on Spirituality and Health:

- Stress Reduction: Practices like mindfulness, prayer, and meditation lower stress and anxiety.[7]
- Mental Health Benefits: Spirituality reduces depression and fosters emotional balance.[8]
- Physical Health Improvements: Better immune function and cardiovascular health are associated with spiritual practices.[9]
- Resilience: Spirituality provides meaning and purpose, enabling people to navigate adversity with hope and strength.[10]

Studies consistently link spirituality to enhanced life satisfaction, emotional stability, and coping skills, affirming its role as a powerful resource for well-being.

## Tapping into Spiritual Strengths

Sharing our spiritual stories isn't just reflection—it's empowerment. Narratives about resilience and strength reshape how we view ourselves and our world, inspiring confidence, resourcefulness, and belonging.[11]

## Reflective Prompts:

- Who in your life gives you strength and energy to overcome obstacles?
- Do you have a belief system that brings meaning and purpose to your life?
- What shared beliefs connect you with others, offering comfort and belonging?
- Where do you find hope and inspiration during challenges?

Answering these questions reveals the spiritual resources sustaining you, enriching your perspective, and strengthening your resilience.

## The Hidden Science of Shamanic Healing

Shamanic healing might sound like something straight out of an ancient myth, but its principles resonate in surprising ways with modern science. At its core, shamanic healing is an intricate dance between the mind, body, spirit, and heart—an integrative approach that seeks to heal the whole person.

A study by Vuckovic and her team in 2010, explored this intersection of ancient wisdom and contemporary science, revealing the profound ways shamanic healing transforms physical, emotional, and spiritual well-being.[12]

## The Core Ideas: How Shamanic Healing Works

Shamanic healing isn't a single remedy or technique; it's a framework with multiple moving parts, each designed to restore balance.

- **Soul Retrieval:** Imagine losing fragments of yourself in moments of trauma. This practice aims to recover those pieces, helping individuals feel whole again.
- **Energy Clearing:** Think of it as decluttering your emotional space—removing harmful energies that can weigh you down or cause distress.
- **Guided Visualization:** Through meditative rituals, participants embark on a journey to self-awareness, connecting past experiences to present healing.

- **Spiritual Connection:** At its heart, shamanic healing strengthens bonds—whether with nature, inner selves, or spirit guides. These connections often become pivotal to recovery.

## The Findings: What Happens When Ancient Wisdom Meets Modern Minds

The study didn't just look at the rituals; it measured their effects on real people with real problems. The results? Strikingly transformative.

- **Emotional and Behavioral Growth:** Participants reported breakthroughs—greater clarity about their life's purpose, improved relationships, and an ability to face challenges with renewed confidence.
- **Physical and Emotional Benefits:** From reduced pain to better sleep and a sense of heightened energy, the healing effects weren't just "in their heads"—they rippled through their entire being.
- **Holistic Integration:** The healing didn't stop when the sessions ended. Participants carried the lessons into their daily lives, incorporating mindfulness and lifestyle changes that reinforced their sense of empowerment.

## The Big Picture: Why Shamanic Healing Matters

Here's the most compelling part: shamanic healing isn't a passive experience. It invites individuals to participate actively in their own recovery, taking ownership of their well-being.

This approach challenges the conventional, "fix-me" model of health care. Instead, it asks: How can we work with the patient—not just on their symptoms, but on their whole self? The answers lie in the spiritual practices, rituals, and personal journeys that form the bedrock of shamanic healing.

## Takeaway: Bridging the Ancient and the Modern

Shamanic healing reminds us of something profound: well-being is not just about treating what's broken but nurturing what makes us whole. It's a partnership— between ancient traditions and modern science, between practitioners and participants, and between the tangible and the transcendent.

The Vuckovic study offers more than insights into shamanic healing; it challenges us to rethink how we define health, healing, and the connection between them. Sometimes, the oldest tools can open the newest doors.

## The Connection Between Spirituality and Well-Being: Key Studies and Findings

| Study | Who Was Studied | What They Found |
|---|---|---|
| Ohajunwa et al., 2021 [13] | 52 participants from village clusters in South Africa | Indigenous African spirituality connects identity, community, and nature. Historical disruptions under-mined this balance, but adaptation restored resilience. |
| **Why It Matters** | **Key Takeaway** | |
| Highlights the need to honor Indigenous perspectives in healthcare for trust and sustainable outcomes. | Spirituality integrates social, spiritual, and environmental health, enhancing community resilience. | |

| Study | Who Was Studied | What They Found |
|---|---|---|
| Nonis et al., 2024 [14] | 129 U.S. business students | Both open-minded thinking and spirituality positively influence well-being, with spirituality having a stronger impact on personal growth and resilience. |
| **Why It Matters** | **Key Takeaway** | |
| Demonstrates spirituality's critical role in reducing stress and improving autonomy and personal development. | Incorporating spirituality enhances well-being in educational and professional contexts. | |

| Study | Who Was Studied | What They Found |
|---|---|---|
| Oxhandler et al., 2021 [15] | 989 U.S. adults receiving mental health care | Religion and spirituality (RS) are viewed as supportive, particularly for coping, but less connected to mental illness struggles. |
| **Why It Matters** | **Key Takeaway** | |
| Suggests therapists should integrate RS into care to improve outcomes and strengthen the therapeutic alliance. | RS supports mental health, offering coping tools and deeper therapeutic connections. | |

# Ancestor Wisdom

This is an invitation—not simply to learn, but to descend into the rich, fertile ground of ancestral wisdom. Here, the teachings of those who came before us rise like an old and familiar song, reminding us that the body, the soul, the heart, and the spirit are not separate, but inextricably linked.

## The Dance of Body and Soul

Our ancestors understood what modern minds often forget: the body and soul are lovers, engaged in a sacred dance. They move together, each step leading and following the other.

As Maimonides, a medieval Jewish philosopher, scholar, and physician, teaches, "The health of the soul cannot be attained without the health of the body."[1] This is no ordinary health; it is wholeness. It is a harmony that sings when we honor both the vessel and the spirit it carries.

Consider the Zapotec wisdom: "In the heart resides your spirit; take care of it, for it is the well of your life."[2] These words speak not only to the physical heart but to the deep well of resilience and vitality within each of us. When we tend to this well, we honor the ancestors who poured their strength and stories into it.

## The Spirit's Quiet Power

And what of the spirit, that part of us that walks when the body falters? It is the ember that refuses to be extinguished, the voice that whispers, *You can go on.* The Maya tell us, "*El espíritu camina donde el cuerpo no puede.*"[3] It reminds us that when we feel broken, it is the spirit that lifts us, carrying us forward through pain, exhaustion, and despair.

Invitation to reflect: How often have you relied on that ember? How has it guided you, warmed you, refused to let you be undone?

## Stories as Medicine

Ancestral wisdom also tells us that stories are medicine. They carry the power to wound and to heal, to break and to mend. As Chimamanda Ngozi Adichie reminds us, "Stories can break the dignity of a people. But stories can also repair that broken dignity."[4]

Our ancestors wove their truths into stories, not just for their own healing but as a gift to the generations yet to come. They knew that stories, like seeds, take root in hearts and minds, growing into forests of understanding and resilience.

Ask yourself: What story has been a balm for your soul? What story have you carried as a gift to others?

## Living the Wisdom

To live with ancestral wisdom is to walk a path of balance—to nourish the body, to honor the spirit, and to gather stories as treasures. This week, let the wisdom of those who came before you guide your steps.

- **Care for your body and soul**: Perhaps with a walk under the open sky or a moment of stillness to breathe deeply.

- **Honor your spirit**: Recall a time when it carried you through a storm, and thank it for its quiet strength.
- **Share a story**: Speak or write it, letting its ripples move outward, a bridge to another's heart.

In these acts, you become the storyteller, the healer, the bearer of light. You keep the ancestors' lessons alive, weaving their threads into the fabric of your own life.

## Wisdom from *La Santera* Sara

For over a decade, *La Santera* Sara's readings were like straight talk from the *abuela* I never knew. I offer them here as affirmations, drawn from my notes of her readings, to encourage you if they resonate with your spirit. My hope is they inspire you to trust your path, embrace your power, and nurture your well-being.

## 2012: Foundations of Self-Love

- *"Piensa en ti. Vive para ti. Lo que es para ti, nadie te lo quita. Quererte tú principalmente."*
(Think of yourself. Live for yourself. What is meant for you, no one can take away. Love yourself first.)
A call to prioritize yourself and trust that life will bring what is yours in due time.
- *"Tú eres espiritual. El miedo nos pone en situaciones difíciles. Ve lo que tú vales. Eres espiritual con muchos valores."*
(You are spiritual. Fear puts us in difficult situations. See your own worth. You are spiritual with strong values.)
A reminder to confront fear and recognize the deep reservoir of strength within.

## 2013: Hope and Protection

- *"Renacimiento, mucha suerte, vienen cosas buenas."*
(Rebirth, lots of luck, and good things are coming.)
Hope that even after hardship, renewal and blessings await.
- *"No comentes mucho las cosas traen envidias."*
(Don't talk too much about things—they bring envy.)
A gentle nudge to guard your plans and protect your energy.

## 2014: Trusting Your Journey

- *"Lo que es para ti, nadie te lo quita."*
(What is meant for you, no one can take away.)
A comforting reminder that destiny is patient and persistent.
- *"Usa tu razonamiento, eres mujer de razón."*
(Use your reasoning—you are a woman of reason.)
A reflection on trusting your intellect and making decisions with clarity.
- *"Estás pisando un éxito. Tú vas a salir adelante, tienes que tener paciencia."*
(You are stepping into success. You will move forward—you just need patience.)
A reminder to remain steadfast and grounded as success unfolds.

## 2015: Staying True to Yourself

- *"No vendo dignidad o tranquilidad. Tú sabes quién eres."*
(I don't sell dignity or peace of mind. You know who you are.)

An affirmation of self-worth and staying true to one's values.

• *"La fe mueve montañas."*
(Faith moves mountains.)
A timeless message about the transformative power of unwavering belief.

• *"Tu éxito está asegurado. No lo dejes atrás por ser necia."*
(Your success is guaranteed. Don't let it slip away by being stubborn.)
Motivation to trust in your path and avoid self-sabotage.

## 2016: Creating Your Own Stability

• *"Todo está en tus manos. Éxito en bienestar, estabilidad, y salud."*
(Everything is in your hands. Success in well-being, stability, and health.)
A reassurance that you hold the keys to creating a balanced, fulfilling life.

• *"Tener más confianza en ti misma. Todo va a cambiar para bien."*
(Have more confidence in yourself. Everything is going to change for the better.)
Encouragement to trust your growth and embrace positive transformation.

• *"Tus espíritus y protectores te cuidan mucho. Buenos pensamientos - te pasan buenas cosas."*
(Your spirits and protectors take good care of you. Good thoughts lead to good outcomes.)
A gentle reminder of unseen guidance and the power of optimism.

## 2017: Beauty in the Present and Future

- *"Tienes una vida tan bonita, en tu vida actual y futuro. No pierdas esperanza y fe."*

(You have such a beautiful life, in your present and your future. Don't lose hope or faith.)

A reflection on cherishing the beauty in your life and holding onto optimism.

- *"Todo lo bueno te regresa en bueno. Hacer las cosas bien por conveniencia tuya. La gente paga aquí. Aquí se pagan las cosas."*

(All good things come back to you in good ways. Do things well for your own benefit. People pay here. Here, everything is repaid.)

A reminder of karma and the balance of actions.

## 2018: Spiritual Cleansing and Protection

- *"Sigue limpiando para proteger tu casa."*

(Keep spiritually cleansing to protect your home.)

Practical advice for spiritual and energetic maintenance.

- *"Tienes protecciones."*

(You have protections.)

Reassurance of the unseen forces keeping you safe.

## 2019: Love and Triumph

- *"Tu mamá fue la única que te entendió. Eres la niña de sus ojos."*

(Your mom was the only one who truly understood you. You were the apple of her eye.)

A reminder of unconditional love and being fully seen by those who care for us.

- *"Siempre estás en la mente que vas a triunfar."*

(You always have the mindset that you will succeed.)
A testament to the power of cultivating a success-oriented mindset.

## 2020: Joy and Renewal

- *"Estás disfrutando; te tocó el momento de disfrutar."*

(You are enjoying yourself; it is your time to enjoy.)
Encouragement to savor moments of joy and celebration.

- *"Límpiate con flores blancas, baños con flores blancas."*

(Cleanse yourself with white flowers, take baths with white flowers.)
A ritual for renewal, clarity, and self-care.

These affirmations are gifts—pearls of wisdom polished by time and shared in the hope that they will find their way into your life, offering guidance and comfort as you step into your own sacred story.

# Tools

The tools in this section are here to invite you into a deeper connection with yourself, your spirituality, and the unique purpose that lights your path. They're designed to help you sit with and navigate life's complexities, untangle the energetic knots that hold you back, and lean into the universe's abundant support. Whether through reflective practices, rituals, or affirmations, use these tools to strengthen your inner resilience, clarify your intentions, and move forward in alignment with your truest self. Think of them as gentle companions, guiding and inspiring your journey toward growth and transformation.

**Tool #1: Reflective Questions About Spirituality**
This tool offers space for reflection, intentional journaling, or deep conversation, guiding you to uncover insights that ground and illuminate your path. Adapted from the Spiritual Assessment Protocol,[1] these prompts expand toward personal spiritual exploration and growth.

**Reflection Questions**

### 1. Belief System
• What beliefs or principles give your life meaning and purpose?
• How do these beliefs influence your everyday decisions and long-term goals?

## 2. Spiritual Practice
• Is there a spiritual practice or ritual that feels renewing or comforting for you?
• How does this practice bring peace or create a sense of grounding in your life?

## 3. Shared Beliefs
• What shared values or beliefs bring you comfort and a sense of belonging with others?
• Can you recall moments when these beliefs strengthened a relationship or created a sense of community?

## 4. Spiritual Force
• Have you ever felt the presence of a spiritual force that comforted or strengthened you?
• How would you describe this force, and when has it been most present in your life?

## 5. Supportive Relationships
• Are there people in your life who inspire or energize you to overcome challenges?
• How have these relationships reinforced your sense of purpose and connection?

## 6. Spiritual Resources
• What practices, rituals, or beliefs help you stay resilient during tough times?
• How have these resources empowered you to keep moving forward?

## 7. Spiritual Mentors
• Has a mentor or guide ever played a significant role in your spiritual journey?

- What lessons or insights did they share, and how do they continue to shape your life today?

## Why Reflect?

Taking the time to explore your spirituality can: [2]

- Build resilience during life's toughest moments.
- Deepen your connections—with yourself, others, and something greater.
- Illuminate your sense of purpose and bring clarity to your path.

When engaging with these reflections you won't necessarily find perfect answers, but rather you'll be giving yourself the space to listen, feel, and discover. You might uncover insights that bring balance, energy, and a renewed sense of direction as you move toward a life rooted in alignment with your deeper self and values.

Take your time. There's no roadmap, no perfect way to do this. Let curiosity and self-compassion guide you as you explore your spirituality and uncover the wisdom it holds for you.

## Tool #2: *Limpias* and Clearing Your Energy with a *Barrida de Limón* (Adapted from Trotter & Chavira's *Curanderismo*)[3]

Our energy—linked to our body, mind, spirit, and heart—is our precious lifeblood. It carries us forward through the rivers of life, guiding us to our purpose. Yet, like a stream cluttered with fallen branches and stones, our energy can become blocked or weighed down. To walk the road with clarity, it helps to clear these obstructions.

The *limpia*, an ancient practice of energy clearing, is a gift passed down through countless generations, rooted in the knowledge that balance and vitality are our birthrights. The *barrida de limón* is a sweeping cleanse with a simple yet potent object (like a lemon, an egg, or sacred herbs like rosemary, basil, or rue) during which negative energy is transferred from the body to an object. These rituals address physical discomfort (headaches, tension), emotional challenges (stress, sadness, or feeling "stuck"), and spiritual blockages.

As one *curandero* put it:*"Some things cannot be explained; they must be experienced."*[4]

## How to Perform a *Barrida de Limón*
If this practice resonates with you, approach it with a heart open wide and set your intention clearly and firmly—cast your prayer into the wind:

### 1. Prepare the Object
• If using a lemon, wash it as though you are washing away the world's dust—thoroughly and with care, using soap or alcohol.
• If using herbs, pause. Speak softly to the plant, asking permission to use its branches. Offer gratitude for its gift, as this exchange is sacred.

### 2. Remove Accessories
• Free your body of rings, watches, or jewelry to allow for a clear, unbroken connection.

### 3. Begin the Ritual
• Stand tall, like the tree of life, or lie down, yielding to the earth's embrace.

• Sweep the lemon or herbs over your body, beginning at your crown—the seat of divine connection—and moving gently down to your feet, where you ground with the earth.
• Cover the entire body, including the front, back, and sides. Pay extra attention to areas where you feel pain or tension.

## 4. Focus Your Mind
• Whisper your intention, let it rise like smoke from a sacred fire:
• Reflect in silence.
• Pray, if prayer is your way.
• Affirm: *"I release what no longer serves me. I welcome peace and vitality."*

## 5. Observe and Reflect
• Stay attuned to sensations and feelings as you move through the ritual. Are there shifts, a softening, a release? Notice any shifts in your energy or mood.

## 6. Repeat and Dispose
• Commit to this practice for three days, honoring its rhythm. Since the lemon absorbs negative energy, it's recommended to use a fresh one each day for the full three-day period.
• When complete, return the lemon or herbs to the earth—buried, surrendered, or burned—far from your home, as though releasing a burden to the wild winds.

## Reflect on Your Experience
After your ritual, take pen to paper and let your spirit speak:

• What emotions, memories, or insights arose during the barrida?
• Did you feel a sense of lightness, clarity, or renewal?
• How did this experience deepen your connection to your cultural roots or spiritual practices?

## Personal Accounts of *Barrida de Limón*

In the whispers of memory and tradition, our bodies carry a way of knowing. I have been sharing the practice of *barridas de limón*—the ancestral ritual of cleansing with a lemon—with graduate students and workshop participants seeking to reconnect with the health practices of those who walked before us. I ask them to approach the ritual as a behavioral scientist might: curious, open-minded, and observant, recording what emerges in the body, the spirit, the heart, and the mind.

What follows are their accounts, the threshold where ancient wisdom and modern experience meet. Each has their own experience and yet all speak to the timeless power of a simple act of healing.

• Reconnecting With Ancestral Wisdom
"As the lemon traced my body, I saw my ancestors in my mind's eye. By the third day, I felt them walking with me, their strength weaving into my own."
• Releasing Heavy Energy
"I had carried a deep sadness for months. With each sweep of the lemon, I imagined the weight lifting.
On the final day, I wept, but it was a cleansing rain, not a storm."

- Finding Comfort in Tradition

"This practice brought me back to my grandmother's kitchen, where the scent of rue and basil mingled with her prayers. It soothed a part of me I hadn't realized needed soothing."

- The Power of Belief

"At first, I doubted. But I leaned in, and by the end, I couldn't deny the shift. My heart felt unburdened, as though the ritual itself had whispered: 'You are free.'"

## A Story of Renewal

*Don* José, a weathered mechanic with hands marked by decades of labor, sank into despair after gallbladder surgery. Convinced his vitality had left him, his wife called for a *curandero*. Over three days, the healer performed *barridas*, sweeping away the shadow that clung to *Don* José's spirit. When asked what the healer had given him (that the doctor had not), *Don* José answered: "*Animo!*" (courage and spirit).[5]

## The Heart of *Limpias*

Whether through the *barrida de limón* or another sacred practice that has meaning for you, the purpose remains the same: to shed what no longer serves, to restore the flow of your energy, and to reconnect you with your spirit's strength and clarity.

Take this moment to reclaim your vitality, explore and embrace the energy-clearing rituals that resonate with you. Your body, mind, spirit, and heart will thank you. As the winds of change sweep through your life, may you remember: *You carry the power to renew yourself. Always.*

# Chapter 3
## The *Tonalli* of Love

"As water reflects the face, so one's life reflects the heart."
—Jewish Proverb

## Introduction

Love is a trip and a gift, isn't it? In love relationships of all kinds, I've experienced as much healing and growth as I have joy and connection. I'm relieved that all my love relationships whisper a confirmation that we don't have to do life alone.

Heartbreak may leave a mark, but it has taught me wisdom, not bitterness. No way will I trade love for cynicism. Risking heartbreak is the price of admission. Thankfully, joyfully, love is worth it. No guarantees, but still, I choose to leap, because wherever we find it, love is a gift.

In *Mexica* philosophy, *tonalli* represents the life force that flows from the heart, connecting us to the universe and the call of our true purpose. It is our inner spark—the energy that makes you, you. When balanced, life feels aligned. When the sacred current is disrupted, everything falls out of sync, our energy wanes, relationships fray, even our body's health begins to show signs of the imbalance. Tending to our *tonalli* is part of staying whole.[1]

## Lessons in Love From My Mom

My mom was my first love, the one who showed me what it means to love and be loved in return. She had a magic about her. She was the kind of woman who could light up a room with her humor and radiance. Loving her wasn't always easy, but even when complicated, it was still the most beautiful thing I remember.

Her humor was sharp, her wit quick. We shared playful banter that made me feel seen. She called me *cucaracha* because I'd hole up in my room after school, studying and watching TV, and only coming out at night for snacks. She nicknamed me *la antena* because, even as a preschooler, I noticed everything (*captabas todo*). My mom saw me completely, quirks and all, and I laughed because she was right.

In high school, I started calling her *mujer* instead of Mom, a playful nickname my friends and I used for each other. "Hey, woman!" She didn't mind or feel disrespected; she accepted it proudly. "*Si soy mujer, y soy orgullosa de lo que significa ser mujer*," she'd say. Sometimes I called her *bruja* because she seemed to know everything about me—what I was thinking, where I'd been. She loved that too. "*Si, soy bruja.*"

That irreverence we shared made her feel more human, more accessible. We spoke to her with the informal *tú*, never the formal *usted* my peers used with their parents. That little *tú* held so much. It meant intimacy, trust, a seat in her inner circle.

### Repeating Her Patterns
Her humor buoyed us both, a balm for the undercurrent of depression I lived with for much of my life. It made me irritable, sleeping too much, and moving through the world tired, my face neutral and unreadable. People like her, funny, smart, and endlessly fun, were my doses of relief, laughter becoming my endorphin-laced escape. But my mom's charisma ruined me for relationships. She was a tough act to follow. In seeking people like her, I repeatedly found my undoing. Her shadow side turned

love into a dance, part connection, part psychological warfare. I started to believe this is just how love was.

Her dramatic displays left little room for my emotions, teaching me early that feelings could be burdensome. I led with my head, dismissing my heart's wisdom as an obstacle to my goals. Drawn to people like my mom (funny, magnetic, emotionally expressive, but often overwhelming), I thought those relationships balanced my stoicism. Healing showed me that ignoring my emotions was self-betrayal. Now, I'm slowly learning and practicing, through thousands of trial and errors, to honor my feelings and strive for balance between heart and mind.

At home, my mom wore the jeans in the family. She emasculated my dad, called the shots, and we all sought her permission for everything. She made the mess in the kitchen; he washed the dishes every night. He'd grumble about her impulsiveness but always went along.

I carried that dynamic into my romantic relationships. I felt like I had to be in charge, and I didn't know how to stop. If I let my partner steer the boat, we'd crash, literally, into the pier, knocking over the sea lions (true story). I convinced myself that being in control was a manifestation of my being a feminist and strong. It gave me a false sense of security. It didn't shield me at all, it left me drained. Even my mom admitted later in life that being in charge all the time was exhausting.

Just like it's hard to defer to a boss you don't trust or respect, it's hard to be a good follower in the metaphorical dance of love when you don't trust or respect the leader.

My salsa instructor once told us, "Even if you have more skills, if you're the follower, you dance his dance. Let him lead." It makes sense: lead, follow, or learn to switch gracefully, because the magic is in the balance and not wrestling for control or stepping on your partner's toes.

After years of leading the dance, I decided to try following. To trust, to respect, to let go. It took devouring forty books on relationships, to truly understand what it meant to be a follower in the dance. I shifted from barking demands to using feeling statements. Before my reading marathon, the scared little girl in me would stomp around declaring, "A woman needs a man like a fish needs a bicycle," and if someone didn't like it, "they could leave." It wasn't strength; it was quasi-power, pseudo-protection.

One former partner once asked, "Why are you such a hard ass?"

"Why are you so sensitive?!" I'd fire back.

Over time, I learned to express my desires differently. Instead of demanding, "You need to drive me to the party," I tried, "It would make me happy if you picked me up for the party." (I later realized the party was just a few blocks from his house, but still.) Not telling a man what to do felt surprisingly liberating. And if he cared about my feelings, it worked. If he didn't, well, at least I knew where I stood.

**Lucky in Love**
I feel lucky to have been in love a few times. On the surface, my type is tall and attractive. I asked *La Santera* Sara why I kept attracting the same type. She told me,

"*Porque lo tienes en tu pensamiento. Somos causa y efecto. Se tiene que exteriorizar.*" Ah, my thoughts become my experiences.

I had my first official boyfriend at twenty-three, which felt like a late start by most standards. Post-divorce, I found myself dating in earnest in my mid-forties, trying every app and meeting all kinds of men - the socially anxious, commitment-phobic, asexual, overly sexual, shy, and arrogant. It was a fun learning experience—and exhausting.

I hung out at cafés and rooftop bars, practicing the art of flirting with my eyes. I went on coffee date after coffee date, testing my skills at "communicating with men." Then one day, I thought to myself, *What's a girl gotta do to get some action?* I swear the Universe listens to my thoughts and conspires on my behalf.

After this phase, I got intentional. I put a picture of an attractive man on my vision board as a symbol of the kind of partner I wanted. When messaging with a documentary film producer I met on a dating app, he invited me to check out his website. While browsing, I came across a picture of the director he worked with. Something about that man caught my attention, and I thought, *How do I meet that guy?* The producer and I never met for the "lemonade" he promised, but fast forward a year later, I was back on the same app. This time, the profile of another man caught my attention. I thought, *I wish he would message me.* And then he did.

As we started texting, he suggested I check out the website for a documentary he had directed. That's when it hit me—he was *that* guy, the director I'd seen on the producer's website a year earlier. The Universe is always listening. My thoughts had become my reality. He even resembled the man I had placed on my vision board.

Some of the men I dated carried a sadness so heavy it bent their shoulders, though they masked it with irritability, a hallmark of depression.[2] Society often teaches men that anger is the only "acceptable" emotion,[3] but I saw their pain. I'd grown up surrounded with this kind of heaviness, so it felt familiar. It made me want to love them into healing. But it wasn't about them. I was trying to rewrite my past. Relationships reflect the cycles we inherit, and healing doesn't come from rescuing others, it comes from finding home in ourselves. For years, I thought I could love others into wholeness, but what I really needed was to love myself whole.

Some of these men were brilliant but stuck, unable to believe they deserved love. One kept asking, "Why are you with me?" Another wondered aloud, "Doesn't it bother you that you have a higher degree than I do?" It didn't, but it sounded like it bothered him.

Still, I saw their strengths: smart, funny, creative, artistic, attentive, and kind. They taught me about music and plays, and I soaked up their warmth. Sensitive, artistic souls—they were the yin to my yang. But in the end, it didn't work out.

Some were anxious, hard-working, and disciplined, also smart, funny, creative, and kind. But their anxiety often expressed itself as people-pleasing, which, blunt as I am, felt inauthentic. I worried I couldn't trust them to be completely honest. Truth is my love language, especially with my family and relationship history. I've learned that trusting my partner to tell me the truth, no matter how hard, is far sexier than superficial niceties.

I also feared I'd walk all over them, even if it wasn't in my nature. One said, "I'm not at your level," and I wish I had been more curious about what that meant to him and how it held him back. Another declared, "If you break up with me, I'll be devastated! No other woman will compare." (For the record, he survived and is probably married now.)

One was both anxious and depressed, like a porcupine who desperately wants a hug but can't soften its quills. And yet, no matter our struggles, they all had one thing in common: they gave unsolicited foot rubs—another one of my love languages. Thank you, men, and thank you, *Yesus!*

Trying to understand them, I consulted *La Santera* Sara for clarity. She described a couple of the men I dated with the same words: *Se sintió siempre menos. Tienen que crecer.* Her explanation helped me realize their insecurities weren't mine to fix, and their struggles didn't define my worth.

When I first brought a man home to meet my mother, she said, *"Nunca te va alcanzar."* I responded, "I don't need him to reach my level, I just need him to love me." Now, I understand exactly what she meant. Just like my daughter with me, I didn't know my mom knew things that I wouldn't understand for years. Oh, a mother's perspicacity.

Some displayed anxious attachment styles, while others leaned toward avoidance. The anxiously attached were attentive but needed constant reassurance of my love and attention. If I didn't text back immediately, they'd spiral into hurt and frustration. I don't live with my phone glued to my eyeball, and the emotional labor of constantly propping them up was exhausting. To protect my own boundaries, I pulled back, which probably made me seem avoidantly attached.

On the other hand, the avoidantly attached left me questioning how they felt about me. That uncertainty made me switch roles, acting anxiously attached myself. I told one of them, "I'm used to being adored!" His joking response? "Well, that ends now," delivered in his deepest, bassiest Barry White voice. *Meow.* When I pressed further, "You don't tell me how you feel about me," he replied, "But I show you." Touché.

Then there was the guy who was kind and attentive but avoided sharing his emotions altogether. I expressed my frustration to him: "I feel like I'm not as important to you as work is. I get that you're driven to work a lot, I've been there, and I love how responsible you are. But I feel like number five on your rotation." He responded in a half-joking way, but mostly I felt dismissed.

Some men reminded me of my mom, exhibiting borderline personality traits I didn't notice until after the breakup. During the relationship, I was "all good" in their eyes, but the moment it ended, I became "all bad." Their black-and-white thinking seemed to justify, at least to them, the cruel things they said and did afterward.

While we were together, they were kind and respectful, but post-breakup, one sneered, "You didn't leave me because of my addiction; you left me because you wanted to jump into bed with other men like the whore that you are." The same man who once said he'd be devastated if we broke up because no other woman would compare, later spat, "I didn't think you were a bimbo," all because I wouldn't reconcile. Looking back, I wasn't just ending relationships, I was dodging bullets.

Whether you're the one initiating the breakup or not, it hurts. I believe all breakups are mutual. One person says the words first, while the other, consciously or unconsciously, telegraphs it through their behavior.

Looking back, I've realized my most cherished relationships ended because we couldn't agree on the terms. One partner had a behavioral addiction, oscillating between acknowledging it and denying it. In the end, he asked, "Why can't you accept me as I am?" A fair question. My answer, just as fair: "Because that would make me co-dependent, and I don't want to live like that." I can be with a man working on his sobriety, but I won't be the caretaker of someone with an active addiction and uninterested in recovery. I've learned that doesn't bring me happiness, and we all deserve to be happy.

A *Mexica* calendar junior-elder had been a lifelong bachelor who valued being "unencumbered." His Mexican Richard Gere looks bought him extra time, but I promised myself I'd walk away if there wasn't a commitment. I kept extending his probationary period, though, and joked while dating him: "What's better than Richard Gere?" Answer: "A Mexican Richard Gere."

Each relationship felt like too much or too little, never just right. Like a Mexican Goldlocks, I kept searching for Mr. Just Right. Eventually, I decided to take a really long break from dating, to give myself all the time and space necessary to heal and grow. I was determined to break the patterns; to level up and own my part in them.

So, I stayed home to read on Friday nights, savoring the quiet, and took myself to the movies on Saturday night. I traveled with friends. I doubled down on my appointments with gifted healers, poured my heart into journaling, and devoured more books. I leaned into *La Santera* Sara's advice, *"Ve lo que tú vales. Todo lo mejor para ti. 'No vendo dignidad o tranquilidad.'"*

Breakups hurt like a MF. But love is a gift, even if the relationship ends. Each one was fun and beautiful in its own way. I knew I'd be okay eventually because I got to keep myself. Whether walking alone or holding hands with someone you love, this is a pretty cool life. Living, learning, and becoming wiser, never cynical or jaded.

**In Recovery**

Breaking cycles requires courage and boundaries. For much of my life, I found myself playing the "strict parent" role in my relationships—fixing, rescuing, and propping others up. Instead of complaining about the Peter Pan types in my life, I decided to stop playing Wendy - and finally grow up myself.

The shift came when I started honoring my feelings and balancing my inner parts. My "Parent" part no longer overshadowed my "Child" part's need for joy. My "Adult" part made decisions in harmony between them. I stopped tying my worth to caretaking others, it turned out to be a liberating step toward healthier relationships and reclaiming my heart.

Reading *Beyond Codependency* by Melody Beattie in my forties was a revelation. A *where-have-you-been-all- my-life* kind of book. Its message felt like manna from heaven. Stop carrying everyone and everything. Find joy, have fun. I underlined furiously, left stars and hearts on every page that resonated, which was every page. One chapter broke down the difference between caretaking and caregiving, and I remember pausing to reflect on how much of my energy had been poured into caretaking. Fixing. Rescuing. Taking responsibility for burdens that weren't mine to carry. For the first time, I saw it clearly. This was a deeply ingrained pattern I had been repeating since childhood, so automatic I didn't even recognize it as a choice. But more than anything, this book handed me something I hadn't even realized I was missing: encouragement to live beyond survival. To heal beyond pain. To rediscover joy, play, and fun because joy isn't selfish. Joy is essential for a fulfilling, balanced life. It confirmed what *La Santera* Sara had been telling me all along:*"Piensa en ti. Vive para ti. Quererte tú principalmente."*

Books like this are not my mother, but they are my closest friends. They sit with me in the moments when I need someone who understands. They offer wisdom without judgment, teaching me lessons in the clearest of ways. I think back to when I first read it, I grabbed it off a shelf at work and it became my companion during lunch breaks, feeling a mix of grief and relief wash over me. Grief for the years I'd spent stuck in those patterns, and relief because now I had a roadmap to move forward.

For years, I poured love into "leaky buckets." People who couldn't hold what I gave. No matter how much I poured, they'd never be full. One mentor's advice landed in my gut where it resonated, settled, and even now, makes me smile: "You like what you like. Just find the healthiest version of it." You feel it too, right?

## Love Within

Reflecting on my relationships, I've come to understand that the love I seek begins within. Self-love is the foundation on which all love rests, something I uncovered by overcoming my family dynamics. My mother offered warmth entangled with manipulation. My father inflicted harm as her doormat. My birth mother kept both me and the world at an emotional distance, while my biological father's absence spoke loudly of being unclaimed, and unseen.

Now, I recognize my power as a creator of possibilities. My vision board celebrates qualities in a partner that truly nourish me: creativity, kindness, attentiveness, and integrity. He is hardworking but balanced, affectionate, and steady. The delights of simple pleasures—a fellow foodie who enjoys museums, my head resting on his shoulder mid-flight. Someone who makes me feel safe in his arms—barrel chest, arm cleavage, and all—but it's his character, his depth, that sustains the dream. I trust and respect him, utterly.

Research affirms that mutual respect fuels lasting love. John and Jane Gottman's studies reveal a man who listens, who shares power, who values his wife's perspective, creates space for love to flourish, and predicts marital success.[4] Love is not about control; it is partnership.

I've earned the confidence I hold today through years of reflection and growth. My daughter, a Taurus with a sharp tongue, often quips, "You think you're right about everything." I smile and reply, "It must be hard for you because I usually am." When she rolls her eyes, I remind her, "You realize people pay good money for my advice?" Without missing a beat, she shoots back, "I'm not paying you." Touché. I laugh—because she's right. And so am I.

## Reclaiming Peace Through Boundaries

Healing is an act of reclamation. The energy I cultivate shapes the world I share with those I love, especially my daughter. I've learned to notice the energy of others, focusing on whether it draws me closer, leaves me neutral, or compels me to step away. Establishing healthy distance is essential to my well-being. I no longer feel guilty for recognizing when a person or situation disrupts my peace. I trust those feelings as warnings. A call to walk away or, when necessary, to run. By honoring my feelings and setting boundaries, I reclaim my peace and open space for healthier, reciprocal connections.

One clear boundary I've set is with addiction. I support sobriety but won't dwell in denial. Relationships are voluntary, and I've grown intentional about whom I share my time and energy with. In this clarity, I've embraced these truths:

- I am not your mother, savior, or victim.
- I can and will step away from harmful behavior.

Healing has taught me that love is a choice, boundaries are love, and peace begins within. By cultivating self-love, I attract relationships grounded in respect and reciprocity. Reclaiming peace is a journey, but it's worth taking for myself and the world I help shape.

## The Medicine of Motherhood

Motherhood has been one of my life's greatest purposes. Becoming a mother expanded my capacity to love and gave me the opportunity to confront my own shadows. I found a dark place deep inside that can come out with exhaustion and no sleep.

Parenting holds up a mirror: Is there anything in your past that is unresolved? Because when your child passes through that unresolved stage, how will you guide them? You are given a second chance to resolve it or repeat the pattern for another generation. There were buried little girl pains, awkwardness, and insecurities that bubbled up when my daughter experienced them – feeling left out, unsure, or small. Those tender places gave us both an opportunity to learn and break patterns. In her youthful wisdom, my daughter coached me: "I don't need you to fix it mom, I just need you to tell me about a time when you felt embarrassed." I often joke that I was born sixty-five years old and have been growing into my age ever since. The apple doesn't fall far from the tree, because I call Paolina *el satélite*. She was even older—probably eighty-five—when she was born.

I've been lucky in relationships, especially with mentors. Reevah Simon became my clinical supervisor in December 1998. I still use what she taught me. Years before I became a mom, she was giving me advice about parenting.

Reevah: What kind of kid were you?
Me: I was a dutiful kid.
Reevah: Be careful.
Me: What do you mean, be careful?!
Reevah: There's gonna be a part of you that admires your child's rebellious attitude against authority. You're gonna admire her attitude because you wish you had been that way. You'll want to align with her against authority, except now that authority will be you.

Her heads-up was right-on. I did not want to subconsciously undermine my own authority with my daughter. Authority is not a bad word to me anymore. What I mean by it is the judicious use of authority, not its abuse. There's a difference and I'm not ambivalent about it. Firm, fair, and caring - that was the balance I aimed for in raising my daughter. When I graduated from UC Berkeley with a master's in social work, I began my career as a child protective services social worker in the Bay Area. Early on, I wrestled with the dilemma of being an agent of social control rather than an agent of social change. That conflict troubled me—

until the day I received a call about an alleged case of physical child abuse.

During the home visit, I encountered a father, no taller than 5 '4, who ruled his household (young wife, two school age children, and a grandmother) with a whip-like rod he had brought from his country of origin. He was dismissive and condescending toward me, but in that moment, I felt a sense of gratitude for the authority vested in me by the state of California to intervene and protect the vulnerable.

The experience helped me start to embrace the judicious use of authority...not too much, not too little. I use it with care, aiming for protection, not harm. The lesson stayed with me as a social worker and as a mother. Authority, used wisely, is a tool for love and safety, for guidance and growth. Otherwise, children wouldn't need us – they'd raise themselves.

## Pregnant & Working

I had always wanted to be a mother, but I carried a fear planted by my mom. She told me it would be hard for me to conceive, reminding me that there were women on my birth mother's side who couldn't have children. Since we believed my mom was a *bruja*, I took her words seriously. Years later, a friend who didn't know about this "family curse" performed a psychic/intuitive health reading. When she scanned my body, she paused at my reproductive organs and said, "I sense fear, but you have nothing to worry about."

Two years later, my pregnancy came as a complete surprise. Six weeks before my wedding, I woke up nauseous and decided to take a test, which turned out positive. This wasn't part of my grand Virgo plan! I had envisioned saving money and carefully preparing to be a stay-at-home mom when the right time came. In hindsight, the timing turned out to be perfect. It gave my mom and daughter two and a half glorious years together. Thank you, *Yesus.*

Throughout my pregnancy, I threw up all day, every day. At home and work, I would sometimes throw up in the bathroom sink when I couldn't stomach throwing up in the toilet. (The school's Plant Manager was a kind friend, so I hope he didn't hate me for that.) I later read that vomiting was a good sign of pregnancy health, which gave me a small sense of relief.

The nausea also made me slow down. As a school social worker, I was used to running around campus, always feeling like I was chasing something. But as the nausea persisted, I sat still and did what was in front of me. My work deepened, and I found a new way to be professional. I started leaving work at 4:30 p.m., instead of working late. I left on time mostly because I needed to get home and crawl into bed as soon as possible. For the first time, life and work imposed physical boundaries on me, and I leaned into them.

**Labor & Delivery**
My labor lasted twenty-four hours and was nothing like I imagined. The prenatal class videos I had watched showcased glaring differences between natural births and medicated ones, and I envisioned myself as having the

experience of the glowing, radiant, unmedicated moms in the class videos.

My water broke at 3 a.m., and by the time I was in the hospital and waiting to dilate fully, I was exhausted. I refused medication until the seasoned nurse said, "Don't be a hero." I finally agreed to tranquilizers and two epidurals. Then begged for a third.

My body told me to walk up and down the long halls of the hospital with their floor to ceiling windows. The staff advised me not to because I was hooked up to a fetal monitor. But my spidey sense just knew it was the right thing for me to do. I think the intermittent walking helped with the dilation.

Since my water broke, I was given the labor-inducing medication, Pitocin, which intensified my contractions to monster levels. By the time I had to push, I was so numb from the epidural and could barely coordinate my muscles like when your lip is numb at the dentist office, and you can't speak clearly. Try as I might, I could only manage to push the eye sockets out of my head. The next day, I looked like a prize fighter.

I tried various birthing positions, but nothing worked. I asked for my options and the doctor suggested suctioning. This terrified my mother. She prayed fervently (not the forceps!). There is nothing like the prayers of a mother. Nothing.

In the hallway, on my way to a sterile room for the suctioning, the epidural wore off, and I could feel the contractions again. The nurse yelled, "Don't push!" but it was the only thing that countered the pain. By the time I got to the sterile room and was transferred onto the bed with stirrups and metal bars I could grip with my hands, it took mere minutes to push my daughter out vaginally. Thank you, *Yesus*!

I couldn't see from where I was, but her dad said he saw the cord wrapped around her neck, and she was blue. The nurse was quick to resolve it, though, and when I spoke to Paolina, she recognized my voice, her cries softened. As her dad admired her, he noted, "She has my dimples!"

Although my prenatal visits had been with midwives, on the day my daughter was born the luck of the draw handed me to a doctor I'll call Dr. L. His name is on my daughter's birth certificate, a cruel footnote to a story I wish I didn't have to tell.

That man decided to shove his whole arm into my body, into my vagina, and into my uterus to remove the placenta. Not just once, but again and again. Each time, I pleaded for him to let me catch my breath. My voice, weak and strained, seemed to fall on deaf ears. When I placed my hand on his arm, to pause, to be heard, he barked: "Never touch my arm again."

I wish I had punched him. But after twenty-four hours of labor, the fight had burned out of me. My then-husband wasn't there—I had asked him to follow Paolina wherever they took her. I wanted eyes on her at all times. I lay there, alone, vulnerable, bullied until the attending physician, a woman thankfully, shot Dr. L a stern look and told him to make the last grab count. I had chosen midwives for my prenatal visits to avoid this. A midwife would not have treated me or my placenta this way.

They say women forget the pain of childbirth. Maybe some do. But I never forgot Dr. L's cruelty in this sacred moment of my life. I have caught my breath now. And this—this is my reckoning. I reclaim my voice, my power, my story because I am the one who decides how this story ends.

Paolina I (for Irene) Acuña-González was born May 8, 2001. At 5 a.m., I found myself alone in the hospital room with her. My mom and her dad were asleep in the waiting room. Paolina was also asleep, likely from the tranquilizers I'd been given, and I was too exhausted to feel anything. When the nurse asked if I wanted to give her the first bath, I couldn't. She looked concerned, maybe worried I wasn't bonding with my baby, but I was just utterly drained. I had given everything I had over the last twenty-four hours. What I needed most in that moment was rest, and so did my people. Motherhood is overwhelming at times, and it truly takes a community to get through it. Every caring hand makes a difference.

**The First Year**
Those early weeks were overwhelming. Breastfeeding every two hours, sleepless nights, and the sheer responsibility of keeping her alive felt like too much. But as we settled into a rhythm, trust and love grew between us.

I let go of my grand plans to read her poetry and a scripture daily, speak Spanish and English, and use cloth diapers. Breastfeeding, though, was my one non-negotiable. It took everything I had. For six weeks, I cried from the pain and sought help from a lactation specialist. I almost quit, but the idea of bottle-feeding, sterilizing bottles, mixing formula, seemed just as hard in the bad state I was in. So, I powered through.

We made it work. For the first four months, I stayed home full-time, then transitioned to part-time work, spending two days a week with Paolina. My mom stepped in to watch her two days a week, and her father adjusted his schedule to take Fridays. Monday dinners became our "staff meetings," where we shared every detail of Paolina's day, her new words in English and Spanish, her little mischiefs (*travesuras*), and her sweet moments (*ternuras*).

My mom told me that when Paolina got too big for her to carry down the stairs, they had a conversation about what to do. Paolina had always been an extra-large baby, and by six months, her pediatrician noted she could easily be mistaken for a one-year-old. My mom claims Paolina came up with the solution: she sat herself down at the top of the stairs and scooted down on her bum. Everything is figure-out-able.

Motherhood brought me face-to-face with my fears. One of them, as blunt as I am, was that I might have an "ugly" baby, and that *I would know it*. I worried I wouldn't see her through the rose-colored glasses of motherhood. Thankfully, I had nothing to fear. She was gorgeous in every way - a perfectly shaped head, big, beautiful eyes, a button nose, red ribbon lips, and not one but two dimples! (Her dad has only one.)

When her first studio portrait at three months old was revealed to me, I shrieked with joy and cried. Looking at it now, though, she resembles a bald businessman, retired, but with a twinkle in his eye and a dimple in his cheek.

I wanted my daughter to have a stay-at-home parent, and I wanted her to always know she was loved. A mentor, Rose Monteiro, a social worker and therapist with more than forty years of private practice experience, said, "No matter the crisis clients came to me with, at the core of it was the same painful question: Did or does my mother love me?"

Secure attachment serves as a protective factor throughout life. Research shows it acts as a buffer against trauma, mediating and moderating the development of PTSD, regardless of the nature of the trauma or the individual's age. It does this by fostering emotional regulation, encouraging supportive relationships, and enabling effective coping mechanisms.[5]

While early relationships lay the groundwork for secure attachment, it's never too late to cultivate it through therapy, personal growth, and supportive connections. As we heal and rewire narratives of fear and uncertainty, we create space for love, trust, and deeper connections with ourselves and others. [6]

I was fortunate to be able to stay home with her. My one job was to care for her, which meant breastfeeding every two hours, twenty-four, seven. One night, she wouldn't stop crying, and I had done everything—changed her, fed her, rocked her. Sleep-deprived and desperate, I turned to her dad and said, "Please take her while I sleep on the couch downstairs, or else I'm afraid I'm going to throw her out the window." He looked alarmed but took the baby. Two hours later, I came back upstairs, refreshed, and found him wide-eyed, holding her. "She hasn't stopped crying," he said. I took over from there. Before being a parent, I couldn't fathom what would make someone hurt their own child, but now I understand that deep, dark place where frustration and exhaustion collide, and it's a miracle we don't give in to the darkness. Again, every caring hand makes a difference. Thank you, *Yesus*. (The readers who are parents get it and are giving me a knowing smile right now. I see you.)

## Parenting Lessons

My opportunity to confront my ambivalence over parental authority happened on a Tuesday when Paolina was two. Thanks to my clinical supervisor whom I mentioned earlier, Reevah, I had learned effective parenting skills to prepare me for this moment.

I was fortunate to be working only part-time then, which allowed me to give Paolina my full, undivided attention when we were together. But Paolina was an only child, and I worried about her being lonely, so I arranged for a neighbor girl, Jenny, to visit and read to her for an hour each week. Paolina loved these visits. She was in her highchair eating breakfast when it came time for Jenny to go home, and Paolina had a meltdown. She flung her bowl across the room, sending breakfast flying—onto the walls, the floor, everywhere. The Virgo in me was livid.

In my mind, I heard Reevah's question: What would she need to do so you wouldn't be mad at her anymore?

So, I took a deep breath, made a rule, and started with empathy: "I get it, Paolina. You were having fun with Jenny, and you didn't want her to leave. That made you sad and angry. But in this family," (my voice dropping to a bassier tone), "we do not throw things, no matter how angry we get."

As soon as her feet hit the ground, she ran. I chased her, knowing there were only so many corners in the house for her to hide. Once I caught her, I brought her back to the mess. With one hand guiding hers to hold a paper towel, we cleaned it up together. She tried to escape more than once, but she was two, and I was thirty-four. She was outnumbered.

I guided her to clean the walls, the floor, every spot where her breakfast had landed. From setting the rule to supervising her cleanup, the whole process took over forty minutes, but that was okay. I wasn't rushed or stressed, and I knew what to do. Truth be told, there was a moment when the spirit of Irene bubbled up within me, and I wanted to strike the table with a leather belt, but since I had the time, the skills, and a strong commitment to a new way of disciplining and parenting, I let the feeling pass.

Then, just as I thought we were done, Paolina walked over to the water dispenser. She glanced back to see if I was watching, then defiantly pulled the lever to spill water on the floor. Round two. Another twenty minutes of chasing, cornering, guiding her hand with a paper towel. I stayed firm. This was my job, and I felt lucky to have the skills to handle it.

I love to tell the story that later in her preschool days, her teacher told me, "It's so interesting, during cleanup time, kids usually cry and refuse to put the toys away, or they put the toys away without crying. But Paolina? She cries *while* putting the toys away." Lesson learned! Paolina and I still laugh about that because it makes sense to both of us. Even now, Paolina knows it's okay to cry while putting the toys away. I figured she wouldn't fully appreciate my structured parenting approach until she was in her thirties, raising children of her own, but I got an early gift when she was in high school: She said, "I get it, mom. You just don't want me to be a jerk." I celebrated with tears of pride and joy.

## Childhood Journey: Identity, Art & Mental Health

When Paolina was four, she woke up one morning excitedly describing a dream in which she was wearing "a blue sparkly dress." I saw this as the perfect opportunity to teach her that the creative process often begins with imagination. We went to the fabric store together, and I encouraged her to pick out the fabric that most resembled the dress in her dream. Then, her *abuelita* brought the vision to life, sewing a dress based on Paolina's memory of its design (a simple off the shoulder look). I still treasure the photo of her modeling it with pride—a tangible reminder of how dreams can take shape in the real world.

In second grade, Paolina entered an art contest sponsored by the PTA in our school district. She created a drawing of a girl wearing an intricately designed dress. Alongside the silhouette, she wrote, "Beauty can be made with your own hands." Her work received an honorable mention and was displayed near downtown—a proud moment for all of us.

Life has been both beautiful and painful for her. She has experienced mental illness—depression, anxiety, and even suicidal ideation—through much of her life. At the same time, she remains the wisest, most imaginative, hard-working, determined, creative, artistic, talented, witty, smart, and adventurous soul I have ever known. Genetics and environment have shaped her, as they shape us all, but she is undeniably extraordinary.

I can't imagine raising her without my education and experience. In many ways, I feel like I earned my license as a clinical social worker (LCSW) just to be her mom. When she struggled with separation anxiety as a child and people stared, I didn't feel embarrassed or ashamed. Instead, I thought to myself, *With all the challenges I could be facing, if crying—a lot—is the hardest part, I'll take it.*

Parenting Paolina has been both the greatest challenge and the greatest privilege of my life. Through her, I've learned that creativity and resilience often go hand in hand, and that love and understanding are the most important tools a parent can possess.

My connection to my daughter has been re-ordering and saving my life ever since she arrived; decisions have been recalibrated by her existence. One late afternoon after work, I was on my way to pick her up from preschool. I drove through a neighborhood near the school where I worked and heard a gunshot. I turned my head to the left and saw a man collapse on the sidewalk. In my rear-view mirror, I saw two young men running away.

Instinct kicked in. My hands tightened on the wheel as I slowed, ready to pull over, call 911, and tend to the man. But then, I saw Paolina's face, her big, worried eyes, waiting for me to pick her up. Daylight-saving time already made her uneasy when I arrived after dark. If I were late... If something happened to me... the thought made my breath catch.

I glanced back at the scene, torn, and then noticed a young woman approach the man lying on the sidewalk. My heart wrestled with itself, but I knew I had to keep driving. I dialed 911 and prayed. My daughter counted on me, and in that moment, my world was her.

I signed her up for art class when she was five because she had been painting since before she could walk. As I accompanied her from the car to class, she would scream and sob. Adults would turn to look at me with judgment in their eyes, as if to say, *What are you doing to that child?* I wanted to scream back: *I'm taking her to art class because she loves art!*

The moment she walked into class, she would stop crying. She was socially anxious and didn't want her peers to see her wailing. After class, she always beamed and asked, "When are you bringing me back?" Sigh. I took it all on the chin. Facing your fears and modeling it is effective exposure therapy.

Every day as we drove home after school, I'd ask her to tell me a story about kindergarten, or first grade, or whatever grade she was in at the time. It became our ritual. One day she was so mad she couldn't speak. Instead, she grabbed a stack of post-it notes and furiously scribbled in her best kindergarten writing skills: "I been tol wat to do." The Taurus in her was livid in the back seat.

She was shy and struggled to join in when her peers played together, so I took her to the park after school to practice socializing. It became our routine, and when we got home, she would record the names of all the kids she had played with on a clipboard—it gave her a sense of progress and accomplishment.

School or separation anxiety was a constant companion throughout her academic journey. Every first day of school, from preschool to college, was marked by lots of tears. The transitions after long school breaks were especially hard—she would wake up with a nervous flutter in her stomach. To help soothe her "belly butterflies," I warmed sand-filled pillows in the microwave, pressing their comforting warmth against her stomach. I knew it would work because it had always worked on mine.

In elementary school, after she told her school counselor that she wanted to die, I took her to the doctor. They referred her to a cognitive coping group—the gold standard for treating depression and anxiety. It was a ten-week program, and I took her every week.

On the first day, she screamed and wailed in the car. She refused to go, yelling, "I have a good life! I don't need to go to therapy!" I gotta admit, I was nervous and unsure of myself. How was I going to get her out of the car, into the elevator, checked in at reception, and upstairs to the waiting room? She was too big to carry.

Those questions swirled in my mind as I went through the motions. I parked the car. Turned off the ignition. Got out. Opened her door. I was still thinking when, suddenly, she stopped screaming. She got out of the car and walked with me the whole way.

I think it was a mix of "this lady always means business" and her social anxiety keeping her from making a scene in front of others. I call it a miracle. Thank you, *Yesus*.

After the group series ended, though, she continued to wrestle with suicidal thoughts. I was depleted, so I asked her dad to step in. He took her to another group—a ten-week social skills program.

During this time, she was waking up at 4 a.m. to get ready for school. She'd set her alarm, race around the house, and finish getting ready hours before school. Then she'd collapse on the couch downstairs and fall asleep watching the news. Getting in her way during those early morning hours was a big mistake. Nothing could stop her.

After twenty weeks of cognitive behavior therapy, her psychiatrist suggested medication. I practically jumped out of my seat to accept it. It didn't take long before her morning routine settled down.

By middle school, her dad and I were divorced, and Paolina's anxiety and depression were at their worst. I took her to see my shaman. She had a spirit animal now to help her. We tried individual therapy, but Paolina didn't take to the cognitive-behavioral approach "I feel like they're blaming me!" she said. She didn't feel like she had the power to change her thoughts or feelings, and what they were asking seemed unreasonable.

Also in middle school, my daughter went on a field trip to the Museum of Contemporary Art in downtown Los Angeles. Standing in front of an abstract collage of assorted objects, the teacher asked, "What do you see?" One student replied, "A shoe." Another added, "A chicken coop." My daughter chimed in, "I see a man running away from his past."

*La antena* gives birth to *el satélite*.

I reached out to a friend for a referral for therapy outside my insurance network. Her son had benefited from therapy after her divorce, and she recommended his therapist. That's how we met Karen. Karen made Paolina feel seen, heard, and understood. Paolina continued seeing her throughout high school and even returned after college.

**My Primary Directive**
Throughout her childhood, it was my job to keep my daughter alive—her life depended on it. Those were my stakes. With multiple episodes of suicidal thoughts and an attempt, I pulled out all the stops—every resource, every ounce of knowledge, skill, and experience I had—fueled by sheer determination, tenacity, and love.

When we brought her home from the hospital as a newborn, I sat next to her in the backseat, hugging her car seat. We drove twenty to thirty miles per hour the entire way. I kept meticulous logs of how long I breastfed her to ensure she was getting enough to eat. And in the middle of the night, when she woke up crying inconsolably, we frantically searched for the fancy digital thermometer. Picture two educated adults struggling to figure out how to use the darn thing at 3 a.m. I've kept an old school thermometer in the house ever since.

Fast forward to February 2021, Paolina, now nineteen years old, was home, taking her college classes online while working part-time in customer service. Over the holidays, she took on too many shifts because no one else wanted them. She thought that's just what you do. Her amygdala convinced her she needed to make money, even as I tried to reassure her that we were fine.

Her anxiety and depression reached a breaking point. From 2019 to 2021, suicide attempts among children and teens aged ten to nineteen increased by 30%, a trend linked to the pandemic's effects. [7]

One morning, I woke up to find an empty bottle of over-the-counter pills on her bathroom sink. Her bedroom door was locked. I knocked and called her name and demanded she open the door. I pounded again and again knowing I wouldn't stop, couldn't stop, until she finally let me in. It felt like an eternity, but I knew I wouldn't stop until she did. I can't even tell you how I got her up and out the door that morning. She was moving slowly, mumbling short answers, shut down, and defiant. Taurus versus Virgo.

At her doctor's appointment, we hit another roadblock: The receptionist, a young woman with an attitude, wouldn't let her up the elevator without an ID. Initially, I walked away, but I quickly returned with a plan. In the crowded waiting area, I said aloud that my daughter had taken pills, it had taken everything to get her there, and asked if there was another way to confirm her identity. When you're desperate to keep your child alive, obstacles, both human and systemic, will test you. That's when you need your clearest, most creative thinking. Your prefrontal cortex needs to be fully online, and for that to happen, your brainstem must be calm, and your limbic system must feel connected.

The receptionist eventually offered a solution but blamed me for walking away earlier. I don't hold it against her. I don't know what she was going through. Maybe she had lost loved ones to the pandemic or was supporting her family on this job.

Because of the rules in place during the pandemic, Paolina went to see the doctor alone. I worried she wouldn't make it to the exam room, that she might harm herself in a random bathroom. I waited outside for four agonizing hours. I called the medical director on duty to share my concerns, only to be dismissed, advising me to ask the doctor how Paolina was doing after the appointment was over.

When Paolina finally came out, the doctor had prescribed something akin to Pepto-Bismol to counteract the effects of the pills she'd taken. A young, male social worker who assessed her mental health suggested she take breaks and go to a neighborhood park when stressed.

I drove home, but my gut told me it wasn't over. It felt like she was still in the eye of the storm and she wasn't safe. Just a block from home, I decided to take her to urgent care instead. Paolina protested, but I told her I wasn't satisfied with the prescription or the advice she'd been given. My mama spidey-sense knew she was still at risk.

Two blocks from a busy intersection, she opened the car door and tried to get out. I stopped the car, held onto her with one hand, and called 911 with the other. Cars lined up behind us. A woman got out of her car to offer help. When the fire truck arrived, a young, white firefighter chastised me for being double-masked, then interviewed Paolina privately. When he finished, he turned to me, questioning aggressively why I was taking her back to the hospital when she didn't want to go.

I stayed eerily calm - laser focused. There was no one for me to call for support; my mom had been gone for nearly two decades. A close family member, who had accompanied me when I dropped off Paolina in her first year at college, was in a medically induced coma due to COVID. I felt alone, but I also felt supported by God. In the quiet of my spirit, I prayed, *Help me get her through this. Don't let anyone stop us.*

Finally, an older Latino LAPD officer arrived. I explained her mental health history and the medications she was on. He ordered her to be hospitalized. Standing on the corner of El Paso Drive and Toland Way, I finally found an ally.

During her five-day hospital stay, she cried a lot. She recalls feeling terrified all the time because it was a new environment, she didn't know how long she would be there, and she was around older patients with severe mental health issues. Without her smartphone and no visitors allowed, she had only a journal and TM. Meditating helped her that week and she continued meditating even when she came home. I'd look out the window and find her sitting cross-legged on the ground, covered in a blanket, head to toe, to protect her from the sun. I was grateful she had this tool in her toolbox for these hard moments. She ended up writing a prize-winning poem about her hospital experience, and I've included it in the *Tools* section of this chapter.

In her junior year at NYU, when I dropped her off at the dorms, it was me who cried this time. The memory of her hospitalization during the pandemic, just a year earlier, still weighed heavily on my mind. I worried every day after returning home, but I knew I couldn't live like that anymore. I decided to put her in God's hands.

I texted her: *I'm going to trust that you'll figure it out.*

Her reply: *Thanks for believing in me, Mom.*

At that moment, a wave of relief washed over me, and I wept. I made the choice to stop worrying about the beautiful heart I had torn from my chest and sent across the country. I trusted that the foundation I had built—with love, patience, and resilience—would carry her. And she took my words as a vote of confidence, not abandonment.

I share this story because I know there are other parents and caregivers out there raising children with mental health challenges. According to the CDC, in 2023, about 40% of high school students experienced persistent feelings of sadness or hopelessness, and 20%

seriously considered suicide.[8] A 2023 survey found that 87% of young people in the US reported regular mental health struggles, with 58% citing anxiety as a primary challenge.[9]

I'm a licensed clinical social worker in California, with decades of experience, and yet, I've had countless moments of feeling helpless as a mom. To every loving parent and caregiver trying to keep their child alive and well, I want to wrap you in a warm blanket of love and tell you, *You are not alone. There are resources. We are on your side (me and the Universe).*

I say this with a lot of trepidation, knowing it could be misunderstood. My mission in life and my greatest wish has been to raise a healthy, happy daughter who is living her purpose. When she became an adult, I told her, "You have to want it more than I do." I deeply believe in her autonomy, her right to self-determination. I know that all I can do is all I can do. There are no guarantees, no way to control everything. I've had to make my peace with that.

## Conclusion

John Bowlby, the father of secure attachment theory, said, "If a community values its children, it must cherish their mothers." I get it now. That's my mission statement. There's no greater role in the community or society than nurturing its foundation: the mothers, the fathers, the caregivers, the hearts that bear the weight of love in all its messy glory. Because love—oh, love—is the thing that explains the impossible. It's the force that moves parents and caregivers to move heaven and earth to keep their children alive and well. And wow, isn't that the most beautiful thing?

If my life were a museum, my relationships are mestiza art. Part pre-Columbian, part post-impressionist, and part avant-garde, provocative, raw, and uncomfortable at times.

The pre-Columbian exhibit houses the monumental Olmec heads and intricate Aztec sun stones, telling stories of enduring rituals, the mysterious, and eternal. It would remind us of the deep roots we carry, the wisdom of those who came before us, and the strength in our foundation.

The post-impressionist section would be alive with Van Gogh's swirling skies and Seurat's deliberate points of light and color. At first, you'd take in the art holistically. The harmony of colors and tones engage your right brain. Then you'd lean in, analyzing the details. Every single dot of light and shadow is constructed with scientific precision, engaging your left brain. This art reaches you through your eyes but lands in your chest, making you sigh.

There would be sculptures, unfinished, jagged, unresolved. They beg to be touched, even at the risk of bleeding. And there'd be installations that make you tilt your head and murmur, "I don't get it," until, days later, the meaning finds you in a conversation, a dream, or a memory.

At the center of it all, there'd be an empty room. The walls would be lined with mirrors reflecting endlessly, countless mothers and daughters across generations. With room for fathers to take their place, standing alongside them. This room would remind visitors that the most important exhibit is the one you carry within yourself. It is the culmination of generations of love and struggle, strength and vulnerability, a living masterpiece that continues to evolve.

The best museums don't leave you unchanged. You leave heavier with emotion but also lighter with understanding. Seeing something honest gives you permission to do the same. Love, in all its complexity, continues to teach me how to let go, how to grow, how to live with a grateful heart, and how to open it even wider. The exhibit isn't finished yet, but I'm proud of the art we're making.

# The Science

## The Science of Loving-Kindness Meditation

Let's start with a question: When was the last time you truly felt safe in your own skin? Trauma has a way of making us forget what peace feels like. It isolates us, leaves us overwhelmed, and severs the connections that help us thrive. But what if there was a way back—a practice that could heal those wounds and reconnect us to joy and loving connections with others?

With just a few minutes a day, the Loving-Kindness Meditation (LKM) can transform not only how you feel about yourself but how you interact with the world around you. Let's dive into some remarkable studies that show how cultivating love and kindness can change your life—from the inside out.

## 1. Healing Trauma: Loving-Kindness Meditation and PTSD[1]

In 2013, researchers explored how LKM could help veterans with PTSD. Picture this: a twelve-week program teaching self-compassion to those who've endured the unimaginable. Here's what they found:

- Veterans reported *fewer PTSD symptoms* and *less depression*.
- They became more mindful, more present.
- And the kicker? Their newfound self-compassion played a huge role in their healing.

**Why this matters:** Traditional treatments for PTSD don't always work. LKM offers something different, a way to soften emotional numbness and build bridges to hope. It's affordable, group-friendly, and welcomed by those wary of medication. Even with its limitations (like no control group), this study planted a flag: LKM is a promising ally for trauma recovery.

## 2. Open Hearts, Better Lives [2]
Another study, in 2008, revealed how LKM does more than ease suffering—it helps people flourish. Participants who practiced LKM for nine weeks reported:

- More love, joy, gratitude, and hope.
- Deeper connections and stronger relationships.
- Better physical health. (Fewer colds, anyone?)

**Here's the magic:** Positive emotions are contagious. When you feel good, it ripples out to your relationships, your work, even your community. LKM isn't just about managing emotions—it's about building emotional wealth. And it's accessible to everyone. No fancy equipment. No gym membership. Just a little time and an open heart.

## 3. The Fountain of Youth, Reimagined[3]
What if I told you LKM could *literally* slow aging? In 2019, researchers discovered that it protects telomeres—the protective caps at the ends of chromosomes that shrink with age. Shorter telomeres are linked to stress, illness, and aging. But for those practicing LKM? The shrinkage slowed.

**Why this matters:** In a world obsessed with anti-aging products, here's something revolutionary: Loving-Kindness Meditation is free, and it works. It's not just about looking younger; it's about staying healthier for longer.

## The Bigger Picture: Love as a Superpower

When you zoom out, the message is clear: LKM is more than a meditation practice—it's a movement toward wholeness. It nurtures self-compassion, strengthens connections, and even slows the clock on cellular aging. But most importantly, it reconnects us to what it means to be human: to love, to grow, to heal. And that, perhaps, is the ultimate science of Loving-Kindness Meditation.

# Ancestor Wisdom

## Love and Relationships

Across centuries and continents, the wisdom of our ancestors whispers to us still, weaving lessons on love that stretch beyond the boundaries of the heart. From the sands of Africa to the mountains of Mesoamerica, from the fires of Jewish homes to the sacred spaces of ceremony, these teachings root us in connection, respect, and balance—within ourselves, with one another, and with the divine.

African Wisdom: *Ubuntu*, the Heartbeat of the People[1]
"I am because we are" is a truth carried on the winds of Africa, where love is not merely an emotion but a living bond, a thread tying each soul to the next. Here, love is relational, a tender offering not just for a partner but for the whole village, for the ancestors who stand behind us and the children yet to come.

- **Familial Love**: Elders remind us that to care for family is to honor the roots that nourish our being. In their voices we hear: *Respect your bloodline; it reflects the sacredness of your own soul.*
- **Romantic Love**: Partnerships are forged with harmony at their core, a dance of two spirits moving to rhythms much older than themselves. Rituals, scented with incense and echoing with ancestral blessings, call forth balance and protection.
- **Communal Love**: Love extends outward, spilling into the communal bowl. The well-being of the many strengthens the joy of the one. Relationships are woven into a tapestry where everyone has a

thread, ensuring the next generation is cradled by many hands.

In the Yoruba tradition, *Shango* and *Oshun*—deities of thunder and sweetness, power and love—teach us about the delicate balance of masculine and feminine forces. Together, they remind us that respect and reciprocity are the sacred glue of all unions.

### *Mexica* Wisdom: Love as a Sacred Mirror[2]

In the *Mexica* tradition, love is not merely of the heart but of the soul, a reflection of the divine order of the universe. *Tonalli*—the vital life force—flows through each of us, binding us to the cosmos and to one another.

- **Romantic Love**: A partnership is not just a union of two; it is a sacred bond, blessed by the deities such as Xochiquetzal, who oversee love and fertility. Together, couples are urged to balance their divine energy, or *teotl*, with the messy, beautiful work of human growth.
- **Family and Community**: Love is inseparable from responsibility to the larger circle. Marriages are ceremonies of commitment not only to a partner but also to the people and the land, reminding us that the well-being of the whole is born in the intimacy of the two.

Key lessons flow like streams from this well of wisdom:

- **Love as Sacred Work**: True love, like tending a fire, requires offerings, patience, and care.

- **Respect for Duality**: What seems opposite—masculine and feminine, strength and vulnerability—are instead partners in the great cosmic dance.
- **Ritual as Renewal**: The act of love is renewed through ceremony, reminding us to adapt, to grow, to cherish.

### Jewish Wisdom: *Chesed*, the Kindness That Binds[3]

*Chesed* (loving kindness) is central to Jewish tradition, rooted in the belief that we are all *B'tzelem Elohim*, created *in the image of God* (Genesis 1:27). As Rabbi Rita Sherwin (personal communication) explains, this concept has been deeply significant in Judaism from the very beginning of the Torah, sparking extensive commentary and discussion. It is closely connected to the Holiness Code, which guides us in embodying divine attributes in our everyday lives. Everything is sacred.

In Hasidic thought, *chesed* is more than an act of generosity—it is a force that binds and sustains, a love that endures. As Rabbi Levi Yitzhak of Berditchev (18th century) beautifully expressed: *"Everyone is wrapped in a holy light, which shines brightest in our hours of love."* Jewish wisdom teaches that true love is not fleeting passion but steadfast compassion—kindness that bends without breaking, stitched with justice, and warmed by the divine spark within every being. *Chesed* is the love that binds us to one another, a reflection of the Divine presence in the world.

But when it comes to love within the home and family, *chesed* is just one of several essential values that sustain relationships. As Jewish scholar Stan Beiner (personal communication) explains, *shalom bayit* (peace in the home) speaks to the importance of marital and family harmony, while *kavod* (honor, dignity, and respect) provides the foundation upon which relationships are built. *Chesed* alone does not hold up a home—it is strengthened by mutual respect, by the sacred responsibility we carry toward those we love.

## Expressions of Love in Jewish Tradition

- **Romantic Love:** The Song of Songs, the poetry of the sacred and the sensual, teaches that romantic love is a divine flame, a connection between souls that mirrors the love of the Creator for Creation.
- **Family Love:** "Honor your father and mother" is more than a commandment; it is a practice, a way of saying to the ancestors, I see you. I carry your story forward.
- **Spiritual Equality:** To see the image of God in every person is to honor the divine in yourself, your partner, and your neighbor.

Jewish family life is woven with these values—kindness, respect, peace, and honor—each thread reinforcing the next. It is not simply about love but about the ways love is practiced, nurtured, and sustained. In the end, *chesed* is not only about grand gestures of kindness but about the small, everyday acts that build a home filled with warmth, trust, and enduring connection.

## Common Threads in Ancestral Wisdom

Across these traditions, love is not a fragile, fleeting thing but a sacred trust, a responsibility, a joy. The elders whisper:

- Sacred Balance: Between the masculine and feminine, the self and the community, the human and the divine.
- Interdependence: Love cannot exist in isolation; it thrives in the rich soil of connection.
- Spiritual Connection: The love between two people mirrors the great love of the universe itself.
- Commitment and Renewal: Relationships, like gardens, flourish through care, attention, and the willingness to grow anew.

These teachings remind us that love is not only about what we feel but about what we do—how we nurture, honor, and hold space for others. In tending to love, we tend to the sacred within ourselves and the world around us.

## Introduction to the Bolero, *Tonalli* of Love

The song, *Tonalli of Love*, emerges from the themes woven through this chapter—love's ability to transform, the wisdom inherited from our ancestors, and the quiet strength we find through healing. Inspired by the Mexica concept of *tonalli*—the soul essence that fuels connection, purpose, and vitality—this bolero reflects the bittersweet cycles of love: its joys, its losses, and the tender renewal that follows.

Rooted in the vibrant cultural tapestry of late 19th-century Cuba, the bolero fuses the poetic lyricism of Spanish traditions with the rich, syncopated rhythms of Afro-Cuban heritage. With its slow, melodic cadence and heartfelt verses, the bolero transcends time and borders, giving voice to the devotion, heartbreak, and deep emotional truths that define love's many faces. For generations, this genre has been a timeless medium for exploring the profound complexities of the human heart, connecting us through shared experiences of longing and resilience.[4]

*Tonalli of Love* continues this legacy, inviting us to reflect on the sacred nature of love—an eternal rhythm that harmonizes our past, present, and future.

## *Tonalli* of Love

**(Verse 1)**
In your laughter, I found my song,
A melody where I belong.
Through shadows deep, you held my light,
A love that warms the coldest night.

**(Chorus)**
Oh, *corazón*, your rhythm's mine,
In your embrace, the stars align.
Through pain and joy, through loss and gain,
Your love has taught me to rise again.

**(Verse 2)**
From my mother's eyes, a flame so bright,
To my daughter's soul, pure as sunlight.
Their voices echo, their wisdom stays,
Guiding my heart through endless days.

**(Bridge)**
The dance of love is bittersweet,
A cycle of wounds, a cycle complete.
Boundaries drawn, the healing flows,
Through every trial, the *tonalli* grows.

**(Chorus)**
Oh, *corazón*, your rhythm's mine,
In your embrace, the stars align.
Through pain and joy, through loss and gain,
Your love has taught me to rise again.

**(Verse 3)**
With every tear, a seed is sown,
In every storm, I've come to know:
Love's not a cage, but wings that free,
A path to my truest destiny.

**(Outro)**
Oh, *corazón*, your beat is true,
A legacy of strength from you.
Through all the cycles, all life's art,
The *tonalli* of love will guard my heart.

# Tools

The tools in this section are crafted to nurture emotional resilience, harmonize your thoughts and actions with your aspirations, and foster self-compassion and meaningful connection. Rooted in a spirit of care and possibility, these practices offer tangible strategies for navigating life's challenges, letting go of negativity, and building momentum toward a life filled with purpose and joy. Through meditation, reflection, and small, intentional steps, these tools provide a pathway to a more balanced, mindful, and intentional existence. Let them guide you in deepening your emotional well-being and stepping boldly into the life you envision.

## Tool #1: Loving-Kindness Meditation (LKM)

Loving-Kindness Meditation (LKM) is a transformative practice that cultivates compassion, love, and goodwill toward yourself and others. Grounded in ancient Buddhist teachings, it has become widely recognized for its profound impact on emotional and spiritual well-being. Research highlights LKM's ability to boost positive emotions such as joy, gratitude, and connection, while fostering resilience and enriching relationships. For instance, Fredrickson et al. (2008) demonstrated that practicing LKM enhances life satisfaction and a sense of purpose, offering a meaningful pathway to greater inner peace and fulfillment. [1]

## The Science and Benefits of LKM

Loving-Kindness Meditation (LKM) is more than an emotionally enriching practice—it's a proven tool for healing and transformation. Studies show its effectiveness in alleviating anxiety, depression, and trauma symptoms,[2] as well as improving physical health by enhancing heart function and resilience. Neuroscientific research highlights LKM's activation of brain regions tied to empathy and emotional regulation, affirming its alignment with our innate capacity to love and connect.[3]

LKM also holds the power to address societal issues by reducing implicit biases. Stell and Farsides (2016) found that even brief LKM sessions decreased racial bias through increased compassion and empathy.[4] Similarly, Kang, Gray, and Dovidio (2014) demonstrated that six weeks of LKM training significantly reduced biases against marginalized groups, underscoring its potential to foster equity and social harmony.[5]

For individuals in high-stress professions, LKM offers a sanctuary from burnout. Seppala et al. (2014) revealed that just ten minutes of LKM can enhance positive emotions and resilience among healthcare providers.[6] Furthermore, Watson's (2023) systematic review found that regular LKM practice decreases burnout and compassion fatigue while nurturing self-compassion and emotional well-being, making it an essential practice for sustaining a balanced and purposeful life.[7]

## How to Practice Loving-Kindness Meditation

Here's an adapted (and adaptable) script for LKM. Feel free to tailor it to your needs:[8]

### 1. Preparation:
• Sit comfortably with your feet on the floor and your spine straight. Close your eyes or keep them softly focused. Take a deep breath in, exhale slowly, and relax your whole body.

## 2. Receiving Love:

• Visualize someone who loves you deeply—a person, pet, or spiritual figure.
• Imagine them standing by your side, sending you wishes of safety, happiness, and well-being.
• Envision yourself surrounded by those who have loved you, all sending you warmth and kindness.

## 3. Sending Love:

• Silently repeat: "May you live with ease, may you be happy, may you be free from pain."
• Extend these wishes to an acquaintance, a neutral person, and even someone you find challenging.

## 4. Expanding Love Globally:

• Visualize the entire globe and send warm wishes to all beings: "Just as I wish to, may you live with ease, happiness, and good health."

## 5. Closing:

• Take a deep breath, exhale, and notice how you feel before opening your eyes.

### Reflect on Your Experience

• How did it feel to send and receive love?
• What emotions arose?
• How does this practice align with your spiritual journey?

For guided versions of Loving-Kindness Meditation, explore the free resources available through the UCLA Mindful Awareness Research Center.

Loving-Kindness Meditation is more than a relaxation technique—it's a gateway to deeper connection, inner peace, and a profound sense of interconnectedness with yourself, others, and the world. Through this practice, you can nurture compassion, dissolve barriers, and embrace a more harmonious way of being.

## Tool #2: Forgiveness Affirmations

There are nearly two hundred research studies on forgiveness, each exploring its depths and nuances. While definitions may vary, here's what forgiveness is not—it's not pardoning, excusing, condoning, denying, forgetting, or even reconciliation. Forgiveness doesn't erase the past, but rather it helps free you so you can move forward. [9] Decades of research show that forgiveness enhances well-being, even for those without religious or spiritual inclinations. [10]

## A Forgiveness Practice

### 1. Make a List:

Identify the people (including yourself) and entities (e.g., organizations) you want to forgive.

### 2. Forgiveness Affirmation: [11]

Imagine saying this to each person or entity:
"I forgive you completely and freely. I release you and let you go. The incident between us is finished forever. I wish the best for you; I wish for you your highest good. I am free, and you are free."

### 3. Reflect:

- How did it feel to say the affirmation?

- How might forgiveness move you closer to your goals?

## Questions for Deeper Reflection

- Have you addressed everyone on your list?
- Do you feel resistant to forgive someone? Could this signal a need for grieving or healing?
- If forgiveness feels challenging, consider writing a letter (which you never have to mail) to the person or entity. Express your emotions fully and honestly—it's a vital step in the forgiveness journey. It helps to say it - all of it. Feel heard and understood, by your own heart.

Forgiveness is a gift you give yourself. By releasing what no longer serves you, you reclaim your energy to focus on joy, purpose, and the life you want to create. It's a practice of freedom and transformation, moving you closer to the inner peace you deserve.

## Tool #3 One of My Daughter's Poems

Poetry holds a peculiar power—it gathers you in, wraps you up in shared experiences, and reminds you that even in your solitude, you are never alone. Poets are humanity's connective tissue, giving shape to our joys, sorrows, and those in-between spaces we don't always have words for.

My daughter's poem finds beauty where it seems impossible, turning the sharp corners of pain into something full of light. Like the poets who carve meaning from the chaos, she has a way of laying it all bare—messy and magnificent, leaving you nodding in recognition.

## Beautiful Things in a Psych Hospital [6]

Fuzzy socks
How their plastic soles grip on cold white linoleum

7 am sunrises
After side sleeping on a marble slab

Ibuprofen stomach aches
The sweet relief of failure

The soreness of a thrice poked vein squeezed into a
blood pressure machine
The warm sting of petrichor eyes

Lying face first in AstroTurf
Absorbing twenty-minute sun

The manic koi fish and her tissue box of broken
crayons
The surprising kindness of a half-plucked porcupine
who finds muses in blueberry muffins

The moments when the tears stop

Black out poems in dry erase marker
One for every day here

Cawing with ravens
Throwing big bellied laughs
In the faces of our abysses

Mom's crackling voice through a toy phone
The metallic timbre of her forgiveness

The air on the west side ward
Smells like recovery and clean linens
Tastes like cafeteria jello and apple juice.

New answers to old questions
The reunion of my head to my body

A doctor's signature on a release form

The final verse of a final poem
"I have accepted the way."

Chapter 4
# Deep-End Lessons on Work and Purpose

I'm not an ambitious b!tch, I'm a b!tch on a mission.
I come in peace, but don't f*ck with me.

## Life Purpose and Work

Am I doing what I came here to do? This is a central question in my life. My only fear would be *not doing what I came here to do*. Thankfully, I'm doing it with God, books, and writing as my foundations. They have guided and supported me in shaping the life I want to live.

Since the sixth grade at Rowan Avenue Elementary in East Los Angeles, I've wanted to be a writer. My teacher, Mr. Prucha, had a poster of an abstract painting on the wall, and I would gaze at it during class activities, almost like meditating. One day, he asked us to write about the painting, and I thought, "Oh! That's easy! I've been imagining this for days." In my mind, the painting showed fall-colored leaves trapped in a frozen stream during winter that were then released again in the spring. He loved my essay and asked to keep it. Years later, when I visited him, I asked for it back, wanting a collection of my early work as a reminder that I am a writer. His sorrowful look as he returned it let me know that he cherished it, too.

As an introverted child, people's behavior often left me confused. Books, however, made sense. They were my refuge. Reading connected me to something greater. Ideas would burst out of my brain like popcorn, and I'd have to furiously scribble them in the margins before they vanished.

In high school, my English teacher, Ms. Roundtree, introduced me to the concept of a transcendental force. She explained that poets and writers drew upon this creative energy to write truthfully. To illustrate, she walked to the chalkboard and drew a long, horizontal line separating the seen and the unseen. "This," she said, "represents the transcendental force—an unseen energy that is always present, always flowing. Writers don't create from nothing; they attune themselves to this energy, drawing inspiration from it." At fifteen, I was skeptical. I asked her, "Do you really believe in the transcendental force?" Her enthusiastic, almost church-like exclamation, "Yes! Yes, I do!" was full of belief and passion. Years later, Lynn, my TM teacher, said that Ms. Roundtree must have practiced TM. Lynn's teacher described the transcendental field as "an unbounded reservoir of creativity, intelligence, peace, and love."

I always dreamed of majoring in English and becoming a writer. However, as the daughter of working-class immigrants, I felt immense pressure to succeed financially. My mother, who dreamed of one day driving a pink Cadillac, often stressed about money. With three older siblings who either hadn't finished high school or college and my younger brother still being a child, it seemed clear that fulfilling these aspirations fell to me, and I felt the weight of her dreams squarely on my shoulders. Despite this pressure, I also felt a deeper, more personal yearning—one that transcended career and financial success. For a high school assignment, I wrote that my ultimate goal was to hear God's voice say, "This is my daughter, whom I love; with whom I am well pleased" (Matthew 3:17).[1]

In high school, I watched television reports about people experiencing homelessness and felt an unshakable desire to help. I wanted to learn medicine, so I could help them to heal. I was torn between becoming a Christian missionary or a doctor—both paths seemed equally important to me, but I didn't know how to choose. I shared this dream with Mr. Prucha, my former teacher. He asked, "Have you heard of Albert Schweitzer?" I shook my head. "He was a Christian medical missionary," he continued, "a doctor who dedicated his life to serving others. You should read about him."

His words planted a seed in my heart. Schweitzer's story, a man who combined faith and healing to bring hope to those in need, ignited something within me, and my vision began to take shape. I would pursue medicine, inspired by Schweitzer's example, blending compassion with action.

In undergrad, I majored in Biology and planned to apply to medical school. However, after a grueling semester with twenty hours of weekly lab courses, I was miserable. Spring in Southern California was calling, but I was stuck indoors. Though I passed most of my courses, Physics and Organic Chemistry tripped me up, and medical school became out of reach. I graduated college in four years at twenty years old and pivoted to new possibilities. I dreamed of joining the Peace Corps to teach science abroad, but that, too, didn't work out. Depressed, I spent a month in bed before deciding to comb through the LA Times classified section for jobs.

My first job was as a health educator at a nonprofit in the San Fernando Valley, earning minimum wage. Within six months, at age twenty-one, I was promoted to AIDS Program Director. The work was incredibly meaningful but also overwhelming. I transformed a small prevention education program into a full-scale clinic for people with HIV during a time when providers were in short supply.

After two intense years, I transitioned to another nonprofit in Hollywood, serving unhoused youth. My supervisor, a seasoned social worker, became a source of inspiration. When we discussed the needs of youth, she helped me understand them by framing their needs through their Erikson stage of psychosocial development: identity vs. role confusion (*Who am I? What do I want to become?*) and intimacy vs. isolation (*How do I balance relationships with independence?*). She also highlighted how early trauma could leave individuals stuck in earlier stages, such as trust vs. mistrust (*Can I trust others and the world?*) or autonomy vs. shame (*Can I do things by myself, or must I always rely on others?*).

Trust vs. mistrust, the first stage of Erikson's theory, forms the foundation for all relationships. When caregivers provide consistent love, safety, and care, infants learn to trust the world as a secure place. Without this, we may carry a deep-seated mistrust that shapes our future interactions. Similarly, autonomy vs. shame emerges as toddlers, when we explore our independence. When caregivers support our efforts, they build confidence in our ability to make choices. But when we are criticized or over-controlled, we may internalize shame and doubt in our abilities. Hearing this framework helped me better understand the layers of trauma our clients carried. Erikson resonated with me, offering a lens through which to see how unmet needs in early stages could ripple into struggles in adolescence and beyond.

At the time, I was young, idealistic, and brimming with enthusiasm. Yet, the work felt what I jokingly termed, "developmentally inappropriate." The responsibilities I carried (overseeing people, programs, and budgets) felt beyond my age and experience; I wasn't fully equipped to manage them. By twenty-three, I was on the fast track to becoming a workaholic, barely keeping my head above water as I tried to learn to swim in the deep end. After two more years, I decided to leave.

In an effort to become better skilled, less overwhelmed, expand my horizons, and take a break from LA, I applied to the Master's in Social Welfare program at UC Berkeley and started in the fall of 1994. Moving from my Silverlake apartment to a tiny studio in North Oakland, I studied children, families, and school social work. My research project on school-based social work outcomes felt daunting until Dr. Kurt Organista reminded me, "It's just an exercise. It's not a dissertation." His words helped me complete the assignment.

Decades later, when I was a doctoral student, I sat with my advisor, Dr. Stuart Kirk, explaining my dissertation research questions and the three phases of my proposed research study. He talked me off the ceiling and said, "You don't have to do a three-volume dissertation." I chose to do the first phase only.

In 2017, I taught a research methods course to MSW students, the one in which completing a research project was a graduation requirement. It was my first time teaching the class, and I'll admit, I was nervous. At one point, I told my students that their anxiety about the research project was stressing me out. So, I invited them to trust themselves and to trust me. I made a commitment: I wouldn't leave a single student behind. And I kept my word. They all completed their projects and graduated.

Much like my own dissertation journey, finishing the research project turned out to be less about the research itself and more about managing anxiety and finding alternatives when we hit a wall. I encouraged my students to stay open to plan B, then plan C, then plan D, and so on. It was about following the green lights—those simple, achievable steps—that guided them to the finish line.

Students started with ambitious research questions, but when recruiting certain participants proved too time-consuming, or the secondary data set they wanted wasn't available, or some other obstacle popped up, I would gently guide them back to a more doable path. Sometimes, I felt like a used car salesman, persuading them to scale down their expectations. But I wasn't selling mediocrity. I was helping them avoid burnout and move forward, much like my mentors had once done for me.

That semester taught me that managing anxiety and staying flexible are the real keys to finishing a big project. If we can stay calm and trusting, open and hopeful, we can always spot a green light on the horizon. Everyone I know who has completed a dissertation or major research project says the same thing: after that experience, it feels like you can do anything. Maturity, I've come to believe, is about learning to manage our anxiety so it doesn't block us from what we are meant to do. Finishing a research project is about learning to persevere, to adapt, and to trust that we'll find our way forward, even when it gets exasperatingly hard.

**Use Your Voice**

Working as a school social worker in an elementary school in South LA, five years post-masters—not quite a beginner but not fully seasoned either—I was approached by a mother from my parenting group. She requested a referral to a provider who could conduct a psychological assessment her immigration lawyer advised her to obtain for her upcoming deportation proceeding in court. Both she and her husband were in the process of being deported to their respective countries of origin, Guatemala and Mexico. Their two school-age children and baby-on-the-way were U.S.-born.

I wanted to help her, but I had no experience with this type of assessment, and I didn't know any psychologists who specialized in immigration cases. I referred her to a local community mental health center, but they turned her away, saying they needed more time than the one month before her court date. I reached out to a psychologist colleague for guidance, but he wasn't aware of anyone specializing in this area either. Meanwhile, the clock was ticking...

When I called my supervisor, she suggested something I wasn't prepared for. She suggested I do it myself. Me! I had never conducted a psychological evaluation for court, and while I had done assessments before, I hadn't performed anything of this magnitude. But given the short time frame, I realized there was no one else to turn to. I was it. I had to take this on, and I immediately asked for help.

Who on a school campus completes evaluations regularly? School psychologists. And luckily, our school psychologist was not only a good friend of mine but also a fellow MSW. Despite her own workload, she agreed to help. I also reached out to the mother's immigration lawyer and asked for a sample evaluation that had been used successfully in previous cases. The forwarded sample was for an elderly man from China.

Armed with the sample and my friend's support, we met with the family's fourth grader to conduct the evaluation. We used standardized psychological tests and biopsychosocial assessment questions to gather the necessary information. I remember sitting with my friend, nervously waiting for the evaluation to print, right before the mother came to collect it for her appointment with the lawyer. We got it done just in time.

The mother went to court, and the judge accepted the assessment, allowing the parents to stay in the country. There was a catch though. The judge scheduled another court hearing a year later and requested that I attend to testify about my evaluation.

By the time the court date rolled around, I had moved on to a high school in the Valley, and the school psychologist had left the district. The Parent Representative from my previous school tracked me down to let me know I was being summoned to court.

It was the cold, quiet morning of January 2, 2004. I was on winter break and bereavement leave, still reeling from my mother's death just weeks earlier. With so much at stake, I wasn't even anxious. I was simply too drained. Emotionally, physically, and spiritually spent, I waited in the hallway to testify. Sleepy and steeped in grief, I silently prayed and held back tears, though I wanted to cry.

As a child, my mom often took me along on her trips to help people cross the border. I was, in a way, her decoy. Once, my mom traveled to Tijuana to pick up a two-year-old girl from her grandmother. Our mission was to bring the toddler to Los Angeles to reunite her with her parents. I can still see the grandmother's face as she handed over her precious child—her eyes filled with love, sorrow, and worry. The little girl cried inconsolably, wailing as we drove away, non-stop crying through lunch, and well into the afternoon. But my mom had a plan. By the time we reached the border, the girl had cried herself to sleep.

I can still see the heartbreaking relief on the girl's mother's face when we handed her back. I had been part of something bigger than myself, and I felt everyone's stake in that moment. The world felt momentarily right again. Witnessing that scene at ten years old forever shaped how I understand immigration, borders, and the lengths people go to for love.

That morning in court, it all felt full circle. I was testifying in a deportation proceeding while grieving the woman who had taught me everything about everything. I decided to dedicate my testimony to her, my mom—the woman who made me her assistant *coyote* before I even understood what that meant. There I was, honoring her legacy in my grief. Of course I was about to testify in a deportation proceeding while mourning my mom. What better way to commemorate her?

I silently told myself, *This one's for you, Irene, You better help me do this, like I helped you.* My mom did things her way, laws and policies be damned. I did things my way—nerdy and professional. Same outcomes, different methods. We were the Dream Team - the outlaw and the straight-up square.

The lawyer for Immigration and Naturalization Services (INS) tried to discredit me as an expert witness, but strangely, I felt nothing - no insecurity, no fear. Just indignation, especially because she was Latina like me. All I could think was, *Does your mom know where you are and what you're doing?*

The judge asked me questions about my grad school background at Berkeley, and the INS lawyer grilled me about whether I was being paid to testify (no) and if I was qualified to diagnose (yes). The judge focused on the children's emotional reactions. I explained how their strong attachment bonds were both helping them cope with the stress of the deportation proceedings and heightening their anxiety about losing those bonds.

In our interviews, the fourth grader had been unable to stop thinking about the court case, sometimes repeating the same sentence over and over. While children are resilient, I explained, losing the very people who help them weather life's storms could have devastating effects.

Then, I went further, as if I was the lawyer arguing the case. Drawing from my grad school course, *Children, Families, and the Law* (thank you, Professor Mary Ann Mason), I argued that U.S. laws, both child welfare and immigration, are grounded in the principle of keeping families together.

Finally, I went for the emotional jugular. What more could I lose? I shared my own experience of loss. Still mourning my mother, I explained how losing a parent can shatter you. *If a thirty-five-year-old woman can be completely undone by the death of her mother, what kind of devastation would it cause for a nine-year-old and a six-year-old?*

That day, I took a risk. I used my voice, stretched my skills to the edge, and leaned on otherworldly assistance. The next day, I got the call. The judge had ordered that the parents could stay. The Latina INS lawyer filed an appeal, but for the moment, we had won.

That experience changed me. I had always been persistent, but this gave me a new level of confidence. No matter the challenge, it's possible to figure things out. Nothing fully prepares you for what may come in the line of duty, but with enough help, you can navigate through it.

Years later, that mother found me on Facebook. She was working at the same elementary school where it all started. Her children were doing well—now sixteen, thirteen, and seven. All I can say is, "Thank you, *Jesus.*"

This one is dedicated to Irene Acuña, the best advocate and role model a girl could ever have. *Amen.*

## When Are You Getting Your PhD?

"*Quien no arriesga, no gana.*" (Who doesn't risk doesn't win.) — Mexican Proverb

*When are you getting your PhD?* The question would arise at the most unexpected moments from unexpected sources - family members, colleagues, or mentors, as if they knew something about my path.

I was married, raising my beautiful eight-year-old daughter, making mortgage payments, and working full-time. A PhD was always a dream, but one I'd labeled "*eventually.*" How could I possibly afford the time, energy, or money?

But the question kept coming, like a gentle nudge from the universe: *When are you getting your PhD?*

When Dr. Brown, a beloved mentor, posed the question and added, "I'll write you a reference letter," her confidence in me felt like a sign. When God calls, I answer. That summer of 2008, I finally decided to apply.

I reassured myself with contingency plans: *If I don't get in, I'll reapply next year. If I get in and can't afford to attend, I'll defer and save up.* The act of applying itself felt like a monumental step.

In moments of doubt, I find solace in stories of perseverance. I thought of Arthur Miller, the acclaimed playwright and Pulitzer Prize winner for *Death of a Salesman,* who faced rejection twice before being accepted into college. He had worked in a warehouse, saving money and building the academic record he needed to finally pursue his dreams.[2] His story was a reminder that trying, even against odds, was always better than living with the regret of not trying.

The process began with requesting a program brochure and transcripts from every school I had ever attended. I started drafting the application essay and collecting all the necessary documents. It felt surprisingly easier than when I had applied for my MSW at Berkeley, maybe because I was older (Forty!) and hopefully wiser than I was at twenty-five. Every step felt exciting at first: deciding to apply, working on the application, telling everyone my plans. Of course, my mind would occasionally wander to, *What if I don't get in?* But I always answered with, *I'll just reapply.*

When a mentor gifted me a session with a reader, I tried to come up with questions: *Will I go back to school? How will I manage?* But, I realized those questions stemmed from fear, so they weren't the right questions. I let my inner voice answer and chose to let God show me how.

The process—applying, overcoming obstacles, managing fears—felt like a little game. How many barriers would I face before I cracked? How many times did I need to overcome them before I realized that no barrier could truly keep me down? They were part of the journey, the test of endurance, persistence, and faith. I had to ask myself: *How much do I trust my dreams? How much do I trust that if God is for me, nothing can be against me?* (Romans 8:28-31).

## Overwhelmed with an "O" of OMG

What seemed like a good idea over summer vacation turned into a *"what-were-you-thinking?"* moment in the fall. I was officially and completely overwhelmed. To cope with the application process, I had avoided thinking too much about what being back in school would really be like. I imagined offshore breezes, marble libraries, and endless reading time. But once I was in it, the reality hit me like a towering wave—I was trying to stay optimistic, so I tried not to call it a tsunami.

Reevah, my longtime clinical supervisor and mentor, always said, "We feel ambivalent about everything." With that in mind, I was feeling all my feelings. In a moment of fear and overwhelm, I'd think to myself, *Oh no! What have I gotten myself into?* Then, after turning in an assignment, I'd say, *I did it. I can do this.* But then I'd be staring down another twenty or more hours of reading thinking, *OMG, how am I going to manage it all?* After completing three weeks of schoolwork, I'd feel reassured. *I'm doing this. I can do this.* Then I'd be lying down because my body would be too exhausted to move thinking, *Why did I sign up for this? Is it too late to quit?* But then, I'd have a great discussion in class and think, *Wow, this is really cool—I get to do this.* On top of it all, I'd been fighting off the flu (worried about H1N1 at the time), and trying to digest everything that was coming at me. It was making my head hurt, both figuratively and literally.

I couldn't help but wonder, *how could I have prepared better for this?* I tend to dive into the deep end with both feet, thinking I'll deal with the emotional consequences later. And boy, do those emotional consequences come. I've always feared that if I focused on my emotions beforehand, I might talk myself out of showing up. So, there I was, paddling through the deluge, hoping for a better way to manage.

Despite the chaos, there was good news too. I was right about carving out time to read, think, and write. At orientation, the professors all agreed that this was part of the experience. And being asked questions like, "What do you want to become an expert at?" felt exhilarating. I was excited to think about what I would immerse myself in, the research questions that would drive me over the next few years. I felt in the right place, doing the right thing.

I learned to ask for help and to lean on my support system. I also tackled self-care in ways that were tried and true for me—through the body. Thank goodness for all the tools that kept me grounded: spirituality, Buddhism, mindfulness. They've saved me more than once. Being stoic is overrated. There's nothing weak about being real. In fact, it takes a whole lot of courage and confidence to be vulnerable, to accept that there's so much we don't know and when we need support.

Here's what helped me get through:

- Self-talk (*One reading/assignment at a time, you can do this*)
- Support from second year doctoral students, professors, family, friends, colleagues, and administrators
- Prayer
- Good quality salmon oil
- Meditation CDs
- Sleep
- Having a job—some sense of normalcy in the midst of the madness
- And, of course, writing

## First Year, Second Quarter

I did it! I made it through the second quarter, and it was even harder than the first. One of my classes was *Epistemology.* I had to look the word up after I registered - just the name sounded intimidating. Every week the reading was dense and deeply philosophical. To tackle it, I'd retreat to tucked-away cafés, creating a little oasis of solitude that felt both isolating and indulgent.

As I strained to focus, keep up, and make sense of the readings, I could almost feel my brain flexing like a muscle, growing stronger under the weight of the challenge. It wasn't easy. It was a test of endurance, week after week. So much sitting and reading and mind stretching. I wrestled with internal temper tantrums, self-doubt, and moments when I wanted to throw up my hands. But somehow, I kept going.

Finals week felt like scaling a mountain without a clear view of the summit. When I told myself, *It will get done*, I didn't believe the words. And yet, there I was—another round finished, still standing, still moving forward.

With spring quarter and its new challenges looming ahead, I paused to celebrate what mattered most: I was still here. It was hard, brutally hard, but I was *really* living. Every step of the way, I felt more alive, more connected to the raw reality of the experience. That pit in my stomach seemed to scream, *This is real! This is really happening!*

Thank you, *Yesus*—again and again and again.

**End of the First Year**

Immersed in writing two, twenty-page papers, one a Community Intervention Proposal and presentation, the other a Policy Implementation Evaluation Proposal, I found myself facing the overwhelming final stretch of the academic year. And then came the comprehensive exams—six grueling, timed essays over two days, covering epistemology, intervention research methods, policy formulation, and evaluation. I kept reminding myself: *It will get done*. This is when I tricked myself into believing it and acted as if it already was—until it was. June 17 marked the finish line.

At brunch one morning with one of my cherished mentors, he said, "Thinking about it is half the work." I let those words sink in as I continued to mull over what I wanted to become an expert in. That single question would inform my research internship, my dissertation topic, my research agenda, and ultimately, my career.

And then, it was over. *We did it!* The first year was behind me. Every time someone asked me about school, it was hard to admit the truth: *the program was beating me up.* But I survived. I passed all my classes, finished the comprehensive exams, and lived to tell the tale. Along the way, I learned about research, evaluation, policy, attachment, secondary traumatic stress, and so much more.

When the cork popped, I cheered. With a dramatic collapse onto the couch, I smiled. With all the pressure off, life suddenly seemed lighter. I wanted to capture that feeling and carry it with me—to keep smiling all year long.

I once read about a study interviewing octogenarians and septuagenarians. A common regret surfaced among them: they wished they had taken more risks. I'm glad I took the risk. Cheers to everyone who shows up, even though the goal seems impossibly far away.

I thought of a quote from Bandura I'd read in an article for class: "Those who persist in threatening situations and master the experience gain efficacy reinforcement, whereas those who avoid threatening situations or cease their activities early reinforce negative efficacy expectations."[3] My romanticized notions of going back to school motivated me to take that first step. I'm glad I didn't realize how hard it would be. My eighty-year-old self is smiling. If you're thinking about taking on a challenge—whatever it is—take the leap of faith. What's the worst that can happen? Mistakes are guaranteed at first, but there's no need to fear them to the point of paralysis. Nobody gets to be perfect. When we're learning something new, we need to be kind and patient with ourselves. It gets better. There's a reason you're dreaming of taking that step. Your heart and imagination are pulling you toward something that will bring you closer to yourself. That's what we're here for. The eighty-year-old in us won't regret it one bit.

But the good and bad always live side by side. That first year, I realized I wanted out of my marriage. The writing was on the wall, but I was overwhelmed. Taking on a divorce seemed impossible. I was already stretched too thin, commuting two hours each way to school because of traffic, sitting in class, sitting at home to study and write papers, sitting in cafés reading articles. Fourteen hours a day of sitting, and I was shortening my life with every page I turned. Yet somehow, I kept going. Every choice, every moment, felt like a piece of the puzzle, assembling a life I could eventually feel proud of.

## Second Year, Fall Quarter (2010)

Things were falling into place at an unbelievable rate—enough to make even a skeptic turn into a believer. I submitted my Doctoral Study Plan and Research Internship Plan, which also served as my Community Project Proposal, and I hoped would become my Dissertation Proposal. It was also my current job assignment—a veritable four-in-one. I began working on these plans the summer before, struggling to conceptualize and write. It all came together in one week, and I turned it in just before midnight, a couple of days ahead of the due date.

I wanted to feel like a badass, but I didn't. I just felt loved—by God. It felt as if, to borrow Brazilian author Paulo Coelho's words, the universe was conspiring to help me accomplish my dream and fulfill my personal legend. If this was possible for me, then it's possible for anyone. The universe wants to conspire to help you, too. As Ed Bacon said to the congregation when he was the minister of All Saints in Pasadena, "God loves you and everyone else."

Walking through campus on a perfect fall day, I smiled and sighed, knowing I was in the right place, doing the right thing, at the right time in my life. The year before felt like an exam, and thankfully, I passed. The question was, *how bad did I want it?* Because it was going to get rough. *Did I want it bad enough, and for the right reasons?*

The first quarter of the second year was a completely different experience. The first pancake is always the worst—burnt on the edges, undercooked in the middle. The first year of anything is like that: full of trial and error, mostly error. It takes a full year just to figure out what you're doing. But once you do, everything starts to come together. It took the entire summer to detox from the storm and stress of that first year. When fall quarter began, I felt like I was finally catching my breath. It was as if I were in a respite quarter—not because the workload had vanished, but because I'd found my rhythm. My class and work assignments started serving double, sometimes even triple duty, which streamlined my time and energy. Everything felt relevant and interconnected.

If I took on a project at work, I'd find a way to make it the topic for a class paper. When I needed a research internship, I realized I could partner with a researcher already conducting a study at work. This synergy made everything feel more manageable and purposeful. I wasn't just surviving—I was thriving.

The first year's readings and assignments were relentless, demanding ten to twelve hours of study each day, seven days a week. By the second year, though, the workload felt lighter, the articles more digestible, and the rhythm of academia less punishing. It was like moving from a stretch of dense nonfiction to a breezy, captivating novel.

The shift was both academic and physical too. I found myself dancing, walking, playing tennis, and hitting the gym more often. The endless hours of sitting were a thing of the past, replaced by movement and vitality. It felt like a whole new day. I was glad I hadn't given in to the nagging thoughts of quitting during those grueling early months. By the second year, the future felt open and hopeful. I was looking forward to what came next, deeply grateful to be putting my talents to use in this way.

I was especially grateful that I had embraced the path of research. It's been about understanding how things worked and finding ways to make them better. My career has been dedicated to working with immigrant and marginalized youth and families, and I've always felt a deep responsibility to give them my best—my sharpest thinking, my strongest skills, the most effective resources and interventions I could find.

Intervention research asks an important question: *What works for whom?* This question fuels my passion because when marginalized youth are excluded from studies, overlooked in research questions, or denied a voice in shaping them, the loss is immeasurable. I believe that those who are most marginalized and vulnerable deserve the very best we have to offer. That's equity. That is leveling the playing field. That is love on a societal scale.

Writing the stories of my life helps me make sense of them and create meaning. Meaning-making is a critical part of healing—moving from disorganization to organization, from chaos to clarity, and finally, putting things to rest. I experienced this process firsthand while working on my dissertation. I wrote over twenty drafts of the problem statement, revising and refining each time. When my advisor asked if all those revisions were frustrating, I said they weren't. In fact, it was a joy to think and write about my research interest. Each draft felt like sculpting. I started with something rough and unformed, then gradually refined it into something clearer, more structured, and elegantly simple. It feels the same writing this book. I felt deep satisfaction while playing with ideas, synthesizing them, and finding the essence of what I wanted to say. One of my professors often challenged us to write about our work in a way that anyone could understand. That push toward simplicity and clarity stretched me as a writer and thinker, helping me grow. Writing is telling stories, creating meaning, and transforming raw, scattered thoughts into something coherent and beautiful.

## Brief Rant on Fear

We all get scared. Trying new things is scary. No one is immune to fear. Sure, we may respond differently - some freeze, some procrastinate, some push through - but the feeling is universal. There's no way around it, no shortcuts. The only path to mastery, competence, or achievement is to go through it.

Do it. Do it. Do it.

It takes hundreds of trials and errors. That's how it works for everyone. Why do you think you are so special that you should be perfect from the start? Or worse, why would you refuse to try at all because you're afraid of failing? Nobody gets to be perfect—ever. And certainly not at the beginning of *anything.*

So, grab hold of your *ovarios* or *cojones* or both if you're lucky. Dare to step into the fear and do the thing. If for no other reason, do it to spite the Evil One whispering in your ear that you can't, that it's impossible.

Hmm. *Don't you just want to prove 'em wrong?*

## Recovering Perfectionist

Perfectionism can be a MF. It holds us back from trying new things, seizing opportunities, loving and forgiving ourselves and others (or at least being compassionate), speaking our mind (whether fully formed or still in progress), and learning. Bump that and FTS. I'm done missing out on the good stuff because I'm hung up on being perfect. I get to be imperfect!

Wouldn't those thoughts make great mantras? Little reminders to drown out the perfectionistic voices in our heads:

- *I get to be imperfect.*
- *This doesn't have to be perfect—it just has to get done.*
- *I've got nothing to prove.*

I can pinpoint the exact moment I hit rock bottom with perfectionism and finally surrendered to my higher power. It was my second year in the doctoral program, during a policy analysis course. At the time, I was juggling parenting, part-time work, full-time coursework, and a brutal commute. I'd nearly finished a twenty-page paper due the next day when my laptop crashed, wiping out everything.

That was it—the breaking point. So, I did the only thing that made sense to my mind-body: I took a nap. I slept for three hours, woke up, and rewrote the entire paper from memory and notes. My new mantra was born: *This doesn't have to be perfect or excellent—it just has to get done.*

Despite all the personal and professional stressors, I finished my doctoral program at a good time-to-degree pace (according to the department graduate assistant). Now, I remind myself every day: *I've got nothing to prove.* Sure, there are moments where I aim for excellence, but for most things? They just need to get done.

There was a professor whose office was near mine. An older faculty member who walked around in a t-shirt, shorts, and flip-flops, seemingly unbothered by professional expectations. His classes had a reputation for easy A's, and he seemed immune to scrutiny. I often joke that I aspire to the confidence of someone like him unburdened by microaggressions, self-doubt, or external expectations. *Tengo derecho*. Perfectionism is a thief robbing joy and weighing down everyone it touches. I refuse to let it control me anymore. I'm free.

## FTS: A Mental Reset

For years, I've taught interns and graduate students one of my favorite cognitive-behavioral tools. It's a simple mental reset; a sharp-edged mantra to hush the inner critic, shake off imposter syndrome, and drown out the static of self-doubt. It's my go-to for unhelpful comments, side-eye microaggressions, or those sneaky, self-defeating thoughts that creep in like an unwelcome draft. And, yes—the language matters. The profanity is the punch. The rage is the reset. It lets the negativity in the air know: I am not the one.

I don't cuss at people—that's never the move. But injustice? That voice in my head that sometimes forgets who I am? That deserves a firm and resounding FTS.

I don't always say it out loud—at least not in polite company. But at home, in my cone of silence, it's fair game. Some days, when an old embarrassment kicks down the door of my memory, I don't just think it—I say it. I might even throw up two middle fingers and pump them in the air for good measure. It's oddly satisfying. Most of the time, though, it's just a quiet mantra. A reminder that someone else's harsh opinion is not my problem, my business, or my burden. Then I keep it moving.

My daughter gets me. For Christmas, she gave me a stamp with this phrase on it. (She had it custom-made, because, of course, she did.) I love that stamp. It sits on my desk like a little guardian, standing watch. I've even gifted some to my students as graduation presents—a parting note that says:

*You don't have to believe every negative thought you think. You don't have to carry every unkind word you hear.*

This phrase, this mindset, is about staying grounded, keeping perspective, and cutting through the noise. It's a declaration, a boundary, a way forward. When the overly harsh inner critic gets loud, when the world tries to shrink me—FTS. In that moment of rage and push back, I stand stronger and I'm free.

# F**K THAT
# $HIT!

## Psychological Warfare in the Workplace: Stories (Mine, Yours, and Everyone Else's)

My stories of psychological warfare in the workplace are also your stories and everyone else's. The names and settings change, but the workplace dynamics have a way of repeating themselves. As long as human beings are involved, there will be a shadow side to interactions.

Say you land a new job and pour your heart into it. You thrive on meaningful work that challenges you, honoring the sacrifices of immigrant parents who crossed borders so you could have these opportunities. You don't take that for granted, yet, you find yourself branded as "too much." Your work ethic earns mixed reactions - some appreciate it, but others envy you ("No one likes a show-off.") or some others grow suspicious ("Why are you making me look bad?" or "What's your angle?").

Unless you're on a team of *A players*, you are the problem. Cue the office mentors, meanies, and allies.

The mentor, or the *A player*, is secure and visionary - they challenge and guide you. They see your potential and take you under their wing. They show you what it feels like to fly.

Then there's the *C player*—in over their head but no less ambitious. They might be an insecure boss who feels threatened by your presence. Beneath their polished exterior lies a fragile ego fed by validation through status symbols — polished suits, the right car, an expensive brand-name university. Your competence doesn't inspire them; it agitates their inner critic. Without a secure foundation to draw from, they weaponize their authority, cutting you down to protect their sense of worth.

You wonder, *Did I misstep? What's wrong with me?* Then you realize, it's not about you. They are threatened. You have to walk around reminding yourself, *It's okay to be who I am.*

Steve Jobs famously believed in hiring *A players*—highly talented, driven, and creative individuals who inspire one another. *A players* thrive in environments that spark innovation and excellence. *C players*, on the other hand, avoid *A players* because they're a constant reminder of their own insecurities. Instead, they surround themselves with *D players*—people who won't challenge or outshine them. It seems like a good idea to keep company with people who make you feel safe rather than exposed. This dynamic stifles innovation, fosters mediocrity, and creates a culture of complacency.[4]

I've worked with all types of leaders and believe toxicity in the workplace is shaped by life's wounds. At the heart of many workplace conflicts is a question that therapy clients often wrestle with: "Was I truly loved?" Unresolved insecurities from childhood—whether rooted in neglect, loss, or other traumas—can seep into professional relationships, coloring how we see others and ourselves. A healed person leads with confidence and grace; a wounded one leads with fear and resentment.

The workplace is a reflection of family patterns and societal ones. *Mal de ojo*, or the "evil eye," captures a truth recognized worldwide: envy is a powerful, universal force. Envy can motivate us to build or tempt us to destroy. In workplaces where collaboration is sacrificed to competition, envy often takes the destructive route.

I reached my breaking point with a *C player* boss. After a weekend of reflection, I decided to stop shrinking myself to make them comfortable. I showed up on Monday with a quiet resolve: *If you want my talents, you'll need to treat me with respect.* While their tone shifted temporarily, the pattern didn't change—we eventually parted ways. Still, the lessons stayed with me: In every workplace, the same dynamics appear until we learn to navigate them differently.

Sibling rivalries, parental approval, and childhood wounds replay in our professional lives, especially unresolved family patterns. We take on roles—whether it's the overachiever, the peacekeeper, or the rebel—without even realizing it. Maybe we play the role like a younger sibling eager to curry favor, using charm and social savvy to gain the attention and protection of stronger allies. Maybe we fill the role of the favored eldest, a well-crafted mentorship persona with charisma, using influence to maintain power. Maybe our relentless drive to succeed is rooted in our shadow—feelings of frustration and resentment can become a barrier, cutting us off from meaningful connection.

Seeing these patterns clearly is the first step to breaking free. Have you learned to navigate them? In your family? At work? The love and hate of sibling rivalry exist in families regardless of age; it's the same in the workplace, but without the love.

## Conclusion

Work and purpose? They're the messy roommates you never asked for but can't live without (like my daughter). They leave dishes in the sink, borrow things from your bathroom without letting you know, and somehow still manage to teach you something about yourself.

The deep end doesn't care if I'm ready to swim. It just waits, daring me to jump, and laughs if I panic. And yet, I do it anyway because what's the alternative? Standing on the edge forever, wondering what it might feel like to float? When I took the leap to go back to school in my forties, I asked myself, *What are you gonna do instead, watch TV and complain about your job?*

The truth is, work is never just about work. It's a mirror, a magnifying glass, a hall of funhouse horrors that reflects every insecurity and every spark of brilliance you have. You flail, you gasp, you choke on the water, and, if you're lucky, you break through. You learn. You grow. You find out that the thing that felt like drowning was actually you becoming something more.

Purpose is the current that drags you into something bigger than yourself, whether you're ready or not. It's confusing, relentless, beautiful, and often completely unfair. But it's also the only thing that makes this whole exhausting cycle worth it.

So here's to the deep end, to the moments that strip you bare and force you to figure out who you really are. Dive in. Swallow the fear. Come out the other side with stories to tell and muscles you didn't know you had. And if you're lucky, maybe a little peace with the chaos.

Because here's the secret no one tells you: The deep end isn't the enemy. It's where you find your purpose. It's where you learn to swim.

# Science & Research

## Workplace Relationships: The Hidden Key to Success

When you think about what makes or breaks a workplace, your mind might jump to productivity, strategy, or leadership. But here's a surprising truth: Workplaces function a lot like marriages. They thrive or crumble based on relationships.

Scientists have begun borrowing tools from marital research to decode workplace dynamics, and the findings are fascinating. Turns out, the same emotional processes that predict a happy marriage—positivity, teamwork, and how conflicts are handled—are just as critical for employee engagement and retention.

Let's explore how thinking of your workplace like a relationship could change the way you approach your job or your team.

### 1. My Lawfully Wedded Workplace[1]

In 2015, a group of researchers adapted a tool originally designed to predict divorce, the Oral History Interview (OHI), to assess workplace relationships, ƒ and what they found was striking.

### The Highlights:

Employees who viewed conflicts through a positive lens and maintained a sense of "we-ness" (shared identity with their team or employer) were significantly less likely to quit. On the flip side, negativity and unresolved conflict spelled trouble.

**Why It Matters:**
Employee turnover isn't just a nuisance; it's expensive and disruptive. Yet most prediction models only get it right about 30% of the time. By focusing on the emotional and relational health of employees, organizations have a new, much sharper tool to tackle retention issues.

**What We Can Learn:**

• A sense of fondness for the organization and a collaborative mindset can keep employees engaged.
• Relationships at work are emotionally significant—just like in marriage.
• To retain employees, businesses need to actively nurture positive dynamics.

**The Study in Numbers:**

• Participants: 46 employees in legal and healthcare sectors.
• Average Tenure: 7 years (ranging from 1 to 35 years).
• Key Insight: Employment relationships, like personal ones, thrive when negativity is kept in check and connection is prioritized.

**2. Predicting Turnover: Lessons from Marriage[2]**
In 2014, another team of researchers took the OHI method into the workplace, but this time with a laser focus on predicting who might leave. Their findings? Positivity and collaboration are retention superpowers, while negativity and language suggesting disconnection ("they" instead of "we") predict higher turnover.

**The Eye-Opener:**
Traditional turnover prediction methods hover around 30% accuracy. By borrowing insights from marital research, this study achieved over 90% accuracy. Imagine what businesses could do with that kind of foresight.

**Big Takeaways:**

• Words matter. Employees who speak positively about their workplace are more likely to stay.
• "We-ness" isn't just a nice idea—it's measurable and critical.
• Approaching workplace dynamics like a relationship offers profound, actionable insights.

**The Study in Numbers:**

• Participants: 7 academic staff with 10–30 years of tenure.
• Accuracy: Relational indicators predicted turnover with 90% precision.

**Workplaces Are Relationships in Disguise**
At the heart of these studies is a simple, profound idea: work means understanding the importance of relationships as well as tasks and goals. It's about relationships. When we invest in building connection, trust, and positivity at work, the benefits ripple out— happier employees, healthier teams, and organizations that retain their talent.

So, here's a question worth asking: How's your workplace relationship doing? Because the answer might hold the key to your next big breakthrough.

# Ancestor Wisdom

"As you teach, you learn." —Jewish Proverb

## Ancestor Wisdom: Transforming Rivalry into Harmony

The ancestors knew something we often forget: that the heart can be both a battlefield and a sanctuary. In the sacred teachings passed down from Latin America and Africa, we find the wisdom to transform rivalry into kinship, competition into celebration, and isolation into interconnection. These teachings invite us to see ourselves not as solitary beings but as threads in an intricate web of life, each one holding and strengthening the other.

### *Ubuntu*: "I Am Because We Are" (Africa)[1]

The philosophy of *Ubuntu* rises like the sun on a shared horizon, illuminating the truth that we are inseparable from the well-being of those around us. When rivalry arises, it is as though the threads of a communal tapestry are pulled taut, threatening to snap. *Ubuntu* teaches us that to harm another is to harm oneself, for the success of one is the success of all.

**Wisdom:** "If you want to go fast, go alone; if you want to go far, go together." This proverb whispers an ancient truth: the solitary path may be swift, but the journey of togetherness endures. *Ubuntu* reminds us to move as one, with hands joined and hearts aligned, knowing that the strength of the collective can overcome any challenge.

### *In Lak'ech Ala K'in*: "I Am Another You" (Mayan Philosophy)[2]

The Mayan wisdom of *In Lak'ech Ala K'in* beckons us to look into the eyes of another and see ourselves reflected. It is a profound call to empathy, a reminder that every thought, word, and action toward others reverberates back to the self. Rivalry, in this light, becomes a wound inflicted upon our own being.

> **Wisdom:** "*In Lak'ech*" invites us to celebrate each other's successes, recognizing that when one grows, the whole garden flourishes. It is a call to honor the divine mirror in every face, to replace envy with admiration, and to dance together in the rhythm of life.

### Respecting the *Orí*: Destiny in Afro-Brazilian Candomblé [5]

In Afro-Brazilian traditions like *Candomblé*, each person's *orí* (destiny) is seen as divinely guided by the *orixás*—spiritual forces that shape our unique paths. Rivalry here is futile, as it disregards the sacred individuality of each journey. Instead, respect for others' paths strengthens communal harmony and spiritual alignment.

> **Wisdom:** "Respect the path of others." This teaching reminds us that envy is unnecessary when each person's journey is sacred. Supporting others honors not only their destiny but the divine forces guiding them.

## Conclusion: A Tapestry of Interdependence

Ancestral wisdom calls us back to the circle, where rivalry is softened by understanding and competition transformed into celebration. These teachings show us that our strength lies in our interdependence, in the sacred truth of *Ubuntu*.

# Tools

The tools in this section invite you to cultivate growth as you navigate relationships and foster meaningful collaboration in the workplace. By reframing rivalry and approaching interactions with compassion and balance, you can nurture healthier dynamics, reduce stress, and thrive in a supportive environment. These practices are here to help you create authentic connections and find harmony in your professional journey.

## Tool #1: Reframing Rivalry and Building Collaboration

Workplace relationships often awaken feelings of rivalry or competition. These emotions, while natural, can become powerful opportunities for growth and connection when reframed with intention. Let these strategies guide you toward building healthier relationships—with your colleagues and with yourself.

### Reframe Rivalry as Inspiration

Rather than seeing others' successes as threats, shift your lens:

- **Find inspiration in others' achievements.** Instead of comparing, admire their strengths as models for your own growth.
- **Turn competition into motivation.** Use it as fuel to explore your potential and stretch beyond your comfort zone.

## *Reflection Questions*

- What can I learn from this person's strengths?
- How can their success inspire me to grow or improve in my own unique way?

## Set Boundaries with Empathy

Boundaries are essential to reducing stress and avoiding unnecessary competition. When approached with empathy, they strengthen relationships rather than divide them.

## Tips for Setting Boundaries

- Redirect overly competitive conversations with grace.
  * "That's an impressive approach you took—I'd love to hear more about how you came up with it!"
- Protect your personal time by stepping away from work emails or chats after hours.
  * "To show up at my best tomorrow, I'm stepping away from emails after 6 p.m."
- Communicate boundaries with compassion:
  * "I value our collaboration, but to stay balanced, I need to focus on family time after 6 p.m.—let's reconnect tomorrow morning!"

## Practice Active Listening

Shift your focus from responding to deeply understanding. Active listening fosters respect, connection, and collaboration.

## Why It Matters

- It reduces competition by creating space for shared understanding.
- You may uncover strengths in others that complement your own.

## How to Practice Active Listening

- Pause before responding to fully absorb what's been said.
- Reflect by summarizing their words or asking thoughtful follow-up questions.

By reframing rivalry, setting boundaries, and practicing active listening, you can transform workplace dynamics into a thriving culture of collaboration.

## Tool #2: Reflection and Connection Practices

Building self-awareness is the foundation of stronger relationships. These journaling prompts, exercises, and affirmations are designed to deepen your workplace connections and align your actions with your values.

## Journaling Prompts

### 1. Explore Insecurities

What insecurities surface when I see someone else succeed? How might these feelings connect to my unacknowledged goals or self-image?

### 2. Cultural Wisdom

What values from my cultural background can guide me to approach rivalry differently? How can I weave these into my daily interactions?

### 3. Celebrate Your Strengths

What unique strengths do I bring to my workplace? How can I focus on these rather than comparing myself to others?

## Activities and Exercises

- **Workplace Gratitude Moments**

Write down one thing you appreciate about a colleague each day. Small acknowledgments—like their creativity or kindness—create a culture of connection.

- **Perspective Swap**

Imagine life from a rival's point of view:
  - What pressures might they feel?
  - How could I support or connect with them?

## Affirmations and Weekly Reflections

- "I celebrate others' success as inspiration for my own growth."
- "There is enough success for everyone; I am worthy of my own achievements."
- "I cultivate cooperation and mutual respect in all my relationships."

## At the end of each week, reflect with honesty:

- Did I respond to challenges with integrity?
- Did I feel envy? How did I redirect it?
- What did my emotions reveal about my aspirations?

Identify one thing you'll do differently next week to foster positive connections.

## A Poem for Reflection: Embracing Shadows

There's light in me, shadow too—
both hum quiet songs beneath my skin.
I see in you the echoes of myself:
the soft fears, the loud ache of pride.
This world teaches us to race,
to grip tight the trophy of 'better than.'
But I'm learning to loosen,
to let my hands hold instead of hoard.
When I lift you, I rise too,
like rivers feeding the same wide ocean.
Rivalry is just a story
we unlearn with every shared embrace.
Each soul burns its own wild flame,
and together,
We are the sun.

When you approach relationships with curiosity, compassion, and courage, you open the door to deeper connections and a more fulfilling professional life.

Chapter 5
**The New Fire Ceremony**

"However far the stream flows, it never forgets its source."
—African Proverb

## Holistic Assessment: Mind, Body, Heart, Spirit

*A estas alturas*, my life is less about reaching a summit and more about finding balance. Maintaining an equilibrium that honors the mind, body, heart, and spirit. For most of my life, I've excelled at two quadrants: spirit and mind. These parts of me feel like strong muscles, so much so that they hold entire chapters of this book (chapter two and chapter four, respectively). But a truly holistic life requires nurturing all the parts of ourselves equally. Anything less creates imbalance.

### Spirit

There's a quiet power that comes from trusting the whispers of my soul. After all, what good is it to gain the world but lose your soul? (Matthew 16:26)

I've learned that when your spiritual coffers are full, the challenges of life seem smaller. It's hard to be overwhelmed by people or situations when your spiritual wealth is abundant. It's like having a vast, untapped reservoir of calm and purpose that shields you from the chaos of the world. Whether it's navigating a minor irritation—a metaphorical speeding ticket—or making monumental life decisions, my connection to spirit has always steadied me.

But this kind of wealth doesn't appear overnight. It's an investment—daily, deliberate, and, often, unseen. My spirituality is about the myriad of consistent practices that keep me grounded and whole, the habits that build resilience and spiritual wealth over a lifetime. It's the reason I feel unshaken in moments of uncertainty. I know where I stand because I know who I am and who has my back.

## Mind

If spirituality is my primary resilience factor, then my mind's tireless ability to come up with creative solutions to problems is my spirit's co-pilot. I'm thankful for my big, creative brain, which has not only helped me navigate tough situations but also dream up and achieve bold visions. No matter what I face, tiny or huge, my brain goes to work to figure it out. Everything is figure-out-able. That's what I've lived, and that's what I believe. That's what I believe, so that's what I've lived.

Books have been my constant companions, filling my mind with infinite possibilities and experiences. Through them, I've lived thousands of lifetimes, absorbed lessons from countless strangers, their lessons becoming my own.

My mind isn't just creative, it's resourceful, and that resourcefulness has helped me scale mountain-tops: earning a PhD at forty-six, achieving tenure in academia where Latinas hold just 2.6% of positions, and building a career that I could one day step away from with pride. I'm grateful for the people, opportunities, and decisions that brought me here.

## Body

For years, I treated my body like a reliable assistant—always there, always waiting, but rarely prioritized. While I nurtured my mind and spirit, my body quietly endured neglect. My sleep habits were the exception; I sleep well and nap with pleasure, no guilt. And there have been decades of monthly massages, a steady act of self-love and self-care. For the most part, however, my body waited in the wings while my mind and spirit took center stage.

That began to change in moments of crisis. During my divorce, when stress rendered me unable to write a single word of my dissertation, I turned to reiki—a practice that unlocked the mental blocks my body had been holding.

Trying hot yoga for the first time was another revelation. Watching retirees glow with vitality reshaped my understanding of aging, inspiring me to invest in my body as much as I had in my mind and spirit. Personal training and Pilates weren't just health practices to me; they were acts of reconciliation with a part of myself I had long ignored.

And yet, I'm still learning. The effects of menopause, pre-diabetes, and sleep apnea remind me that the body demands constant attention. Perhaps these topics belong in the second edition of this book, but for now, they're chapters in progress.

## Heart

When my daughter once called me "a robot—the most logical person she knows," she wasn't wrong. For much of my life, I dismissed emotions as inconvenient obstacles to productivity. My upbringing reinforced this belief. My mother's emotional outbursts felt excessive to me, and I saw how fear paralyzed those around me. My solution was to channel everything into action, until my body refused to keep up.

Emotions, I've since learned, aren't roadblocks. They're messengers. They carry truths that can't be accessed any other way. And so, I've begun the work of unfreezing them, of listening to the wisdom I once ignored. It's not easy; my heart is a muscle long out of practice. But growth isn't linear. It's beautifully discontinuous. And in this, I've come to understand people evolve in bursts, and the areas we neglect eventually demand our attention.

Life has humbled me into empathy. When I used to ask, *"How could they do that?"* the Universe, with its sharp sense of irony, would hand me a situation in which I'd do exactly that. These experiences taught me that judgment dissolves in the face of lived experience. The more I recognized the unseen backstories influencing people's actions, the easier it became to let go of judgment. These days, I focus on listening rather than fixing. I strive to lead with compassion, empathy, and understanding instead of rushing to offer solutions. Or at least, that's what I'm working on.

## Balance

At its core, balance is about harmony. It's about honoring the mind, body, heart, and spirit—not equally all the time, but with an awareness that all parts matter.

For years, my Parent ego state over-functioned, trying to take care of everyone. Eric Berne, a psychologist, created this concept in Transactional Analysis (TA).[1] Even if you have never heard or read about TA, it is a helpful metaphor (so play along). The Parent (nurturing and critical), Adult (the boss who makes the final decisions), and Child (playful, rebellious, curious) parts in us reflect the ways we navigate life. I lived mostly in the Parent state, constantly rescuing, fixing, and sacrificing. My hard-won lesson is that it's not sustainable to always be in that mode. Over time, I wasn't just tired—I was exhausted and depleted. My worth had become tangled in how much I gave to others - family, work, friends, volunteering in the community - and it came at the cost of my own well-being.

Patterns take root early. We carry them like invisible backpacks, rarely stopping to check what's inside. My breaking point came when I realized my exhaustion wasn't just happening to me. *I was creating it.* Something had to give. I began a slow, intentional shift from putting myself last to prioritizing my needs. Not in a selfish way, but out of self-respect. Taking care of myself wasn't just good for me: it was good for the people I loved. My daughter didn't need a burned-out, depleted version of me. Happy mom, happy daughter. Depressed mom, depressed daughter. *Temenos que durar.* We have to last.

When we over-rely on the Parent ego state (constantly feeling responsible for everyone else) we lose touch with the Child ego state (the part of us that craves joy and spontaneity). The imbalance doesn't just affect us; it ripples into the lives of those around us. By stepping back from the urge to fix and rescue, we create opportunities for others to take ownership of their choices. And that's where balance begins. When we commit to it, everyone benefits.

So, what's the antidote? More joy in our lives. By rediscovering play and fun, I began to rewrite my story. I moved from "mothering the world" to showing up for myself first.[2] Once you experience the joy and balance that come from prioritizing your well-being, there's no going back to over-giving. I became more present, compassionate, and calm. And yes, I started living my best life.

What holds us back from balance? Is it guilt? Fear? The belief that being the one who saves the day is noble and right, even as it erodes our well-being? Recognizing those barriers is the first step toward equilibrium.

The antidote to self-neglect is self-love, self-respect, self-worth, and self-care. It's about learning to trust yourself enough to create a life that feels whole. But if self-neglect is all we've ever known, balance can feel foreign, even impossible, or wrong. We don't know what we don't know, and that's okay. Wherever you are on this journey, baby steps count. Feel your way.

If you're stuck in Parent mode, the prescription is simple: have more fun. Make space for joy, even in small, doable ways. It could be as simple as laughing with a friend, walking barefoot in the grass, or a long carefree nap. Once you start taking care of yourself every day and consistently, it feels so good you won't want to stop.

On the flip side, if you lean too far into the Child ego state—losing accountability or leaving responsibilities for others to clean up—the remedy is structure and routine. Start small. Set achievable goals and celebrate every step forward.

True balance lies in the integration of all three ego states. By blending the playfulness of the Child, the wisdom of the Parent, and the grounded leadership of the Adult, we create a life that's fulfilling and stable. When our Adult part decides to attend to both our Parent and Child needs, instead of privileging one over the other, we make balanced choices and live in a way that feels sustainable. Our ancestors understood this. They knew that balance was the key to a life of meaning, connection, health, and joy.

## Semi-Retirement!
For years, work consumed so much of my life that stepping back felt unimaginable. How do you pause something that defines your rhythm, your purpose, your very identity? But when the time came, the idea of letting go didn't feel daunting—it felt liberating. I was ready for a new chapter, one marked by freedom, rest, and rediscovery. And yet, the shift wasn't without its challenges.

## Preparing for the Transition
Retirement (or semi-retirement) is a monumental transition. It means being released from working for money everyday, and it also means releasing everything work represents: the camaraderie of colleagues, the sense of mastery, the predictable structure of a daily routine. Letting go can feel like being a trapeze artist, suspended in midair, unable to release the bar until the next one swings into reach.

For me, transitions are often catalyzed by what I call "birth or death pangs." It's that undeniable discomfort that builds, slowly but steadily, until there's little choice but to move forward. Without those pangs, I might have stayed in the comfort of the familiar, missing the possibilities waiting on the other side. But I was ready. I was ready for more naps, more travel, passion projects like this book, and precious time with my daughter and friends.

I'll never forget a pivotal hypnotherapy session. The therapist guided me into a deep state of relaxation and said, "Nobody needs anything from you. Nobody wants anything from you." Those words hit me like a wave. I felt my whole body sink into the liberation of the words. As a recovering Wendy—someone who had long taken responsibility for the Peter Pan's of my world–I had built my identity and self-worth around caretaking and being needed. But in that moment, those words unlocked something inside me. I realized my worth could exist apart from being indispensable, that I could live a life built on freedom, not obligation. Now, I protect that realization fiercely, carving out space to savor the independence (*¡Ajúa!*) I worked so hard to achieve.

### Recovery & Freedom

Stepping into semi-retirement has been a profound act of recovery, and I'm all kinds of grateful. After decades of overworking and over-giving, I've reclaimed the balance I once thought impossible. I let myself sit with the quiet of inactivity and nothingness, and my nervous system finally exhaled.

Reflecting on my career, I see the trade-offs clearly. Working in public agencies and large bureaucratic institutions provided stability and a sense of purpose, but it also stifled my creativity and passion for innovation.

Semi-retirement has allowed me to find a middle ground—a happy medium. With part-time consulting gigs and plenty of white space on my planner, I've struck a balance in my relationship with work. It's moved from proving my worth or chasing an endless to-do list to joy, curiosity, and living intentionally.

When I think about this chapter of my life, I feel immense gratitude for the lessons work taught me, for the freedom I now savor, and for the journey that brought me here. Semi-retirement is a choice to live life on my terms, to embrace joy without guilt, and to honor the rhythm that feels right for me.

## Community & Connection

At this stage in my life, I'm learning to honor the delicate balance between love, work, and play. For an introvert like me, the pandemic's stay-at-home orders were manageable—at first. I thrive in the quiet spaces of remote work, where solitude fuels my creativity. But even I felt the restlessness creep in as the weeks turned into months and years. That's when I knew I needed something more, something deeper. I reached out to the juiciest, most inspiring women I know and invited them to form a circle—a sacred space where we could gather, connect, and hold each other through life's inevitable ups and downs.

On May 15, 2022, we met for the first time, and we haven't stopped since. The circle has grown and evolved, just as we have. In the beginning, we gathered around the new moon, then the full moon, marking our cycles of shedding and initiating. We meet in each other's homes, retreat to mountain cabins, attend spiritual events, and invite healers to join us. This circle has become my little *familia*, my chosen community—a group of *chingonas* who create sacred space for each other through the *peticiones* and *testimonios* of our lives.

One of my friends described what this group means in a group chat recently:
"Every moment spent with you all fills my heart and energizes my spirit. Honestly, I feel so blessed to be a part of this circle and grow alongside each one of you. As I move more and more into my most authentic self, witnessing you all doing the same is inspiring and a testimony to how spirit provides. This whole thread made my day. Also, Ale, your home is one of my favorite places I've been so far. It feels warm, and loved, and magical."

These words are a reminder of what we've created together—a safe, magical space where we can show up fully as ourselves, *la pura neta y puro amor*. It's a gift I treasure.

Beyond this circle, I've been lucky to find friendships across generations. Older friends mentor me like the *tías* I wish had stayed longer, offering wisdom, perspective, and a gentle push when I need it. Younger friends bring a sense of adventure to my life, filling it with spontaneity and curiosity. They're my fellow wanderlusts—my study buddies for travel and exploration. Together, we've unearthed relics, wandered through museums, and explored historical sites for no other reason than because we can, because they're there, and because we were together.

## Passion Projects

In this chapter of my life, I find myself journeying into the marrow of my passions—exploring the curiosities and callings that once whispered softly but now beckon with urgency. One such calling is my "32 States of Mexico in 32 Months" project. It is not just a journey of geography; it is a pilgrimage of spirit, memory, and blood. With every state I visit, I gather threads—stories, artifacts, and connections—that weave together the tapestry of my heritage.

In the deserts and mountains of San Luis Potosí and Zacatecas, I discovered *queso de tuna*, a candy crafted from the cactus fruit. It is a small miracle—sunlight transfigured into sweetness, a reminder that even the harshest landscapes yield treasures for those who know where to look.

My growing *rebozo* collection is a celebration of regional artistry. There are delicate hand-crafted silk shawls from Santa María made by generations of craftsmen and their silk fringes intricately hand-braided by wives and mothers in their spare time. They shimmer like water under the moonlight. Then there are the vibrant, earthy dyed wool *ponchos* of Chiapas. From Puebla, I've acquired *mañanitas* (short capes worn draped over the shoulders as a decorative outer garment) that are hand-embroidered using cross-stitch with traditional designs. In Oaxaca, the *rebozos* are known for their vibrant colors, handwoven using pedal looms, reflecting their textile traditions. Every one of these coverings holds the essence of the people who created it.

On my last trip, I stood in the land of my mother's birth, Chihuahua, and held in my hands the weavings of *Rarámuri* women (they were called *Tarahumara* by the Spanish). Holding their weavings felt like holding a piece of history. Every thread carries the stories of the land, the traditions of their people.

My friend Jenny Viveros, LCSW, whose roots trace back to Michoacán, Mexico, is another keeper of these stories. She introduced me to the unique marvels of her state's *rebozos*. Woven on a backstrap loom by Purépecha artisans, these *rebozos* are adorned with vibrantly dyed feathers and sequins embedded among rich colors, creating stunning pieces of wearable art. In her healing practice, Jenny incorporates these *rebozos* into therapy, wrapping women in their embrace and gently asking, *"What does this feel like to you?"* The responses echo the archetypal feminine: *It feels like a hug from my grandmother. It feels like being swaddled.* These answers speak to the ancestral memory held within these textiles—not just as objects but as cultural symbols. They are bridges between the practical and the sacred, the past and the present.

The *rebozo* is a wild and loyal thing. It serves without complaint, shielding you from the rain; carrying babies, groceries, and firewood; adorning women in dance, ritual, and ceremony; comforting the weary and the grieving; gracing altars and heirlooms; supporting during labor; adjusting hips postpartum; and grounding the body during a *manteada*—a massage performed with a *rebozo* for physical alignment, emotional comfort, and spiritual healing.[3] The *rebozo* is both cloak and companion, ordinary and extraordinary—a perfect manifestation of the sacred in the everyday, a fusion of form and function.

But even this journey of discovery has not been without its lessons. Monthly trips became an act of endurance, even with Dramamine and compression socks in tow. My body, wise and unyielding, whispered, *This is too much*. I listened. I adjusted. Now, I travel quarterly, giving myself the gift of slowing down, of savoring the beauty without rushing past it.

One day, when the map of my journey is complete, I will write of these experiences as a collection of soul-stories. I will write of the artistry I have witnessed, the resilience I have marveled at, and the joy of rediscovering the roots that anchor me. For now, I move forward, one state at a time, each step a prayer, each story a thread, weaving me closer to the wild, ancient essence of who I am.

## My Purpose

Several years ago, a dear friend, Tina, gave me a bookstore gift card for my birthday because she knows me. She's a fellow Virgo. Anyway, with that gift card, I bought Jack Canfield's book, *The Success Principles*.[4] In chapter two, Jack directs the reader to "write your purpose." This is what I wrote, years ago: "My purpose is to use my passion and creativity to inspire and illuminate for others what we came here to do - and love ourselves and others in the process."

I was sitting next to Paolina while I wrote it. She was reading her own book, so I turned to her and asked: "What's your purpose?" She answered: "To tell real people of color stories. To bring more representation in a meaningful way. To put us in fantastical plots, give us superpowers, send us on sci-fi adventures."

I am a mom, and I am a writer. I am fulfilling my purpose. And Paolina, she is a writer, a poet, performer, a designer of worlds both imagined and tangible (including costume and set design), and she can provide craft service too. She jokes she is amassing skills for the apocalypse. She is a deep thinker with big feelings - exquisite on the stage, potent on the page.

She and her high school BFFs - all Black and Brown women, college graduates, storytellers - just finished a short film, *Tough Cookies*, about the cutthroat competition of scout cookie sales. Now they're dreaming bigger - an all-women production company. Storytelling. Creation. Representation. The revolution begins in storytelling.

Turns out, the antidote to anxiety is creativity[5] because when we are creating—painting, writing, dancing, building, imagining—we are somewhere else. We step out of the endless loop, out of overthinking, out of fear. Anxiety lives in the survival brain, the part that scans for danger, keeps us on high alert. But creativity? Creativity lives in the possibility brain.

When we are making something, we shift. We move from panic to presence, from fear to flow. Anxiety tightens; creativity expands. Anxiety repeats the same tired story; creativity writes a new one. When we are creating, we are living, and nothing quiets anxiety quite like being fully alive.

Heart's desires. Universe conspiring. Thank you, *Yesus*.

## Financial Preparedness & Literacy

Financial health, I've realized, is deeply tied to emotional and spiritual well-being. Learning to manage my finances goes beyond numbers; it's part of the larger journey of creating balance in my life—honoring the resources I have as a reflection of my own worth.

*How did I retire young?* Earn more, spend less, and always prioritize what matters most. Freedom and time over material possessions—these are the values that shaped my intentionally low-maintenance lifestyle. And defining my "freedom number," the amount I truly need to live comfortably, was a game-changer.

Here's what I lived: The more I worked, the more I spent—compensating for exhaustion with things I didn't need. But once I found peace within myself, I needed less. For my Virgo sensibilities, clutter is chaos. Living with less saves money and reclaims power.

Being debt-free is everything. I tackled my credit cards and made a rule: If I can't afford it outright, I don't buy it. Paying off my balance every month is non-negotiable. Keeping expenses low is a way of life. I regularly evaluate my spending—cutting what I don't need, like six months of cable, and keeping what truly matters, like personal training, because muscles in menopause and quality of life matters.

My financial literacy started with books. Jerrold Mundis's *How to Get Out of Debt* was a wake-up call. It showed me the emotional roots of overspending and gave me practical tools to take control[6] (and I've included these in the Tools section of this chapter). Thomas J. Stanley and William D. Danko's *The Millionaire Next Door* drove home this truth: Wealth doesn't come from looking rich; it comes from consistency and smart choices over time.[7] Their book emphasizes that net worth (what you own minus what you owe) is far more important than income when it comes to building true financial stability. It even suggests that teachers, with their modest but steady incomes, can find it easier to become millionaires than professionals who feel pressured to keep up appearances. Finally, it highlighted a critical insight: The more time I dedicate to learning, planning, and thinking about money management, the greater my chances of building and maintaining lasting wealth.

Then there's Suze Orman. As a fellow social worker, her message hit home. Live within your means. Save for emergencies. Avoid debt. Prepare for the future.[8] The wisdom she shared that stays with me as a guiding principle and mantra is "People come first, then money" Don't twist it. Whether it's paying employees a fair wage, donating to your community, or choosing values over profit, the message is simple: your decisions reflect your priorities.

I read countless books, but I'll share one more: *My Money Journey: How 30 People Found Financial Freedom—and You Can Too*, edited by Jonathan Clements. What struck me most was the recurring emphasis on index funds—simple, effective tools praised for their low costs, ease of access, diversification, and alignment with long-term goals.[9]

You don't need to be a Wall Street wizard to build wealth. I started with an index fund, thanks to a family friend who walked me through a straightforward app. Apps like

Fidelity or Vanguard make it easy—no jargon, no high minimums, no excuses. I walked my teenage nephews through the same steps, because building financial stability is for everyone, not just the elite.

What I've learned is that financial health is about freedom. It's about aligning money with personal values, living below my means, and embracing simplicity. Wealth grows through consistent, intentional choices, step by step, and living a life true to my priorities.

**Part-Time Work With a Purpose**
Now that I have pensions and lifetime health benefits, I work part-time, which is code for "I can finally breathe." Freedom is everything, absolutely everything. It's the feeling you get when you toss off a too-tight bra at the end of a long day—only the day is your whole career.

Full-time work? Hard pass.

These days, I've found ways to make part-time consulting not only feasible but downright lucrative. A dear friend once gave me the kind of advice that made me feel equal parts terrified and alive:

"To set your consulting fee, think of your dream number—and then double it."

*Jaja!* I laughed because what else can you do with that kind of audacity? But I tried it. And it worked. It stretched me to think bigger, bolder. To stand up straighter. To let my confidence match the quality of my work and the decades of experience behind it.

## Dreams & Reality Checks

When my daughter was applying to college, I laid out what I thought were reasonable parameters.

"I can afford a UC or CSU," I told her. She nodded and applied to one of each nearby.

But then she said, "NYU is my dream school."

At that moment, I just knew—that's where she was going. Sure enough, she applied for early, early admission and got in. Early.

I wasn't born with a trust fund, but I've learned to live as if the universe has a big, beautiful purse slung over its shoulder, overflowing with everything I need. And somehow, it always comes through. Thank you, *Yesus.* With her scholarships, a little creative budgeting, and a lot of faith, I made it work. Every year, I took out parent loans to fill in the gaps, knowing that if she was bold enough to dream this big, I had to be bold enough to back her. Four years later, she graduated on time—just as I retired.

And then came the email.

My first loan payment: over a thousand dollars a month.

I felt that number press on my chest, but instead of spiraling, I did what any semi-retired mother-slash-therapist would do: I took a deep breath and started brainstorming.

How could I manage this responsibility and still keep my trips to Mexico? (Because let's be honest, my trips to Mexico are non-negotiable.)

## Launching My Private Practice

That's when I decided to launch a private practice using a telehealth platform.

I started small, seeing just a few clients a week to find my rhythm. Telehealth allowed me to ease in (no full-on cannonball), just a steady wade into the waters. I experimented with three platforms:

- **Rula** and **growtherapy** - User-friendly with a consistent flow of referrals.
- **Headway** - Higher reimbursements but required more hustle (self-marketing, securing my own HIPAA-compliant platform).

Onboarding with all three at once, I found myself asking, *Why do I do this?* Then it hit me. I'm the problem, it's me. Overworking is a familiar temptation. For those curious, I still use all three. Hit me up for a referral to any one of them.

I learned quickly that private practice is as much business as it is therapy. Partnering with a skilled accountant to establish my S-corp helped me navigate taxes and set up my business structure in a way that made sense for me. There are other options, of course, but this was the best fit for my needs. Staying connected to professional networks kept me grounded in what can be a solitary journey.

## The Work That Fills My Soul

But the most rewarding part? Helping people navigate anxiety. Anxiety is one of the most common mental health struggles—and a frequent reason people seek therapy. It is shaped by genetics and environment - nature and nurture. I've seen it up close, not just as a therapist but as a parent.

I'll never forget the moment my two-year-old daughter sat on the steps, her head hanging low, and whispered, "I'm bad." My heart shattered into a thousand pieces on the floor. My eyes opened to the depth of anxiety—not as some abstract diagnosis, but as a lived, visceral experience that had taken hold of someone I loved more than my own life. And unlike my reaction (typically frustration) to colleagues whose anxiety I sometimes saw as barriers to progress, my reaction to Paolina was different. This was my girl. My beloved. In pain. I wanted to understand it, figure out how to help her make sense of it. Her moments of anxiety taught me to see it for what it really is: a desperate signal that something inside us feels unsafe, unseen, or unheard. I wanted to help her find a way out. I'm sad to say it took longer than I would have hoped. And yes, there was a mama bear part of me that wanted to beat up the inner critic in her amygdala that was lying to her every day.

## What Anxiety Teaches Us

Understanding my daughter changed me. It made me a better therapist, a better listener, and a better human. Every time I sit with a client struggling with anxiety, I think of that little girl sitting on the steps.

And I remind myself:
*It's not about fixing.*
*It's about understanding.*
*It's about compassion.*
*It's about healing.*

One of my favorite questions to ask clients is, "What are you telling yourself?"

The answers often reveal the hidden scripts shaping their pain:

- *Am I not worthy of having someone love me?*
- *Feeling like I'm not good enough is a constant in my head.*
- *People are staring at me—I need to leave as soon as possible.*
- *How could I be so dumb? How could I let that happen?*
- *This isn't good enough. I'm not good enough.*

When we slow down the thought train, we see that it's not the external event (the break up, walking into a new class, making any kind of misstep, passing an annual employee evaluation) that creates suffering, it's the story we tell ourselves about it. These thoughts make sense. They were built in the context of trauma, an amygdala on overdrive, or years of conditioning.

The amygdala, the brain's alarm system, scans for threats, triggers emotional responses like fear and anxiety.[10] When shaped by trauma, it overreacts, even to situations that may no longer be dangerous but still feel that way.[11]

Years of conditioning—the messages we've absorbed from childhood, culture, or from repeated experiences that cut deep – reinforce these patterns. Certain thoughts, fears or reactions become automatic, even when they no longer serve us.[12] And it's not just experience. Sometimes, the amygdala is wired for overdrive before we even get here. Genetic loading and epigenetics (the stress, fear, and adversity carried by those who came before us) lingers, shaping how we move through the world, priming us to be more reactive to threats that haven't even arrived.[13]

Dr. Daniel Amen, a psychiatrist and brain health expert, has studied anxiety through SPECT brain imaging. He found that when the basal ganglia (a part of the brain involved with movement, motivation, and habit) becomes overactive, anxiety takes over. It's like a car stuck in overdrive (*como un carro accelerado*), always running, always bracing for impact.[14]

And it's not just the brain, it's the whole self - psychological, social, and spiritual. Dr. Amen advocates for a holistic approach because healing means looking at the whole picture.[15]

The amygdala is the alarm, detecting threats, setting off the sirens. The basal ganglia, when overactive, is the loop, keeping the worry running, the muscles tense, the mind stuck on repeat.[16] Anxiety isn't just one thing. It's layers. A system. But when we start to understand the system, we can start to change it.

When clients say their fears out loud, they get to decide:
"Do I still believe this?"
"Does this still serve me?"

"Is there another way to think about this—one that is more true, more kind, more helpful?"

But before any of that can happen, they need to feel heard. They need to feel understood. My favorite intervention for this is saying, "I get it. That makes sense." Because healing starts with empathy and acceptance—with feeling seen and understood, knowing *I am not out here alone. I am not the only one who feels this way.*

Anxiety isn't just in thoughts, it lives in the body. It's the tension in your stomach, the pressure at your temples, the tightness curling in your toes. It grabs your shoulders, stiffens your jaw, settles deep in your chest. It speaks before your mind finds the words.

That's why I use:

- Progressive muscle relaxation—so the body remembers what it's like to release.[17]
- Loving-kindness meditation—so the heart softens, even toward itself.[18]
- Breath-counting meditation—so the mind can slow down, just for a moment.[19]
- Hypnotherapy—so we can rewrite the stories buried deep.[20]

What the mind imagines, the body responds to. When the body finds ease, the mind follows, and it's easier to think, breathe, and live like this.

Finally, mirror neurons are also at play. When I show up to a therapy session rested, regulated, grounded, like after a nap, after meditation, the energy I bring into the room shapes the energy that meets me. I become the affect regulator—the steady presence that signals safety, calm, and possibility. Their brain syncs with mine. Their nervous system takes its cue from mine.[21]

I've been on depression medication since my third year in the doctoral program. My psychologist read me as a caretaker. My psychiatrist saw my deep distress and offered me medication—first Zoloft, then Prozac, 20 mg a day. She said she'd wean me off in six months, but I said: "Don't you dare. Let me get all the way through the dissertation defense." And I did.

After graduation, there was a period when I had no health insurance, so—no medication. I felt it creeping back, the irritability, the exhaustion, the slow unraveling. Especially at work. When I secured a full-time job, I went back on my meds and never looked back. I am so grateful that I had this option through my transition into menopause; it has worked so well for me.

I talk about it openly because the world is filled with stories about medication—stories of struggle, stories of side effects, stories of things not going right, and I want my story to stand next to those stories so people know there isn't just one experience, there are a range of possibilities.

I don't force, I guide. I don't dictate, I invite. I help clients explore their options, see things in new ways, and then they decide for themselves—what feels true, what feels right, what serves them best.

**Money Mindset & Gratitude**

I'm "on retainer" for God. That's how I view my relationship to work and purpose now.

Just as a lawyer on retainer is ready to handle legal matters when needed, being "on retainer for God" means I'm always standing by, tuned in, ready to respond to divine assignments. I'm not hustling or striving, I'm attuned to my higher purpose and show up whenever, wherever I'm called. Saying I'm "on retainer for God" means I trust that my needs—financial, emotional, spiritual—will be met as I go about fulfilling my purpose. It's a way of living that demands faith in divine provision and timing, so I can focus on serving instead of spiraling into anxiety about how the bills will get paid. (Spoiler alert: They always do.)

I'm not just working for money anymore. My work is guided by intuition and a higher calling. I'm aligning my actions with what I believe to be God's will—and the greater good. To anyone who thinks I'm overly ambitious, like I said before: I'm not an ambitious b!tch. I'm a b!tch on a mission.

God whispers: *This person needs your support. That situation needs your time and energy.* And so I listen. Whatever the call, I show up. God handles the logistics—expenses, resources, energy—and I take the assignments as they come. Like writing this book. This is one of those assignments. So here I am, showing up, one story, one bit of science, one pearl of wisdom from the ancestors, and one tool at a time.

## We Are All One
The older I grow, the more I find meaning integrating the lessons of my life into a cohesive whole. Integration feels both beautiful and essential—not just for me, but for all of us. We are interconnected, reflections of one another, bound by a shared humanity. To embrace this unity is to honor the harmony that calls us to live with respect, compassion, and mutual care.

## In Lak'ech
The Mayan phrase *In Lak'ech*—"I am you, you are me"—is a reminder of this sacred truth and the inescapable bond we share. Luis Valdez offers a poetic interpretation of this ancient philosophy:

"You are my other me.
If I do harm to you,
I do harm to myself.
If I love and respect you,
I love and respect myself."[22]

These words, so deep and important, urge us to see others as extensions of ourselves. Compassion becomes not just an action but a way of being.

## A Universal Truth
The recognition of oneness is a shared truth across time, geography, and cultures. The Christian scriptures express this concept beautifully in Paul's letter to the Galatians: "There is neither Jew nor Gentile, neither slave nor free, nor is there male and female, for you are all one in Christ Jesus." (Galatians 3:28)

The Huichol people of Mexico articulate a similar reverence for life's interconnectedness through their sacred symbols—the maize, the deer, the peyote. Ramón Medina Silva's words remind us of the unity that underpins all existence:

"The maize of five colors, the deer, the peyote.
These are our symbols. One cannot be without the other,
Each is the heart of the other, the essence.
They are a unity, they are one, they are ourselves."[23]

It's a worldview that invites us to honor not only our connections to one another but also to the earth and all it sustains.

## Ubuntu

The South African concept of *Ubuntu*, as explained by Archbishop Desmond Tutu, offers yet another lens on our shared humanity: "*Ubuntu* is the essence of being human. It speaks about our interconnectedness. You can't exist as a human being in isolation. You can't be human all by yourself."[24]

This interconnectedness calls us to a life of generosity and grace, recognizing that we flourish not in isolation but through relationships, through seeing and being seen.

## The Path to Wellness

Whether expressed as *In Lak'ech*, *Ubuntu*, or through sacred texts, the message is the same: we are inextricably connected. Each choice we make—to love instead of divide, to honor rather than harm—affirms this connection.

Integration is the process of embracing this truth, and wholeness is its reward. To see others fully is to see ourselves. To love others deeply is to love ourselves more completely. As anthropologist Barbara Meyerhoff observed of the Huichol people: "Wholeness is a dynamic condition of balance in which opposites exist without neutralizing each other, a tension between components that does not blur their essential separateness."[25]

In my life, this balance is the thread running through everything. It is the tension that turns dualities into complements, brokenness into beauty, separateness into unity.

This is my whole story, a journey of integration told in free verse:

# I Am Everything

I am my mother's daughter, even though not born from her womb.
I carry her wisdom, her sacrifices, her fire.

I am a mother, standing in awe of my daughter's brilliance: her wit, her creativity, her dreams, as big as New York, as far-reaching as London.
I marvel at her, knowing she will soar far beyond what she's dreamed, and my heart will watch her go, proud and steady.

I have tasted love - the sweetness that lingers and the ache, knowing there is still so much more love to savor.
I am an orphan, untethered yet held together by the arms of my chosen family, by the hands of all the communities where belonging finds me.

I am Chicana, roots deep, proud, and planted in the earth.
I trace my ancestors across oceans and deserts, across borders and time.
I plant seeds not just for me but for the seven generations to come.

I lead with my head, but my heart – oh, my heart finally speaks, finally sings, even if off-key.
I am grounded in my body – strong and soft, fierce and tender, reaching wholeness, maintaining my health.

I am shy, but brave enough to dance — sober and alone, eyes open or closed, in the middle of a crowd or in the quiet of my room.
I crave the world's wonder, but I cherish the cozy nights with a book, a blanket, and snacks.

I am deeply analytical, my mind a sharp, soaring eagle — seeing the forest, the trees, seeing even in the dark with the eyes of a jaguar.
I am disciplined and spontaneous, charting goals but leaving space for the wild, for naps, for life to surprise me.

I am a writer.
I pour memoir and metaphor, science, and soul into the world.
I think deeply but love the small fun of flipping through magazines at a newsstand, connecting human stories through celebrities - no guilt, all pleasure.

I am a healer.
I stand in science, but I move guided by ancestral whispers in my intuition.
I am a storyteller, weaving tales of pain, love, hope, and discovery.

I am a teacher, planting seeds of change —
in classrooms, in therapy rooms, or the reflective places where growth takes root.
I am a lifelong learner, curious about the stars, the ancestors, and the soul.

I am a connector – I link people, ideas, communities, because I know the energy of unity, the beauty of collaboration.
I am a nurturer and a fighter, crafting places for healing while challenging systems that oppress.

I am a seeker of truth.
I am analytical, but I believe what I cannot see.

I am an advocate for change – in families, in communities, in systems too long broken and biased.
I believe in healing, in justice, and in the boundless possibilities of what can be.

I am both the calm and the storm - flowing like water and powerful as fire.

I am Alejandra.
Forever unfolding.
Forever becoming.
Alejandra.

## Conclusion

This book marks a kind of personal rebirth, my own New Fire Ceremony. It is a collection of Stones, Flowers, and Lessons Learned from a life fully lived.

Writing it has been a profound form of healing that I didn't know I still needed. Chapter by chapter, I confronted my past as if looking into a mirror, allowing myself to reconcile my dualities. It is no small thing for me to confront and embrace my opposites: the personal and universal, the pain and the beauty, the struggle and the renewal. In doing so, I found a deeper wholeness - an integration of unanswered questions and pieces of my story. Like the Huichol's sacred wholeness, this book holds opposites in balance.

This book's completion is a full-circle moment. Less than a year ago, I met my writing coach at the LA Times Festival of Books. Now, I prepare to release these pages into the world at that same event. Part of me could spend eternity revising these words. In my head, I'm already working on the second edition, that's the story I tell myself in order to let go.

Letting this book go feels vulnerable, almost perilous, and yet strangely liberating. It is no longer mine to hold. It's time to let go, trust its journey, and allow it to fulfill its purpose. My hope is that the lessons within will guide you toward your own path of healing, growth, and self-discovery - allowing you to love yourself to wholeness.

This book is not my baby, I have a baby and she's twenty-four. Yet, it's a creation, borne of my mind, my heart, my tears, and my *tonalli*, my essence. These stories are lived and re-lived truths I've worn thin by turning them over and over in my hands.

At its core, this book is about balance: finding it, losing it, holding it, and knowing when to let it go. And now that it's done, I feel both lighter and heavier, like I'm standing in two places at once. Maybe that's what wholeness is—not an arrival, but an ongoing tension, a recognition we are the root and the bloom, the thing reaching, and the thing already found.

When I wrote this, I imagined you—yes, you—holding these pages, searching for something you may not even realize you're looking for. I don't have definitive answers; life isn't *either/or*—it's *both/and*, and *it depends*. What I offer are stories, lessons learned, and moments that nearly broke me but somehow, miraculously, didn't.

I was lucky to have my mother Irene, a *Santera* named Sara, a library of books as another mother, and a deep trust in my inner voice—the voice of God, my ancestors, and my intuition.

I hope you find something here—something that resonates, comforts, or reassures you that you are not alone in the wondrous, tragic, and beautiful journey of being human.

And so, this is me letting go. Trusting its journey. Trusting you. Full circle, indeed.

# Science and Research

## Retirement: A Crossroad of Opportunities and Challenges

Retirement is often painted as a golden age of freedom and relaxation, but the reality is more nuanced. For some, leaving the workforce brings joy and well-being. For others, it ushers in new challenges—mental health struggles, cognitive decline, or diminished life satisfaction. So what makes the difference? Research sheds light on how individual circumstances, social supports, and broader systems shape this major life transition.

Let's dive into three key studies that explore the mental, emotional, and cognitive dimensions of retirement, offering insights into how we can thrive during this phase of life.

## 1. Mental Well-Being in the Workplace and Beyond[1]

Before we retire, our mental health is already being shaped by what happens at work. A 2023 study revealed that the well-being of older workers (ages 50–65) hinges on several factors:

### What They Found:

- Supportive working conditions—both physical and social—boost mental health.
- Financial stability and psychological resources help mitigate stress.
- On the flip side, job demands that outweigh rewards or lack of control at work take a toll.

**Why It Matters:**

As retirement ages rise, creating age-friendly workplaces is more critical than ever. Workers need environments that protect their mental health while extending their careers.

**Key Takeaways:**

- Positive job conditions aren't just nice to have—they're essential for mental well-being.
- Inequities in workplace demands versus rewards drive disparities in mental health.
- Tailored policies can help workers transition to retirement with better emotional resilience.

**Who Was Studied:**

This meta-analysis examined 23 studies across the US, EU, and Nordic countries, capturing diverse workplace experiences.

## 2. Life Satisfaction: Who Thrives and Why?[2]

Not all retirees experience the same level of happiness. A 2017 study explored how education, race, and gender intersect to shape life satisfaction (LS) over time, uncovering surprising patterns.

**What They Found:**

- Education improves life satisfaction, particularly for women.
- Hispanic individuals reported the highest LS at most education levels, followed by non-Hispanic Whites. African Americans faced the lowest LS overall.

• Economic upheavals, like the Great Recession, hit older workers (50–59) and the oldest old (80+) hardest.

**Why It Matters:**
Retirement isn't a one-size-fits-all experience. Social and economic inequities mean some groups face far greater challenges to achieving happiness.

**Key Takeaways:**

• Education is a powerful driver of life satisfaction, especially for women.
• Cultural strengths, such as those seen in the Hispanic community, can buffer against socioeconomic adversity ("Hispanic Paradox").
• Persistent racial and economic disparities demand more equitable policies.

**Who Was Studied:**
This analysis included over 16,000 participants from the US Health and Retirement Study, representing diverse racial and ethnic backgrounds.

### 3. The "Mental Retirement" Hypothesis[3]
Retirement may come with an unexpected cost: faster cognitive decline. A 2017 study confirmed that stepping away from the workforce often means stepping away from the mental challenges that keep the brain sharp.

## What They Found:

- Retirees showed twice the rate of cognitive decline compared to non-retirees.
- Those with poorer health, wealth, and cognitive function before retirement were hit hardest.
- On average, retirees experienced a 3.7% loss in cognitive functioning each year.

## Why It Matters:

Cognitive engagement is crucial for healthy aging. Without it, retirement can accelerate aging, particularly for those who were already vulnerable.

## Key Takeaways:

- Staying mentally active post-retirement is vital for slowing cognitive decline.
- Inequities in health and wealth amplify the risks of aging poorly.
- Policies and programs that promote lifelong learning and social engagement could transform the retirement experience.

## Who Was Studied:

This research followed nearly 19,000 older adults over two decades, offering a comprehensive view of cognitive aging in retirement.

## Retirement Done Right: What We Can Learn

These studies reveal that retirement is more than an exit from the workforce—it's a profound shift that tests our mental, emotional, and cognitive resilience. But it's also an opportunity to thrive, if we plan thoughtfully and address inequities along the way.

Here's how to make retirement a time of growth and fulfillment:

- For Individuals: Stay mentally and socially engaged. Lifelong learning, hobbies, and community connections matter.
- For Organizations: Create age-friendly workplaces and support employees as they transition to retirement.
- For Society: Address disparities in health, wealth, and education to ensure all retirees can age with dignity and purpose.

Retirement, like any major life event, is a chance to rewrite your story. How you prepare—and the support you receive—makes all the difference.

# Ancestor Wisdom

I've always tried to pass down to my daughter the best wisdom I inherited from my mom—not just the big life lessons, but the subtle, symbolic ones too, the kind that shape how we move through the world. Lessons about beauty, power, and self-expression.

My mom had a strict rule: as a minor, I wasn't allowed to wear red nail polish or red lipstick. I carried that rule forward with my own daughter from birth to eighteen— not to stifle her creativity, but to protect her in a world that too often sees young women as prey.

When I was in college, I learned that the ancient Egyptians used rouge to mimic the natural flush of arousal. Suddenly, my mom's rules about makeup made sense—not just as an arbitrary line drawn in the sand but as her way of navigating a world where femininity could be both weaponized and misunderstood. It wasn't just about lipstick or nail polish; it was about what those symbols represented—and how the world might interpret them.

My daughter, Paolina, wrote a poem called *Red Lipstick*[1] and performed it in a short film, surrounded by fifteen dancers in vibrant red dresses. That performance was her declaration—an assertion of her power, resilience, and autonomy. Through her art, she realized something profound: red isn't just a color; it's a story. It's the story of women like her *Tita,* her maternal grandmother Irene, who wore crimson as an emblem of courage, and women like me, who learned to balance self-expression with self-preservation.

Her poem weaves together the strength of generations— her *Tita*'s boldness, my cautious guidance, and her own fiery determination to claim her space in the world. And in that tapestry of words, she reminds me of what it means to navigate a world that often misinterprets the symbols of our strength.

## Red Lipstick
By Paolina Acuña-Gonzalez

Sophomore year, my mom finally let me wear makeup.
But first waved a primrose fingernail in front of my face
And warned, "Never wear red lipstick"
"Why?"
"It mimics the blush of a woman having an orgasm, boys will get the wrong idea."
"But Mom, high school boys don't know what a girl having a real orgasm looks like."
My Mother, modern Lady Macbeth furiously dabbing away at the same red spot.
It hadn't always been there.
My *Abuelita* was never fully dressed without a crest of crimson courage painted on her lips,
A stripe of feminine fury.
Reminder of monthly bloody battle victories.
The marks she'd leave emboldened on her foes.
Either from peace or powerful rage.
I promised my mom:
"When I'm 18, I'll walk out of here clad in a red dress, with matching shoes, fruit punch-stained lips.
Dye my hair in popped cherry jam.
Don rose-tinted glasses.
Rename myself Ms. Scarlet.
Paint the town that primary color.

What are you going to do about it?"

Mom replied, "What are men going to think your intentions are?"

"My intentions are to walk down the street in a dress I like, feeling like the Summer Queen of Strawberries. Who the hell cares what they think!"

Little did I know, my mom's lessons weren't superstitions. They were cautionary tales.

Of men turning womanly-wielded weapons into weaknesses.

Drawing wine-tinted targets on our backs.

Fathers claiming ownership of what never belonged to them.

Now I understand.

She's scared that soon I'll have

The title of woman tied to my neck

With the world ready to pull the other end.

So with this, I assure her:

When someday I'll have to leave her

And walk down the streets of a city I don't recognize,

I promise to draw my mouth a ruby heart

And carry a matching taser.

# Tools

This section is an invitation—to embrace truth, tap into your strengths, and grow resilience as you move toward your dreams. Rooted in themes of honesty, connection, hope, and empowerment, these tools offer practical steps to guide your journey. Whether you're reflecting on your progress, designing a wellness plan, or taking charge of your finances, each tool is a companion for balance, clarity, and fulfillment. Let these practices inspire your steps forward and remind you to celebrate along the way.

## Tool #1: Honoring the Truth

"We're only as sick as our secrets."
– Alcoholics Anonymous
"Then you will know the truth, and the truth will set you free."
– John 8:32

When I've felt stuck, I've learned that the way forward begins with truth. Truth-telling can be uncomfortable, even scary—but the freedom it offers is deliciously full of peace and joy. It starts with knowing myself and being honest with myself.

For years, I believed being stoic was strength. I thought suppressing my emotions and hiding my needs made me noble, but I've learned that being stoic about my feelings often disguises fear and keeps me from living authentically. Speaking the truth—first to ourselves—requires courage and vulnerability. On the other side of that leap lies trust, healing, and growth.

## An Experiment in Truth

Ready to strengthen your integrity? Try this exercise:

1. Commit to truth-telling for two full days (day and night). Be honest with yourself and others, even when it feels difficult.

2. Celebrate each small step. Remember, courage isn't about eliminating fear but acting despite it.

## Reflection Questions:

• How long were you able to stick to truth-telling—minutes, hours, or days?

• How did it feel before, during, and after? Where did these feelings show up in your body?

• Would you try this again? Why or why not?

## Tool #2: Creating Your Wellness Plan

Your well-being is unique to you. A wellness plan is a personal map—a collection of practices and strategies that help you feel balanced and whole. Below are tools that have supported me over the years. Take what resonates, leave what doesn't, and trust yourself to create your own path.

My Wellness Essentials:

• **Prayer and Meditation**: Moments of stillness bring me clarity and peace.

• **Supportive Relationships**: Trusted loved ones offer strength and connection.

• **Healthy Eating**: I listen to my body, choosing whole foods and avoiding triggers like seed oils.

- **Restorative Sleep**: Sleep is sacred, and chamomile or peppermint tea, baths, and journaling help me unwind before bed.
- **Joyful Movement**: Walking, dancing, and strength training keep me grounded and energized.
- **Forgiveness**: Letting go of resentment frees my spirit.
- **Therapy**: A safe space for healing and self-discovery.
- **Energy Healing**: Yoga, acupuncture, and massage help release stress and restore balance.
- **Creative Self-Care**: Pampering through haircuts or facials reminds me to honor my worth.
- **Shamanic Practices**: Soul retrieval has reconnected me to parts of myself I thought were lost.
- **Hypnotherapy**: Exploring my inner world through hypnosis has been a gift.

## A Final Note:

Healing takes patience, courage, and love. Listen to your body. Honor your spirit. Trust your inner wisdom.

## Tool #3: Reclaiming Financial Freedom

Inspired by *How to Get Out of Debt, Stay Out of Debt, and Live Prosperously* by Jerrold Mundis,[1] this tool offers actionable steps to take control of your finances and cultivate a positive relationship with money.

## Step 1: Understanding the Problem

- Uncover the Root Causes: Reflect on emotional and societal factors influencing your spending.
- Recognize the Impact: Debt isn't just financial—it's emotional. Awareness can fuel change.
- Adopt a Structured Plan: Groups like Debtors Anonymous can offer a framework for recovery.

## Step 2: Taking Control

- Commit to No New Debt: Pause credit card use and live on cash or debit.
- Track Your Spending: Log daily expenses for clarity and control.
- Create a Spending Plan: Balance essentials, savings, and joy to avoid burnout.
- Prioritize Repayment: Use the snowball or avalanche method to tackle debts strategically.
- Celebrate Progress: Acknowledge every step forward, no matter how small.

## Step 3: Shifting Your Mindset

- Notice Triggers: Replace overspending habits with healthy coping strategies.
- Practice Gratitude: Celebrate small financial wins.
- Set Clear Goals: Break big goals into manageable steps.
- Find a Community: Support groups or like-minded friends can help you stay accountable.
- Staying the Course: Progress takes time. Be patient, persistent, and kind to yourself.

## Tool #4: Reflecting on Your Journey

Take a moment to pause and honor how far you've come. These reflection questions can help you celebrate and chart your next steps.

- What has improved since you started this journey?
- What have you learned about yourself?
- What changes are you most proud of?

## Celebrate Your Wins:

What do you want to celebrate today? Big or small, every milestone matters. Write it down. Honor your growth.

# Steps to Blooming Workbook

Now that we've explored stories and ideas that root us in earlier chapters, this workbook invites you to wear something comfortable and dance with those lessons. Through reflection and intention, you'll have the chance to make those concepts your own. Let this be a guide as you lean into the beauty of living fully. Together, we'll plant seeds of joy and watch them grow, one baby step at a time.

## Step 1: Goal Setting

Let's start with setting intentions—a grounding activity for your journey of healing, growth, and fulfilling your heart's desires. This is your opportunity to sit with your dreams, to truly see them, to let them rise up like the first light of dawn. Transformation begins here, with the courage to imagine a different future. By reflecting on your hopes and naming them, you open a door to possibility and purpose.

This exercise is an invitation: anchor yourself in hope, water your vision with boldness, and step into the garden of your becoming. Let's dream, reflect, and grow. The time is now. Let's begin!

## Reflect and Set Your Goal

Choose one part of your life—or one corner of your community—and ask yourself:"What do I truly, deeply, soulfully desire to do, be, or have?"

Let joy take your hand and lead your imagination. Wander through the whispers of trees, feel the rhythm of the wind, or simply close your eyes and let your thoughts dance like wildflowers in an open field. Trust what arises—those desires are the song of your heart, calling you home.

When your vision takes shape, honor it. Write it, sketch it, breathe it into being. Let it live outside of you, ready to grow.

## Why Set Goals?

Every step we take is guided by purpose, every action fueled by desire.[1] Setting meaningful goals focuses our attention, lights a fire under our efforts, and inspires us to dream boldly. A high, specific goal doesn't just capture your mind—it stirs your heart, ignites your spirit, and connects you to what truly matters.

Goals are an expression of your values, your needs, your vision. They rally communities, spark unity, and inspire action. They help us measure progress, adjust our course, and persist with grace and tenacity until the dream is realized.[2]

Be bold and audacious enough to aim high—the higher the goal, the greater your performance.[3] Goals tied to purpose and legacy generate the energy to push forward, even when the path is steep. Imagine your ideal life ten or fifteen years from now. What will your legacy be? What gives your life meaning? [4]

More than a thousand studies prove it: setting a clear, challenging goal improves performance and satisfaction.[5] So go ahead—dream big, dig deep, and let your goals guide you home.

## Writing Your Goal

Write your goal as a positive statement—focus on what you want to create, not what you want to avoid. For instance:

- When preparing for an important school or professional license exam, instead of: "Don't miss answering more than three questions," say: "Solve at least 12 questions."

Words shape your thoughts and behaviors, so choose ones that uplift and inspire.

If your goal excites you—if thinking about it brings a smile, you're on the right track! Write your goal as if it's already happening.

## Examples of Inspiring Goals:

- I am finishing my screenplay by July 4th.
- I am building a supportive group of women friends in my community.
- I am celebrating passing my social work licensure exam on August 1.
- I am creating a financial freedom fund that allows me to work on my terms.
- I am in a loving, committed, and respectful relationship.

Pause and reflect—how does writing this goal feel? Exciting? Nerve-racking? Inspiring? Let your emotions guide you.

**Emotions and Goal Setting**

Goals awaken the soul and stir up feelings—fear, joy, doubt, hope, excitement, even a bittersweet nostalgia. These emotions are your teachers, whispering truths about who you are and what you long for. Let them rise up. Hold them gently. Let them flow without judgment.

Close your eyes and step into your dream. What do you feel? Can you see it, taste it, hear it, touch it, as if it's already yours? Imagine the pride swelling in your chest, the joy lighting up your spirit, the deep satisfaction of knowing you did it.

Now, write it down. Speak it into being. Describe this moment as if it's already here, as if the dream has unfolded and the story is yours to tell.

**Here's what others have said about reaching their goals:**

- "I feel warm and nostalgic."
- "It fills me with satisfaction and peace."
- "I'm energized and motivated."
- "It connects me to my spirituality and fills me with love."

**Goal Setting: A Journey to Yourself**

Goal setting is a journey to uncover who you are, what you love, and what lights your way. It's a path to self-discovery, purpose, and joy. So dream big. Reflect deeply. Commit fully to the vision that makes your soul sing.

## Step 2: Recognizing the Barriers to Your Goals

In 2012, self-reflection became my anchor in a sea of chaos. I was balancing PhD studies, navigating a divorce, working part-time, and raising my middle-school-aged daughter. Life felt overwhelming, but I knew that if I wanted to finish my dissertation and reach my dreams, I had to confront the fears and limiting beliefs holding me back.

My fears were loud—echoes of uncertainty and doubt. I was scared of what I couldn't control and afraid that others wouldn't support me. These thoughts left me feeling small and powerless. When political and institutional challenges threatened my ability to collect data, the doubts crept in: *Will I gather enough data for my study? Will the staff at these institutions stand with me or against me?*

I worried that my dissertation—and my degree— might never come to fruition. Then, in 2013, I picked up a worksheet and faced those fears head-on. Writing down my worries, challenging them, and reimagining my possibilities changed everything. That simple act of self-reflection became a turning point, shifting me from limitation to hope, from fear to action.

Now, I invite you to walk this path with me. Engage in this exercise. Confront your fears. Reclaim your power. Are you ready to change your life, even a little bit?

## Identifying Barriers

Let's take a moment to uncover what's holding you back—the doubts, fears, and beliefs standing between you and your goal. These reflections aren't meant to judge or blame but to shine a light on what's been hidden, so you can move forward with clarity and courage.

Begin by settling into yourself: take a few deep breaths, feel your feet on the ground, or go for a quiet, meditative walk. When you're ready, explore these questions:

- What's kept your goal just out of reach? What reasons or justifications come to mind?
- What beliefs about your goal might be holding you back?
- What have others said about why your dream hasn't come true?
- Are there family, community, cultural, or religious expectations you feel you're breaking by pursuing this?
- Do you worry about losing someone or something if you achieve your goal?
- Does any part of your body whisper, "Don't do this"? Listen without judgment—we'll clear this up together later.
- What makes you hesitate, seek permission, or wait for approval to move forward?
- Do you believe you deserve your goal? What stories do you tell yourself?

Take your time. Let these questions unfold naturally. Write as much or as little as you want, whatever feels right, and come back to your answers next week—you might uncover something new.

## Examples of Limiting Beliefs

Here are some common beliefs that can hold people back:

- *I'd like to speak at a conference, but I don't have enough experience.*
- *I had hoped to be further along by now, but unexpected hurdles got in the way.*

## Understanding Emotional Responses

Limiting beliefs don't just stand in our way—they stir the waters of our emotions, leaving ripples of fear, doubt, or even anger. Take a moment to reflect: How do your beliefs make you feel? Write it down, let it out.

Here are some feelings that often surface with limiting beliefs:

- Fear
- Guilt
- Stress
- Sadness
- Overwhelm
- Insecurity
- Trapped
- Frustration
- Defeat
- Anger
- Doubt
- Doom

It's okay to feel these things. Let them rise, sit with them for a while. Emotions are natural—they carry messages, they teach us where to look, what to heal, and how to move forward. Acknowledging what you feel is the first step toward freedom. And remember: you are not alone in this. You have the power, the strength, and the grace to rewrite your story and claim the life you've imagined.

## A Personal Reflection

This practice of confronting my own limiting beliefs gave me the clarity and strength to persevere. It wasn't easy, but by shifting my mindset and choosing to believe in my possibilities, I reclaimed my power. In 2014, I walked across that stage and graduated—a triumph born from hard work and a willingness to face my fears.

Now it's your turn: What limiting beliefs will you transform? What possibilities will you choose to embrace? The power is already within you—waiting to be claimed.

## Step 3: Credible Affirmations – Rewriting Your Narrative

Feeling stuck or powerless can weigh you down, but affirmations can help you rise up. During one of the hardest chapters of my life—writing my dissertation while navigating a divorce and raising my daughter—affirmations became my lifeline. They whispered strength to me when I felt weak, reassured me when doubt crept in, and reminded me of my power within.

The first affirmation I embraced came from *The Alchemist* by Paulo Coelho: *"When you want something, all the universe conspires in helping you to achieve it."* [6] Other affirmations came from *La Santera* Sara, who read my cards, and some were drawn from the Bible. For me, spirituality has always been my anchor, keeping me grounded in strength and faith.

Now it's your turn to rewrite your story. Take the limiting beliefs you've identified—the barriers, the doubts, the why-nots—and flip them. Turn those blocks into affirmations of possibility, statements of truth you want to believe. You can create one powerful affirmation that speaks to all your challenges or write individual affirmations for each barrier. Let your heart guide you.

Write your affirmations here:

Once you've written your affirmations, sit with them. On a scale from 1 to 10, ask yourself if you believe you can achieve your goal.

1: "I'm skeptical—I hardly believe this."
10: "I believe this with my whole heart."

For affirmations scoring five or below, revise them until they feel authentic. Tweak the words, make them more specific, or ground them in truths you already know.

**Need inspiration? Here are a few affirmations others have used:**

- I am worthy of love, acceptance, and respect.
- Even though it's scary, I believe I can achieve this goal.
- I have everything I need to succeed.
- I am capable and wise enough to make a difference.

- I've done hard things before and can do them again—more easily this time.
- My thoughts become my reality.
- I have the right to get exactly what I want out of life.

Now, speak your affirmations aloud. How do they make you feel? Strong? Hopeful? Encouraged? Nervous but excited? Write it down. Feel the shift.

Write how your affirmations make you feel:

Your story is yours to rewrite. Let your affirmations be the pen that shapes a new chapter.

## The Science Behind Affirmations

When you replace the limits in your mind with positive visions of yourself, success begins to bloom. Changing your beliefs is possible—and powerful. Self-affirmations, or reflecting on your values, strengths, and qualities, have been shown in hundreds of studies to reduce stress, boost well-being, improve academic outcomes, and even encourage healthier habits like eating more fruits and vegetables.[7, 8]

Self-affirming moments can be as simple as receiving positive feedback or reflecting on the best parts of who you are. Expressing your core values, even in small ways, is a powerful act. Research shows self-affirmations help you stay grounded and confident, even when life shakes your foundation. [9]

## Imagine Your Future Self

Close your eyes and picture the version of you who has achieved your goal. What do they look like? How do they feel?

Write your visualization here:

Now listen—does your future self have any words of wisdom, reassurance, or encouragement for the you of today? Write those messages here:

Affirmations grow stronger with repetition. Speak them often, let them echo in your mind, and place them where they'll remind you daily:

- On your bathroom mirror
- Inside your car's sun visor
- In your journal
- On an index card in your wallet

Number of times I've repeated my affirmations:
Places I'll post my affirmations:

This is the beginning of a new chapter in your story. With every affirmation, you're rewriting your narrative, stepping into your power, and building a brighter, more empowered future—one word at a time.

## Step 4: Acknowledging Ambivalence

Change—yes, even the good kind—has a way of stirring up ambivalence, it's just the nature of change. We're funny creatures like that, built to hope for and fear the same things. We might dream about reaching our goal and, at the same time, worry about what comes next. That's just how we're wired.

Think about it: we love and hate our parents. If your boss told you about a promotion with a BIG raise, you'd feel proud and elated—but maybe a little nervous, too. BIG raise? What's the catch?

The truth is, achieving a goal comes with pros and cons. Mixed feelings are normal, even when the goal is meaningful and life-changing. And here's the beauty of it: research shows that pursuing goals you truly care about is key to your well-being, even when ambivalence sneaks in.[10]

So, when you're stuck or need motivation, don't shy away from your ambivalence. Reflect on it. Let it teach you about what you value and what you fear. That's how you move forward—with all your feelings in tow.

## Reflecting on Ambivalence

### 1. Acknowledge Your Feelings

Take time to notice all the feelings you have about your goal—both positive and negative. Listen to them without judgment. Mixed emotions don't mean you're not committed; they mean you care deeply.

Write your worries, fears, doubts, and concerns here:
• Example: I'm afraid I won't meet my own high expectations.
• Example: I worry I'll face rejection.

### 2. Lighten the Load

Writing down your concerns can help reduce their emotional weight. What once felt overwhelming may seem more manageable when you see it on paper. Reflect on these questions:
• What happens when you write your concerns down?
• Do they seem smaller or more approachable?
• Do you notice any patterns or recurring fears?

## 3. Address Your Concerns

Take time to reflect on your worries and consider how you can reframe or address them.

Write your thoughts here:

•   Example: I'll break my goal into smaller, manageable steps to avoid feeling overwhelmed.

•   Example: I'll remind myself that rejection is part of growth.

## 4. Explore Possible Outcomes

Think about the potential outcomes of pursuing your goal—both positive and negative.

Reflect on these questions:

•   What positive outcomes do you expect from achieving your goal?

•   Example: I'll feel proud of myself and gain new opportunities.

•   What negative outcomes do you expect from achieving your goal?

•   Example: I may have less free time.

•   What positive outcomes do you expect from staying the same?

•   Example: I won't face the fear of failure.

•   What negative outcomes do you expect from staying the same?

•   Example: I may regret not taking this chance.

## 5. Reflect on Past Successes

Think about a time when you accomplished a goal. Reflect on the process and the emotions involved. Write your reflections here:
• What choices and values inspired you?
• How did it feel physically and emotionally to achieve your goal?
• What lessons can you carry forward from that experience?

### Moving Forward

Ambivalence isn't a barrier—it's a signal that your goal truly matters to you. By acknowledging your mixed feelings and reflecting on them thoughtfully, you can transform ambivalence into clarity and purposeful action.

Use these reflections as a foundation to move forward with confidence and self-compassion. Ambivalence can be a powerful teacher, showing you what matters most and giving you the tools to navigate change with intention.

### Step 5: Partnering with the Universe [11]

Achieving meaningful goals often brings moments of overwhelm, pressure, or even loneliness. During these times, embracing the idea of partnering with the Universe can provide profound relief and inspiration.

By "Universe," I mean whatever higher force resonates with you—God, Creator, Ancestors, Higher Power, or the interconnected flow of life.

| Me | Universe |
|---|---|
| **What** specifically do I really want? State it in the positive. | **How** is it going to happen? |
| **Why** do I want it? Write 100 reasons. | **When**? |
| **Who** am I really? **What** is my true purpose? | |

## What Does It Mean to Partner With the Universe?

In this partnership, your role is to focus on the **what**, **why**, and **who** of your goal. Leave the **how** and **when** to the Universe. When your goal aligns with your authentic self and life's purpose, it often feels as if the Universe is conspiring in your favor.

As Paulo Coelho beautifully wrote in *The Alchemist*: "And when you want something, all the Universe conspires in helping you to achieve it." [12]

This perspective reminds us that success isn't solely about personal effort. It also involves external support—resources, relationships, and synchronicities that lie beyond our control.

## Reflecting and Revising Your Goal

Take a moment to refine your goal by answering these questions:

## 1. What Specifically Do You Want?

State your goal in positive terms. Focus on what you want to create or achieve rather than what you want to avoid.

• For example: "I am building a career I love" instead of "I want to stop feeling stuck."

Write your goal here:

## 2. Why Do You Want It?

Reflect on your deepest motivations. Why does this goal matter to you?

Write your reasons here:

## 3. Who Are You, and What Is Your Purpose?

Consider how this goal aligns with your authentic self and your contribution to the world. Ask yourself: Does this goal reflect my values, passions, and strengths?

How will achieving this goal help me fulfill my purpose?

Write your reflections here:

## Declaring Your Partnership With the Universe

If you're ready to embrace this partnership, declare your intention aloud. Speaking your goal into existence is a powerful act of commitment.

For example, you might say, "I trust the Universe to work with me in achieving this goal. I commit to focusing on my role and allowing the Universe to guide the rest."

To formalize your commitment, sign your partnership agreement.

## Partnership Agreement

I trust the Universe to support me in achieving my goal. I commit to focusing on what, why, and who, and I will allow the Universe to take care of how and when.

- Name: _____
- Signature: _____
- Date: _____

## Trusting the Process

This partnership serves as a powerful reminder: You are not alone in your journey.

- Trust that the Universe is guiding you.
- Stay in your lane, focusing on your role.
- Let go of the need to control every detail.

By declaring your intention, refining your goal, and aligning with your purpose, you invite the Universe to meet you halfway. Together, you can create something extraordinary.

## Step 6: One Hundred Reasons Why You Want, Deserve, and Need to Achieve This Goal

This is your homework—however long it takes, however many moments of reflection it demands. Write one hundred reasons why this goal matters, why you deserve it, why it's essential to make it real. Let the reasons flow, even if they begin to sound like affirmations. Let the reasons rewire, reorient, and retrain your mind to think expansively about your dreams.

This exercise isn't just about writing—it's about building. Brick by brick, reason by reason, you're creating a foundation so strong it becomes unshakable. With every reason, you reframe your mindset, fortify your belief in yourself, and ignite unstoppable momentum.

Don't rush. Let this process unfold over days or weeks. Give yourself the grace to reflect, to dig deep, and to let your truth rise naturally. Repetition is welcome—each reason, like a steady heartbeat, strengthens your commitment and carries you closer to the life you're building.

### Prompt

*Why do you want and deserve this goal?* Write your answers here:

Keep going. Let the reasons flow. By the time you reach one hundred, you'll see your goal in a whole new light— one filled with power, purpose, and possibility.

## Examples to Spark Your List

- Because it's for my own good.
- Because I love myself.
- I deserve to feel that rush of aliveness.
- I want to feel great about my health.
- Because why the f$%# not?
- I'm ready to release the messages I've been told about not being good enough.
- Because I want autonomy over my life.
- I deserve a community that uplifts me.
- It will make my life more fun and enriching.
- This goal has been calling to me for years.
- Because I want peace and security.
- Because I need to love myself first and foremost.
- My quality of life will improve.
- I deserve nurturing relationships that meet my adult needs.
- Because it's my birthright.
- Because I want to model strength and joy for my kids.
- Because I have the power to change my life.
- The Universe has already aligned this for me.
- Because my body and spirit will be so happy!
- Because discomfort and challenge are the birthplace of growth.
- Because I've done the work of healing, and I'm ready.
- Because I survived, and now I thrive.
- This is my primetime!

## Why Does This Exercise Work?

- **Subconscious Programming**

By repeatedly identifying reasons, you train your brain to view your goal as achievable, meaningful, and essential.

- **Building Momentum**

The more reasons you uncover, the stronger your belief and excitement grow.

- **Affirmations in Action**

Each reason acts as a mini-affirmation, reinforcing positive thoughts and motivation.

## Pro Tip: Top Ten Reasons

Once your list is complete, choose your top ten reasons and write them on sticky notes or display them somewhere visible. Use these as daily reminders to stay focused and inspired. Whenever doubt or discouragement creeps in, revisit your list to reconnect with your "why" and reignite your commitment.

This is your moment to anchor yourself in purpose and possibility. You are capable, deserving, and ready.

## Step 7: Think, Feel, Do[13]

Our thoughts and feelings are deeply interconnected. How we think about a goal shapes how we feel, and how we feel influences what we do, or don't do. But here's the beautiful truth: by recognizing this dynamic, we can shift it. Align our thoughts, emotions, and actions with what truly matters, and watch how our path opens up.

## The Power of Thought Patterns

Let's consider an example. Let's say your goal is, "I really, really want to get married in a year's time to the right person for me."

**Negative Thought:** "Who do you think you are? That's not gonna happen."
**Feeling:** Embarrassed or dejected.
**Likely Action:** Withdrawing, isolating, or stopping dating altogether.

**Positive Reframe:** "Why not? I'm willing to dream big! This is the prime time of my life!"
**Feeling:** Hopeful, inspired, and excited.
**Likely Action:** Meeting new people, engaging joyfully, and going on dates.

**Cautious Thought:** "I really want this, but I'm worried I might be disappointed. I don't want to give up, so I'll try even though I'm scared."
**Feeling:** Nervous but determined.
**Likely Action:** Taking small, meaningful steps— like going on a date, pausing to rebuild confidence, and trying again.

Every thought holds power. Each can uplift you, hold you back, or challenge you to move forward, even when you're unsure. The key? Choose thoughts that inspire action and reflect the faith you have in yourself and your dreams.

## Reflect on Your Thoughts

Take a moment to pause and listen to the whispers in your mind. What automatic negative thoughts come up when you think about your goal?
Write them here:

How do these thoughts make you feel?
Write your feelings here:

What actions are these thoughts and feelings leading you to take—or avoid?
Write your actions here:

## Reframe Your Thoughts

Now it's time to rewrite the story. Challenge those doubts and fears. What could you say to yourself instead? How can you create a narrative that lifts you up instead of one that holds you down?
Write your reframed thoughts here:

## Practice Makes Progress

Shifting your thoughts is like planting seeds. Each time you choose a more supportive thought, you're nurturing a garden of positive feelings and purposeful actions. With practice, this shift becomes second nature. You'll find your thoughts, feelings, and actions aligning with the life you're building—one small, powerful choice at a time.

You hold the pen. You have the power. Choose thoughts that serve you. Start today.

## Step 8: Brainstorm a To-Do List – Baby Steps Toward Your Goal

When I was in my doctoral program, I was ready to take action—ready to brainstorm the baby steps that would lead me to my goal: "I am filing my dissertation by June 2, 2014!" Each new idea found its way onto my growing to-do list, and I made sure to include one essential step: "Repeat affirmations at least three times a day!" Because words have power, and I was speaking my future into existence.

## Planning (Tiny Baby) Action Steps

The beauty of goal setting is turning a wish into something real—it's alchemy in motion, step by step. Focus on the actions, and watch the overwhelm melt away. It's not the size of the leap but the rhythm of the stride that gets you there. Systems and habits set the tempo, steady and sure. Inspired actions are the spark, the magic pulling you closer to the goal than you ever dreamed.

They say 80% of success is just showing up. So, I ask you: What are you willing to show up for? What can you commit to today? Every time you show up, you give yourself a chance to meet the right moment at the right time. Small steps, full attention—they're the seeds of transformation, waiting to bloom.

Let's dream it together: systems to guide you, habits to ground you, and actions to ignite you. Regardless of judgment and fear. Just the courage to begin, again and again. Showing up is the rhythm of becoming.
Write your action steps here:

Take a moment—breathe deeply, do a victory dance, or whatever gets you inspired—and commit to one baby step this week. It doesn't have to be big; it just has to move you forward.

## A Journey of Baby Steps

As the Chinese proverb says, "A journey of 1,000 miles begins with a single (baby) step."

Complete this sentence:

*This week, I will...*

_____

Sign your name:

This is your first step toward the life you're creating. Show up for it. Believe every small step is building momentum toward your success.

## Examples of Baby Steps

Need some inspiration? Here are examples of small, achievable actions others have taken:

- Read affirmations daily.
- Visualize your goal and how it feels to achieve it.
- Spend time learning about your goal.
- Journal your intentions.
- Reach out to friends for support or encouragement.
- Practice yoga or self-care activities.
- Make an appointment with a therapist.
- Meditate on nurturing relationships.
- Take one small action daily toward your goal.
- Take time to love yourself enough to take more baby steps.
- Eat more greens and approach your goal with joy.

- Watch your portion control, get an accountability partner, and journal four times a week.
- Write for thirty minutes daily, even if it's just brainstorming ideas.

## Tune Into Yourself

Pause for a moment. Breathe. Reflect.

- What is your spirit whispering about your next step?
- What is your body saying as you commit to action?
- What does your heart long for, and what does your mind need to feel at ease?

Listen closely. These messages are your guide, your inner compass pointing you toward what's true and necessary. Honor them, and let them shape your next move.

## Step 9: Tracking Progress and Scaling Confidence

Tracking your progress and scaling your confidence are essential parts of achieving your goal. This step invites you to reflect on where you are now, to identify ways to build your confidence, and to visualize your success.

## 1: Confidence Check

On a scale of 1 to 10 (where 1 = very little confidence and 10 = all the confidence in the world), rate your confidence level about achieving your goal.

My current confidence level: _____

What tells you that you are at this number?

Write down the evidence, feelings, or thoughts that reflect why you're at this confidence level:

## 2: Moving the Needle

What would it take to raise your confidence by just one point?

What about by half a point?

Even small changes can make a big difference. Reflect on manageable actions or shifts in perspective that could elevate your confidence.

## 3: Aligning Spirit, Body, Heart, and Mind

How does it feel to focus all parts of yourself—spirit, body, heart, and mind—on your goal?

Reflect on any sensations, emotions, or thoughts that arise.

## 4: Visualization With a Loved One

Imagine a loved one—whether a pet, friend, family member, or mentor—standing beside you as you achieve your goal. Now, rate your confidence level again:

What do you notice when you visualize this? Write about any shifts in your feelings, body sensations, or outlook

## 5: Embodying Achievement

Take a moment to visualize yourself having achieved your goal. How does your body feel at that moment?

Pay attention to any physical sensations, such as:

- Warmth
- Tension
- Lightness

Reflect on any emotions that surface.

## Examples From Others

Here's how others have described their confidence and progress:

- 10: I have every confidence my goal(s) will manifest in the fullness of time.
- 8: Continuing to take baby steps, harnessing the power of connection with others, and prioritizing how I spend my time.
- 2: I'm really lacking confidence right now. I think it would help if I found someone to plan with.

## Action Idea: Baby Steps

Sometimes big goals can feel overwhelming. Breaking them down into "baby steps" can make them feel more achievable. For example:

**Goal:** Becoming an Acapulco cliff diver

- **Baby Step 1:** Watch videos of cliff divers to understand the techniques.
- **Baby Step 2:** Practice diving from a low height into water to build skills and confidence.
- **Baby Step 3:** Visualize standing confidently on the cliff, preparing to leap.

## Tip: Add an Artistic Touch

Incorporate a creative element to prime your mind for success:

- Create a vision board.
- Add a doodle or artistic affirmation to your journal.
- Use symbolic imagery to remind yourself of your goal.

By tracking your progress and scaling your confidence incrementally, you'll build the resilience and belief needed to achieve your dreams. Small steps, consistent reflection, and visualization will carry you forward.

## Step 10: What's Better (Even a Little Bit)?

Making progress on your goals gives life meaning—it fuels your well-being and purpose.[14] But when you set high goals, false starts and mistakes are part of the process. They're not failures; they're proof you're showing up, trying, and learning—the precursors to growth and achievement.

Progress is built on tiny, meaningful shifts. As you work toward your goal, take time to celebrate those steps, no matter how small they may seem. Reflection helps you recognize how far you've come, even if the changes feel subtle.

Starting something new can feel vulnerable, like being a freshman all over again. We crave mastery and control, but the truth is, getting from point A (beginner) to point B (mastery) is a journey paved with trial, error, and resilience. Every stumble is a step forward, and every step forward deserves to be honored.

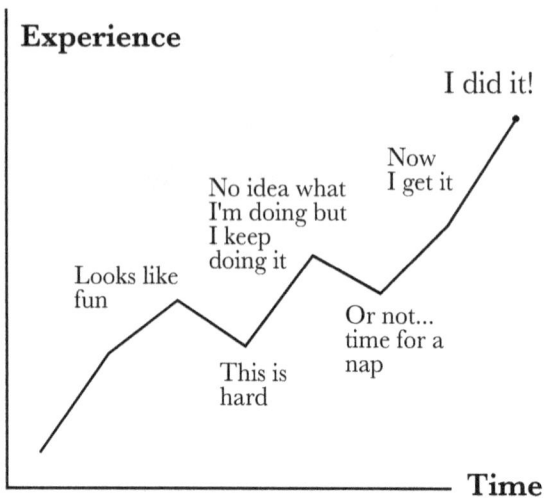

## Reflect on Your Journey

Pause for a moment. Take stock of how far you've come and what's changed since you began this journey.

Ask yourself:

- What's one thing that's better in your life since starting this goal?
- What have you learned about yourself or the goal-setting process?
- How much closer are you to your goal? What percentage have you achieved?

Even the smallest shifts matter. Notice the improvements in your life, your mindset, or your habits. Progress is progress, no matter the size.

What's better? Write your reflections here:

Celebrate those shifts—they're proof you're moving forward, one step at a time.

## Examples of What Others Said Was Better

Here's what others who have participated in workshops I led using these steps have noticed as they tracked their progress toward their goal:

- Deeply realizing that it will all work out, without me needing to control any of it.
- Connecting to nature.
- Love.
- Gratitude!
- Slowing down.
- The space for healing.
- Showing up for myself.
- Being intentional at least once a day.
- *My damn boundaries!!! Finally getting better at that.*
- My outlook and attitude toward the near future.
- Actually doing the work that gets me closer to my goal!

- Playing with my child more; riding scooters outside almost every day. Tiring, but fun.
- Genuine, deep conversations with my son at mealtimes, without any screens nearby. Complete attention on each other.
- Peace of mind and sense of calm.
- Learning about myself and putting trust in God.
- Feeling more secure about my goal—I now believe it can be accomplished.

## Keep the Momentum Going

Now that you've reflected on what's better, let's keep that energy flowing. Progress is like a wave—you just have to ride it.

Ask yourself: What's your next step? Write your next actionable step here:

## Examples of the Next Steps of Others

Need some inspiration? Here are ideas for small, intentional actions others have taken:

- Thinking of a goal that feels authentic to me now, is less daunting, and makes me smile.
- Practicing creative visualization.
- Finding ways to experience more laughter.
- Practicing my mantras.
- Making sure I'm sticking to facts in terms of my thoughts—I don't want my goal to be derailed by whack thinking!

## Tip: Celebrate Every Small Step

Every victory, no matter how small, is worth honoring. Revisit this exercise often to track your growth and reconnect with your progress. Each reflection builds a foundation of confidence, propelling you closer to your goal. You are capable, deserving, and making progress— one meaningful shift at a time. Keep showing up for yourself, and the momentum will carry you forward.

## Step 11: Factors for Change[15]

It's said that people recover, grow, or move forward because of four key factors. The largest piece—40%— comes from your own strengths, talents, skills, and resources. Another 30% comes from the relationships you build with your therapist or support network— relationships rooted in trust, empathy, warmth, and acceptance. Then there's the 15% that comes from the power of belief: hope, self-efficacy, and optimism about the possibility of change. The final 15%? It's about using the right technique.

Let's focus on three of these transformative elements:

1. Your strengths and resources.
2. The relationships that support and uplift you.
3. The hope that fuels your journey.

These are the foundations of change, and they are already within reach. Let's build on them together.

## Strengths and Resources [16]

Your personal strengths are the foundation of your resilience and progress. Take a moment to identify the qualities that have helped you navigate challenges in the past.

## Examples of strengths to inspire you:

- Building positive relationships
- Service to others or a cause
- Decision-making and impulse control
- Humor and adaptability
- Optimism and inner drive
- Creativity and perseverance

## Your Strengths:

- Add any additional strengths or talents not listed above.
- How have you used these strengths to overcome challenges or achieve goals in the past?
- How can these strengths help you with your current goal?

Write your reflections here:

## The Power of Connection

We are wired to connect—we are social beings at our core. Even when we're chasing a dream we deeply desire, having someone who understands and encourages us can make all the difference. Pursuing our heart's desire and sustaining change aren't solitary acts; they're anchored in high-quality, resonant relationships.

Research shows that these rich, meaningful connections ease career transitions, strengthen our sense of identity, and build the kind of trust that helps us learn and grow from failure. But it doesn't stop there—resonant relationships are good for the body as well as the soul. They improve immune function, boost cardiovascular health, and support patterns of neuroendocrine activity that build resilience and engagement at work. [17]

Relationships that resonate deeply don't just support us—they transform us, reminding us that we are never alone in our journey.

## Reflection Questions:

• Who are the people you trust to support and encourage you?
• Who can you freely express yourself to—those who truly "get" you?

Write your answers here:

## The Power of Hope [18]

Hope—those positive expectations about the possibility of change—is a vital force for transformation. It's more than just wishing; hope is the belief in your ability to find pathways to your goals and the motivation to follow them.

Hope theory breaks down like this:

- **Pathway thoughts** are the routes we create to reach our goals and our confidence in being able to navigate them.
- **Agency thoughts** are the drive—the motivation—that keeps us moving along those routes.
- **Goals** are the anchors of hope, providing direction and purpose, especially when they are both valuable and uncertain.
- **Barriers** are the obstacles that block our way. When faced with them, we can either give up or tap into our pathway thoughts to forge new routes.

Higher hope is consistently linked to better outcomes—academics, athletics, physical health, mental health, and even therapy. Those with high hope don't see barriers as stop signs. They see them as challenges, opportunities to problem-solve, to create, and to keep going. Hope is both a feeling and a practice. It's the mindset that says, "I can find a way, and I'll keep moving until I do."

## Reflection Questions:

- On a scale of 1 to 10, how hopeful are you about achieving your goal?
- What tells you that you're at that number?

• Can you recall a time when you successfully overcame similar challenges?

Write your reflections here:

## Step 12: Celebrating Milestones and Achievements

Celebrating milestones is a powerful way to acknowledge your progress, stay motivated, and reinforce your belief in your ability to succeed. Write about the moments when you felt closer to your goal, the date you achieved your goal, and how you felt in that moment.

### Reflection Questions:

• What specific milestones have you reached so far?
• What emotions did you experience as you moved closer to your goal?
• What did achieving your goal teach you about yourself?

Write your reflections here:

## Example: Celebrating Success

- "I felt an overwhelming sense of pride and gratitude when I finally completed my goal. It reminded me of my strength and resilience and how far I've come."
- "Reaching my goal showed me that I am capable of more than I ever believed."

## Closing Tip: Honor Your Journey

Every milestone—big or small—is worth celebrating. By reflecting on your progress and achievements, you're solidifying your belief in your potential and paving the way for future success. You're not just achieving goals; you're becoming the person who achieves them.

# References

## Introduction: Autobiographical Storytelling as Medicine

[1] Schauer, M., Neuner, F., & Elbert, T. (2011). Narrative Exposure Therapy: A Short-Term Treatment for Traumatic Stress Disorders (2nd ed.). Hogrefe Publishing.

[2] Wang, S., & Wang, S. (2024). Effects of narrative exposure therapy for treating depressive and anxiety symptoms: A systematic review and meta-analysis. *Psychiatry Investigation*, 21(1), 1–11. https://doi.org/10.30773/pi.2023.0281

[3] Neuner, F., Onyut, P. L., Ertl, V., Odenwald, M., Schauer, E., & Elbert, T. (2008). Treatment of posttraumatic stress disorder by trained lay counselors in an African refugee settlement: A randomized controlled trial. *Journal of Consulting and Clinical Psychology*, 76(4), 686–694. https://doi.org/10.1037/0022-006X.76.4.686

## My Introduction Using Location of Self

[1] Watts-Jones, T. D. (2010). Location of self: Opening the door to dialogue on intersectionality in the therapy process. *Family Process*, 49(3), 405–420. https://doi.org/10.1111/j.1545-5300.2010.01330.x

[2] Watts-Jones, p. 409.

[3] Caballero, G. (2017). Choguita Rarámuri (Tarahumara) language description and documentation. *Language Documentation & Conservation*, 11, 224–262.

[4] Miller, W. R. (1996). A note on extinct languages of northwest Mexico of supposed Uto-Aztecan affiliation. *International Journal of American Linguistics, 62*(2), 258–261.

[5] Merrill, W. L., & Burgess, D. R. (2014). Ralámuli kinship terminology. *Anthropological Linguistics, 56*(3–4), 229–258.

[6] Indigenous Mexico. (n.d.). *Indigenous Zacatecas: From contact to the present day*. Retrieved March 3, 2025, from https://www.indigenousmexico.org/articles/indigenous-zacatecas-from-contact-to-the-present-day

[7] Instituto Nacional de Estadística y Geografía (INEGI). (2020). *Censo de Población y Vivienda 2020*. Retrieved from https://www.inegi.org.mx/programas/ccpv/2020/

[8] Gonzalez-Barrera, A. (2016, March 1). *Afro-Latino: A deeply rooted identity among U.S. Hispanics*. Pew Research Center. https://www.pewresearch.org/short-reads/2016/03/01/afro-latino-a-deeply-rooted-identity-among-u-s-hispanics/

[9] Gonzalez-Barrera, A. (2016, March 1). *Afro-Latino: A deeply rooted identity among U.S. Hispanics*. Pew Research Center. https://www.pewresearch.org/short-reads/2016/03/01/afro-latino-a-deeply-rooted-identity-among-u-s-hispanics/

[10] MacNell, L., Driscoll, A., & Hunt, A. N. (2015). What's in a name: Exposing gender bias in student ratings of teaching. *Innovative Higher Education, 40*(4), 291–303. https://doi.org/10.1007/s10755-014-9313-4

# Chapter 1: Tan-tararán Its All About My Mom

[1] Park, C. L. (2010). Making sense of the meaning literature: An integrative review of meaning making and its effects on adjustment to stressful life events. *Psychological Bulletin*, *136*(2), 257–301. https://doi.org/10.1037/a0018301

[2] Pennebaker, J. W., & Seagal, J. D. (1999). Forming a story: The health benefits of narrative. *Journal of Clinical Psychology*, *55*(10), 1243–1254. https://doi.org/10.1002/(SICI)1097-4679(199910)55:10<1243::AID-JCLP6>3.0.CO;2-N

[3] Doyle, K. (1998, October 2). *Tlatelolco Massacre: Declassified U.S. Documents on Mexico and the Events of 1968*. National Security Archive Electronic Briefing Book No. 10.

[4] "Tommie Smith and John Carlos raise their fists at the 1968 Olympics." *History.com*, A&E Television Networks, October 16, 1968.

[5] American Psychiatric Association. (2022). *Diagnostic and statistical manual of mental disorders* (5th ed., text rev.). Arlington, VA: American Psychiatric Publishing. https://doi.org/10.1176/appi.books.9780890425787

[6] Linehan, M. M. (1993). *Cognitive-behavioral treatment of borderline personality disorder*. Guilford Press.

[7] Furst, J. L. M. (1995). *The natural history of the soul in ancient Mexico*. Yale University Press.

[8] See Endnote 7

[9] Holy Bible, New International Version. (2011). Zondervan. (Original work published 1978)

[10] Lovett (2004): *Child sexual abuse disclosure: Maternal response and other variables impacting the victim.*

[11] Giovanni, N. (1975). *The women and the men*. William Morrow & Company.

**Science & Research**

[1] Acuna, M. A. (2014). *How we talk about it: Stressful life events, family communication, and PTSD among public school adolescents*. University of California, Los Angeles.

[2] Pennebaker, J. W., & Beall, S. K. (1986). Confronting a traumatic event: Toward an understanding of inhibition and disease. *Journal of Abnormal Psychology, 95*(3), 274–281. https://doi.org/10.1037/0021-843X.95.3.274

[3] Pennebaker, J. W. (1993). Putting stress into words: Health, linguistic, and therapeutic implications. *Behaviour Research and Therapy, 31*(6), 539–548. https://doi.org/10.1016/0005-7967(93)90105-4

[4] Felitti, V. J., & Anda, R. F. (2009). The relationship of adverse childhood experiences to adult medical disease, psychiatric disorders, and sexual behavior: Implications for healthcare. In R. Lanius & E. Vermetten (Eds.), *The hidden epidemic: The impact of early life trauma on health and disease* (p. 91). Cambridge University Press.

[5] Bowlby, J. (1988). *A secure base: Parent-child attachment and healthy human development*. Basic Books.

[6] Bryant, R. A. (2023). Attachment processes in posttraumatic stress disorder: A review of mechanisms to advance theories and treatments. *Clinical Psychology Review, 99*, 102228.

## Ancestor Wisdom

[1] Mbiti, J. S. (1990). *African religions and philosophy* (2nd ed.). Heinemann.

[2] Olupona, J. K. (2011). *City of 201 gods: Ile-Ife in time, space, and the imagination*. University of California Press.

[3] Falicov, C. J. (2001). *Latino families in therapy: A guide to multicultural practice*. Guilford Press.

[4] National Park Service. (n.d.). *Corridos: Stories told through song*. U.S. Department of the Interior. Retrieved January 22, 2025, from https://www.nps.gov/articles/corridos-stories-told-through-song.htm

## Tools

[1] Felitti, V. J., Anda, R. F., Nordenberg, D., Williamson, D. F., Spitz, A. M., Edwards, V., Koss, M. P., & Marks, J. S. (1998). Relationship of childhood abuse and household dysfunction to many of the leading causes of death in adults: The Adverse Childhood Experiences (ACE) Study. *American Journal of Preventive Medicine, 14*(4), 245–258. https://doi.org/10.1016/S0749-3797(98)00017-8

[2] California Department of Public Health. (n.d.). *Prevalence of Adverse Childhood Experiences (Adult Retrospective; CA Only)*. Retrieved January 22, 2025, from Kidsdata.org

[3] Centers for Disease Control and Prevention. (n.d.). *Adverse childhood experiences (ACEs): Preventing early trauma to improve health outcomes*. Retrieved from https://www.cdc. gov/violenceprevention/aces/index.html

[4] Cronholm, P. F., Forke, C. M., Wade, R., Bair-Merritt, M. H., Davis, M., Harkins-Schwarz, M., Pachter, L. M., & Fein, J. A. (2015). Adverse childhood experiences: Expanding the concept of adversity. *American Journal of Preventive Medicine, 49*(3), 354–361.

## Chapter 2: The Still, Small Voice

[1] Siegel, D. J. (2012). *The developing mind: How relationships and the brain interact to shape who we are* (2nd ed.). Guilford Press.

[2] Harper, D. (n.d.). *Confidence*. In *Online Etymology Dictionary*. Retrieved January 22, 2025, from Etymology Online

[3, 4] Holy Bible, New International Version. (2011). Zondervan. (Original work published 1973)

[5] Russell, S. (2012, January 3). 'Being Gay Is a Gift from God': The Gift That Keeps On Giving. *HuffPost*.

[6] Lawton, K. (2008, July 18). Reverend Ed Bacon. *Religion & Ethics NewsWeekly*. PBS.

[7] Hanh, T. N. (1991). *Peace is every step: The path of mindfulness in everyday life*. Bantam Books.

[8] Harner, M. (1980). *The way of the shaman: A guide to power and healing*. Harper & Row.

[9] Myerhoff, B. G. (1974). *Peyote hunt: The sacred journey of the Huichol Indians*. Cornell University Press.

[10] Eliade, M. (1964). *Shamanism: Archaic techniques of ecstasy* (W. R. Trask, Trans.). Princeton University Press. (Original work published 1951)

[11] Myerhoff, p.74.

[12] Myerhoff, p.52.

[13] Fowler Museum at UCLA. (2000). *Art and power in the Central African savanna*. University of California Press.

[14] Eliade, M. (1964). *Shamanism: Archaic techniques of ecstasy* (W. R. Trask, Trans.). Princeton University Press. (Original work published 1951)

[15] Price, J. (2006). *Does a Spouse Slow You Down?: Marriage and Graduate Student Outcomes*. Cornell Higher Education Research Institute. eCommons

[16] Demme, J. (Director). (1998). *Beloved* [Film]. Touchstone Pictures.

[17] Morrison, T. (1987). *Beloved*. Alfred A. Knopf.

[18] van der Kolk, B. (2014). *The body keeps the score: Brain, mind, and body in the healing of trauma.* Penguin Books.

[19] Murphy, J. M., & Sanford, M. M. (2001). *Osun across the waters: A Yoruba goddess in Africa and the Americas.* Indiana University Press.

[20] Bai, Z., Chang, J., Chen, C., Li, P., & Yang, K. (2015). Investigating the effect of transcendental meditation on blood pressure: A systematic review and meta-analysis. *Journal of Human Hypertension*, 29(11), 653–662. https://doi.org/10.1038/jhh.2015.6

[21] Infante, J. R., Peran, F., Martinez, M., Roldan, A., Poyatos, R., Ruiz, C., & Garrido, F. (1998). ACTH and beta-endorphin in transcendental meditation. *Physiology & Behavior*, 64(3), 311–315. https://doi.org/10.1016/S0031-9384(98)00057-0

[22] Travis, F., & Arenander, A. (2006). Cross-sectional and longitudinal study of effects of transcendental meditation practice on interhemispheric frontal asymmetry and frontal coherence. *International Journal of Neuroscience*, 116(12), 1519–1538. https://doi.org/10.1080/00207450600575482

[23] Orme-Johnson, D. W., & Barnes, V. A. (2014). Effects of the transcendental meditation technique on trait anxiety: A meta-analysis of randomized controlled trials. *The Journal of Alternative and Complementary Medicine*, 20(5), 330–341. https://doi.org/10.1089/acm.2013.0204

[24] Nidich, S. I., Rainforth, M. V., Haaga, D. A., Hagelin, J., Salerno, J. W., Travis, F., & Schneider, R. H. (2009). A randomized controlled trial on effects of the transcendental meditation program on blood pressure, psychological distress, and coping in young adults. *American Journal of Hypertension*, 22(12), 1326–1331. https://doi.org/10.1038/ajh.2009.184

[25] Grosswald, S. J., Stixrud, W. R., Travis, F., & Bateh, M. A. (2008). Use of the transcendental meditation technique to reduce symptoms of attention deficit hyperactivity disorder (ADHD) by reducing stress and anxiety: An exploratory study. *Current Issues in Education*, 10(2). https://cie.asu.edu/ojs/index.php/cieatasu/article/view/1605

[26] Alexander, C. N., Langer, E. J., Newman, R. I., Chandler, H. M., & Davies, J. L. (1989). Transcendental meditation, mindfulness, and longevity: An experimental study with the elderly. *Journal of Personality and Social Psychology*, 57(6), 950–964. https://doi.org/10.1037/0022-3514.57.6.950

[27] Lynch, D. (2006). *Catching the big fish: Meditation, consciousness, and creativity*. TarcherPerigee.

[28] Holy Bible, New International Version. (2011). Zondervan. (Original work published 1973)

[29] Carson, C. (Ed.). (1998). *The autobiography of Martin Luther King, Jr.* Warner Books.

[30] Masten, A. S. (2014). *Ordinary magic: Resilience in development*. Guilford Press.

## Science and Research

[1] Beckett, C., & Johnson, P. (1995). Spirituality in Social Work: The Journey from Fringe to Mainstream. Social Work, 40(3), 385–393.

[2] Canda, E. R. (1989). Spirituality as a Vital Dimension in Social Work Practice: The Art of Transcendence. Social Work, 34(2), 93–100.

[3] Cowley, A. S., & Derezotes, D. S. (1994). Transpersonal Psychology and Social Work Education. Journal of Social Work Education, 30(1), 32–41.

[4] Statista Research Department. (2023). Which nationalities consider religion most important?. Statista. Retrieved January 22, 2025, from https://www.statista.com/chart/4189/which-nationalities-consider-religion-most-important/

[5] Pew Research Center. (2018, November 20). Where Americans find meaning in life. Pew Research Center.

[6] Musgrave, C. F., Allen, C. E., & Allen, G. J. (2002). Spirituality and health for women of color. American Journal of Public Health, 92(4), 557–560.

[7] Koenig, H. G. (2012). Religion, Spirituality, and Health: The Research and Clinical Implications. ISRN Psychiatry.

[8] Koenig, H. G. (2012). Religion, Spirituality, and Health: The Research and Clinical Implications. ISRN Psychiatry.

[9] Koenig, H. G. (2012). Religion, Spirituality, and Health: The Research and Clinical Implications. ISRN Psychiatry.

[10] Pargament, K. I. (2011). Spiritually Integrated Psychotherapy: Understanding and Addressing the Sacred. Guilford Press.

[11] Saleebey, D. (1997). The strengths perspective in social work practice (2nd ed.). Longman.

[12] Vuckovic, N., Schneider, J., Williams, L. A., & Ramirez, M. (2010). Journey into healing: The transformative experience of shamanic healing on women with temporomandibular joint disorders. Explore, 6(6), 371–379.

[13] Ohajunwa, C., Mji, G., & Chimbala-Kalenga, R. (2021). Framing Wellbeing Through Spirituality, Space, History, and Context: Lessons from an Indigenous African Community. Wellbeing, Space and Society, 2, 100042. Stellenbosch University

[14] Nonis, S. A., Jernigan, S., & Young, M. (2024). What Predicts Well-Being: Connectedness to Oneself, Nature, Others, or God? Cogent Psychology, 11(1), 2371024. Taylor & Francis Online

[15] Oxhandler, H. K., Pargament, K. I., Pearce, M. J., Vieten, C., & Moffatt, K. M. (2021). The relevance of religion and spirituality to mental health: A national survey of current clients' views. Social Work, 66(3), 254–266. https://doi.org/10.1093/sw/swab025

## Ancestor Wisdom

[1] Maimonides. (1993). *The Guide for the Perplexed* (M. Friedländer, Trans.). Dover Publications. (Original work published 1190)

[2] Parsons, E. C. (1936). *Mitla: Town of the souls, and other Zapotec-speaking pueblos of Oaxaca, Mexico.* University of Chicago Press.

[3] Tedlock, D. (1996). *Popol Vuh: The Mayan book of the dawn of life.* Simon & Schuster.

[4] Adichie, C. N. (2009, July). *The danger of a single story* [Video]. TED Conferences. Retrieved January 22, 2025, from https://www.ted.com/talks/chimamanda_ngozi_adichie_the_danger_of_a_single_story

## Tools

[1] Ortiz, L., & Langer, N. (2002). Spiritual assessment protocol for elderly clients in long-term care. *Annals of Long-Term Care*, 10(11), 34–39.

[2] *Suggested Reading:*

• Pargament, K. I. (2011). *Spiritually integrated psychotherapy: Understanding and addressing the sacred.* Guilford Press.

• Koenig, H. G. (2012). *Religion, spirituality, and health: The research and clinical implications.* ISRN Psychiatry.

[3] Trotter, R. T., & Chavira, J. A. (1997). *Curanderismo: Mexican American folk healing* (2nd ed.). University of Georgia Press.

[4] Trotter & Chavira, p. 11.

[5] Trotter & Chavira, p. 172.

## Chapter 3: The *Tonalli* of Love

[1] For a discussion on tonalli and the soul in Mexica philosophy, see León-Portilla, M. (1990). Aztec thought and culture: A study of the ancient Nahuatl mind. University of Oklahoma Press; and Furst, J. L. M. (1995). The natural history of the soul in ancient Mexico. Yale University Press.

[2] American Psychiatric Association. (2022). Diagnostic and statistical manual of mental disorders (5th ed., text rev.). Arlington, VA: American Psychiatric Publishing. https://doi.org/10.1176/appi.books.9780890425787

[3] hooks, b. (2004). The will to change: Men, masculinity, and love. Atria Books.

[4] Gottman, J. M., & Silver, N. (2015). The seven principles for making marriage work: A practical guide from the country's foremost relationship expert. Harmony Books.

[5] Bryant, R. A. (2023). Attachment and PTSD: A comprehensive review. Journal of Traumatic Stress, 36(1), 35–50.

[6] Levine, A., & Heller, R. (2010). Attached: The new science of adult attachment and how it can help you find—and keep—love. TarcherPerigee.

[7] University of Virginia. (2023). *COVID-19 pandemic led to increase in suicide attempts among kids and teens, study shows*. UVA Today. Retrieved January 26, 2025, from https://news.virginia.edu/content/covid-19-pandemic-led-increase-suicide-attempts-kids-teens-study-shows

[8] Centers for Disease Control and Prevention. (2023). *Youth mental health: Trends and statistics*. Retrieved January 26, 2025, from https://www.cdc.gov/healthy-youth/mental-health/index.html

[9] Statista. (2023). *Share of U.S. youth experiencing mental health challenges, by type*. Retrieved January 26, 2025, from https://www.statista.com/statistics/1412704/mental-health-challenges-among-us-youth-by-type/

**Science**

[1] Kearney, D. J., Malte, C. A., McManus, C., Martinez, M. E., Felleman, B., & Simpson, T. L. (2013). Loving-kindness meditation for posttraumatic stress disorder: A pilot study. Journal of Traumatic Stress, 26(4), 426–434. Carolyn McManus

[2] Fredrickson, B. L., Cohn, M. A., Coffey, K. A., Pek, J., & Finkel, S. M. (2008). Open hearts build lives: Positive emotions, induced through loving-kindness meditation, build consequential personal resources. Journal of Personality and Social Psychology, 95(5), 1045–1062.

[3] Le Nguyen, K. D., Lin, J., Algoe, S. B., Brantley, M. M., Kim, S. L., Brantley, J., Salzberg, S., & Fredrickson, B. L. (2019). Lovng-kindness meditation slows biological aging in novices: Evidence from a 12-week randomized controlled trial. Psychoneuroendocrinology, 108, 20–27.

## Ancestor Wisdom

[1] *Suggested Reading:*

- Mbiti, J. S. (1990). African religions and philosophy (2nd ed.). Heinemann.
- Tutu, D. (1999). No future without forgiveness. Doubleday.
- Gyekye, K. (1997). Tradition and modernity: Philosophical reflections on the African experience. Oxford University Press.
- Drewal, H. J., & Drewal, J. P. (1990). Gelede: Art and female power among the Yoruba. Indiana University Press.
- Abimbola, W. (1997). Ifa: An exposition of Ifa literary corpus. Athelia Henrietta Press.
- Senghor, L. S. (1964). On African socialism. Praeger.

[2] *Suggested Reading:*

- León-Portilla, M. (1990). Aztec thought and culture: A study of the ancient Nahuatl mind. University of Oklahoma Press.
- McKeever Furst, J. L. (1995). The natural history of the soul in ancient Mexico. Yale University Press.
- Read, K. E. (1998). Time and sacrifice in the Aztec cosmos. Indiana University Press.

- Miller, M. E., & Taube, K. (1993). The gods and symbols of ancient Mexico and the Maya: An illustrated dictionary of Mesoamerican religion. Thames & Hudson.
- Sahagún, B. de. (1981). Florentine Codex: General history of the things of New Spain, Book 2—The ceremonies. University of Utah Press.

[3] *Suggested Reading:*

- Dorff, E. N., & Newman, L. E. (2008). Jewish choices, Jewish voices: Social justice. Jewish Publication Society.
- Sacks, J. (2002). To heal a fractured world: The ethics of responsibility. Schocken Books.
- Pope, M. H. (1977). Song of Songs: A new translation with introduction and commentary (Vol. 7C). Yale University Press.
- Leibowitz, N. (1995). Studies in the Song of Songs. World Zionist Organization.
- Telushkin, J. (1994). Jewish literacy: The most important things to know about the Jewish religion, its people, and its history. William Morrow.
- Diamant, A. (2001). The new Jewish wedding. Simon & Schuster.
- Schwartz, R. H. (2002). Judaism and global survival. Lantern Books.

[4] Boggs, V. G. (1992). Salsiology: Afro-Cuban music and the evolution of salsa in New York City. Greenwood Press.

**Tools**

[1] Fredrickson, B. L., Cohn, M. A., Coffey, K. A., Pek, J., & Finkel, S. M. (2008). Open hearts build lives: Positive emotions, induced through loving-kindness meditation, build consequential personal resources. Journal of Personality and Social Psychology, 95(5), 1045–1062. https://doi.org/10.1037/a0013262

[2] Hofmann, S. G., Grossman, P., & Hinton, D. E. (2011). Loving-kindness and compassion meditation: Potential for psychological interventions. Clinical Psychology Review, 31(7), 1126–1132.

[3] Lutz, A., Brefczynski-Lewis, J., Johnstone, T., & Davidson, R. J. (2008). Regulation of the neural circuitry of emotion by compassion meditation: Effects of meditative expertise. PLoS ONE, 3(3), e1897. https://doi.org/10.1371/journal.pone.0001897

[4] Stell, A. J., & Farsides, T. (2016). Brief loving-kindness meditation reduces racial bias, mediated by positive other-regarding emotions. Motivation and Emotion, 40(1), 140–147. https://doi.org/10.1007/s11031-015-9514-x

[5] Kang, Y., Gray, J. R., & Dovidio, J. F. (2014). The nurturing effect of loving-kindness meditation on implicit intergroup bias. Psychological Science, 25(7), 1377–1385. https://doi.org/10.1177/0956797614532671

[6] Seppala, E. M., Hutcherson, C. A., Nguyen, D. T. H., Doty, J. R., & Gross, J. J. (2014). Loving-kindness meditation: A tool to improve healthcare provider well-

being. Clinical Journal of Oncology Nursing, 18(5), 566–567. https://doi.org/10.1188/14.CJON.566-567

[7] Watson, T., Watts, L., Waters, R., & Hodgson, D. (2023). The benefits of loving-kindness meditation for helping professionals: A systematic review. Health & Social Care in the Community. Wiley Online Library

[8] Salzberg, S. (1995). Loving-kindness: The revolutionary art of happiness. Shambhala Publications.

[9] Harris, A. H. S., Luskin, F., Norman, S. B., Standard, S., Bruning, J., Evans, S., & Thoresen, C. E. (2006). *Effects of a group forgiveness intervention on forgiveness, perceived stress, and trait-anger. Journal of Clinical Psychology*, 62(6), 715–733. https://doi.org/10.1002/jclp.20264

[10] Akhtar, S., & Barlow, J. (2016). Forgiveness therapy for the promotion of mental well-being: A systematic review and meta-analysis. Trauma, Violence, & Abuse, 19(1), 107–122. https://doi.org/10.1177/1524838016637079

[11] Domino, C. (2009). The law of forgiveness: Tap into the positive power of forgiveness—and attract good things to your life. Berkley Books.

[12] Acuña-González, P.I. (2021). *Beautiful Things in a Psych Hospital*. Unpublished manuscript.

## Chapter 4: Deep-End Lessons on Work and Purpose

[1] Holy Bible, New International Version. (2011). Zondervan. (Original work published 1978)

2 Doe, J. (2005, March 10). Arthur Miller's early life: A tale of perseverance. *Los Angeles Times*.

3 Bandura, A. (1977). Self-efficacy: Toward a unifying theory of behavioral change. *Psychological Review, 84*(2), 191–215. https://doi.org/10.1037/0033-295X.84.2.191

4 Isaacson, W. (2011). *Steve Jobs*. Simon & Schuster.

## Science

1 Alony, I., Hasan, H., Sense, A., & Jones, M. (2015). My lawfully wedded workplace: Identifying relational similarities of marriage and employment. *Journal of Organizational Change Management, 28*(3), 407–425. https://doi.org/10.1108/JOCM-09-2014-0173

2 Alony, I., Hasan, H., & Sense, A. (2014). Predicting turnover based on relationship diagnosis – Lessons from marital research. *Proceedings of Informing Science & IT Education Conference (InSITE) 2014* (pp. 25-37). Retrieved from http://Proceedings.InformingScience.org/InSITE2014/InSITE14p025-037Alony0638.pdf

## Ancestor Wisdom

1 Battle, M. (2009). *Ubuntu: I in you and you in me*. Seabury Books.

2 Vergara, M. Á., & Cotter, M. (2007). *The sacred energies of the sun and moon: Shamanic rites of passage*. Bear & Company.

3 Apffel-Marglin, F., & PRATEC (Eds.). (1998). *The spirit of regeneration: Andean culture confronting Western notions of development*. Zed Books.

4 Anzaldúa, G. (1987). *Borderlands/La Frontera: The new mestiza*. Aunt Lute Books.

5 Verger, P. (1997). *Orixás: The gods of Africa in Brazil*. Albin Michel.

## Chapter 5: The New Fire Ceremony

1 Berne, E. (1964). *Games people play: The psychology of human relationships*. Grove Press.

2 Beattie, M. (1989). *Beyond codependency: And getting better all the time*. Harper & Row.

3 Gabriel, J. (2015). Touching bellies, touching lives: Midwives of Southern Mexico tell their stories. Waveland Press.

4 Canfield, J. (2015). *The success principles: How to get from where you are to where you want to be*. HarperCollins.

5 Barnett KS, Vasiu F. How the arts heal: a review of the neural mechanisms behind the therapeutic effects of creative arts on mental and physical health. Front Behav Neurosci. 2024 Oct 2; 18:1422361. doi: 10.3389/fnbeh.2024.1422361. PMID: 39416439; PMCID: PMC11480958.

[6] Mundis, J. (2012). *How to get out of debt, stay out of debt, and live prosperously* (Rev. ed.). Bantam Books. (I read the first edition printed in 1988!)

[7] Stanley, T. J., & Danko, W. D. (1996). *The millionaire next door: The surprising secrets of America's wealthy.* Longstreet Press.

[8] Orman, S. (1997). *The 9 steps to financial freedom: Practical and spiritual steps so you can stop worrying.* Crown Publishers.

[9] Clements, J. (Ed.). (2023). *My money journey: How 30 people found financial freedom—and you can too.* Harriman House.

[10] Fox, A. S., & Shackman, A. J. (2019). The central extended amygdala in fear and anxiety: Closing the gap between mechanistic and human studies. *Physiological Reviews*, 99(2), 561–605. https://doi.org/10.1152/physrev.00018.2018

[11] Henrico CASA. (n.d.). Trauma and the brain: An overactive amygdala. *Henrico CASA*. Retrieved from https://henricocasa.org/brain-amygdala

[12] Flouri, E., & Panourgia, C. (2014). Negative automatic thoughts and emotional and behavioural problems in adolescence. *Child and Adolescent Mental Health*, 19(1), 46–51. https://doi.org/10.1111/camh.12004

[13] Márquez, C., Poirier, G. L., Cordero, M. I., Larsen, M. H., Groner, A., Marquis, J., & Sandi, C. (2013). Peripuberty stress leads to abnormal aggression, altered amygdala and orbitofrontal reactivity, and increased

prefrontal MAOA gene expression. *Translational Psychiatry*, 3(4), e216. https://doi.org/10.1038/tp.2012.144

[14] Amen, D. G. (1998). *Change your brain, change your life: The breakthrough program for conquering anxiety, depression, obsessiveness, anger, and impulsiveness*. Three Rivers Press.

[15] Amen, D. G. (2021, May 5). *A holistic approach to mental health* [Video]. YouTube. https://www.youtube.com/watch?v=UAfinP5JN4c

[16] Martin EI, Ressler KJ, Binder E, Nemeroff CB. The neurobiology of anxiety disorders: brain imaging, genetics, and psychoneuroendocrinology. Psychiatr Clin North Am. 2009 Sep;32(3):549-75. doi: 10.1016/j.psc.2009.05.004. PMID: 19716990; PMCID: PMC3684250.

[17] Toussaint, L., Nguyen, Q. A., Roettger, C., Dixon, K., Offenbächer, M., Kohls, N., ... & Sirois, F. (2021). Effectiveness of progressive muscle relaxation, deep breathing, and guided imagery in promoting psychological and physiological states of relaxation. *Evidence-Based Complementary and Alternative Medicine*, *2021*(1), 5924040.

[18] Reilly, E. B., & Stuyvenberg, C. L. (2023). A meta-analysis of loving-kindness meditations on self-compassion. *Mindfulness*, *14*(10), 2299-2310.

[19] Levinson, D. B., Stoll, E. L., Kindy, S. D., Merry, H. L., & Davidson, R. J. (2014). A mind you can count on: validating breath counting as a behavioral measure of mindfulness. *Frontiers in Psychology*, 5, 1202. https://doi.org/10.3389/fpsyg.2014.01202

[20] Jiang, H., White, M. P., Greicius, M. D., Waelde, L. C., & Spiegel, D. (2017). Brain activity and functional connectivity associated with hypnosis. *Cerebral Cortex*, 27(8), 4083–4093. https://doi.org/10.1093/cercor/bhw220

[21] Siegel, D. J. (2006). An interpersonal neurobiology approach to psychotherapy: Awareness, mirror neurons, and neural plasticity in the development of well-being. *Psychiatric Annals*, 36(4), 248–256. https://doi.org/10.3928/00485713-20060401-10

[22] Valdez, L. (2010). *Mummified deer*. Arte Público Press.

[23] Meyerhoff, p. 15.

[24] Tutu, D. (1999). *No future without forgiveness*. Image.

[25] Meyerhoff, p. 74.

## Science

[1] Amilon, A., Siren, A., Larsen, M., & Holt, H. (2024). Mental Wellbeing Among Workers Approaching Retirement: A Scoping Review. *Nordic Journal of Working Life Studies*.

[2] Zhang, W., Braun, K. L., & Wu, Y. Y. (2017). The educational, racial and gender crossovers in life satisfaction: Findings from the longitudinal Health and Retirement Study. *Archives of Gerontology and Geriatrics*, *73*, 60-68.

[3] Clouston, S. A., & Denier, N. (2017). Mental retirement and health selection: Analyses from the US Health and Retirement Study. *Social Science & Medicine, 178*, 78-86.

## Ancestor Wisdom

[1] López Estrada, C. (Ed.). (2021). *Summertime: Odes to LA.* Odes2la, LLC.

## Tools

[1] Mundis, J. (2012). *How to get out of debt, stay out of debt, and live prosperously* (Rev. ed.). Bantam Books.

## Steps to Blooming Workbook

[1] Hurn, J., Kneebone, I., & Cropley, M. (2006). Goal setting as an outcome measure: a systematic review. *Clinical rehabilitation, 20*(9), 756-772.

[2] Latham, G. P. (2023). Motivate employee performance through goal setting. *Principles of Organizational Behavior: The Handbook of Evidence-Based Management 3rd Edition*, 83-111.

[3] Latham, G. P., & Locke, E. A. (2006). Enhancing the benefits and overcoming the pitfalls of goal setting. *Organizational dynamics, 35*(4), 332-340.

[4] Mosteo, L. P., Batista-Foguet, J. M., Mckeever, J. D., & Serlavós, R. (2016). Understanding cognitive-emotional processing through a coaching process: The influence of coaching on vision, goal-directed energy, and resilience. *The Journal of Applied Behavioral Science, 52*(1), 64-96.

[5] Latham, G. P., & Locke, E. A. (2018). Goal setting theory: Controversies and resolutions. *Handbook of industrial, work & organizational psychology*, *1*, 103-124.

[6] Coelho, P. (1993). *The alchemist* (A. R. Clarke, Trans.). HarperOne. (Original work published 1988)

[7] Epton, T., Harris, P. R., Kane, R., van Koningsbruggen, G. M., & Sheeran, P. (2015). The impact of self-affirmation on health-behavior change: a meta-analysis. *Health psychology*, *34*(3), 187.

[8] Dutcher, J. M., Creswell, J. D., Pacilio, L. E., Harris, P. R., Klein, W. M., Levine, J. M., ... & Eisenberger, N. I. (2016). Self-affirmation activates the ventral striatum: a possible reward-related mechanism for self-affirmation. *Psychological Science*, *27*(4), 455-466.

[9] Schmeichel, B. J., & Vohs, K. (2009). Self-affirmation and self-control: affirming core values counteracts ego depletion. *Journal of personality and social psychology*, *96*(4), 770.

[10] Moberly, N. J., & Dickson, J. M. (2018). Goal conflict, ambivalence and psychological distress: concurrent and longitudinal relationships. *Personality and Individual Differences*, *129*, 38-42.

[11] *Suggested Reading:*

- Hicks, E., & Hicks, J. (2004). Ask and it is given: Learning to manifest your desires. Hay House.Byrne, R. (2006). The secret. Atria Books/Beyond Words.

- Chopra, D. (1994). The seven spiritual laws of success: A practical guide to the fulfillment of your dreams. Amber-Allen Publishing.
- Bernstein, G. (2016). The universe has your back: Transform fear to faith. Hay House.

[12] Coelho, P. (1993). *The alchemist* (A. R. Clarke, Trans.). HarperOne. (Original work published 1988)

[13] *Suggested Reading:*

- Beck, A. T. (1979). *Cognitive therapy and the emotional disorders.* Penguin.
- Seligman, M. E. P. (2011). *Flourish: A visionary new understanding of happiness and well-being.* Atria Books.

[14] Moberly, N. J., & Dickson, J. M. (2018). Goal conflict, ambivalence and psychological distress: concurrent and longitudinal relationships. *Personality and Individual Differences, 129*, 38-42.

[15] Lambert, M. J. (1992). Psychotherapy outcome research: Implications for integrative and eclectic therapists. In J. C. Norcross, & M. R. Goldfried (Eds.), Handbook of psychotherapy integration (pp. 94–129). Basic Books.

[16] Adapted from the book, Resiliency in Schools: Making It Happen for Students and Educators by Nan Henderson and Mike Milstein, published by Corwin Press, Thousand Oaks, CA (2003, revised ed.).

[17] Mosteo, L. P., Batista-Foguet, J. M., Mckeever, J. D., & Serlavós, R. (2016). Understanding cognitive-emotional processing through a coaching process: The influence of

coaching on vision, goal-directed energy, and resilience. *The Journal of Applied Behavioral Science*, *52*(1), 64-96.

[18] Snyder, C. R., Harris, C., Anderson, J. R., Holleran, S. A., Irving, L. M., Sigmon, S. T., ... & Harney, P. (1991). The will and the ways: development and validation of an individual-differences measure of hope. *Journal of personality and social psychology*, *60*(4), 570.

# Acknowledgments

I would like to acknowledge and thank:

## Personal Support

• My family, friends, colleagues, and women's circle for their support, wisdom, and love.
• My mentors and students, who have inspired me to keep growing and sharing.
• My love relationships of all kinds, for teaching me about connection and vulnerability.

## Creative and Professional Contributors

• Lynn Kaplan, Jenny Viveros, Maxine Amondo, and Dawn Robert-Forbes for adding depth to my stories and essays.
• Louie Curiel for encouragement and insights.
• Zach Sherwin for connecting me to Rabbi Rita Sherwin, whose guidance enriched this work.
• Arlene Schenir for connecting me to educator and author, Stan Beiner whose scholarship and insights proved valuable.
• Trini Rodriguez for reading an early, much longer draft and giving me the words of affirmation to keep going and then writing a forward that made me cry happy tears.
• Ruben Rodriguez and Anne Marie Wells for their help in editing.
• Davina Agudelo for coaching me with writing prompts and biweekly sessions that helped shape this book.

- Carlos Mendoza for creating the book cover of a writer's dream.
- Alegria Publishing for their support in bringing this vision to life.

## Inspiration

- Psalm Sto. Domingo and Alejandra Martinez for encouraging me to finish so they could read it. Picturing that was inspiring.
- Nikki Giovanni and Sandra Cisneros for their poetry, prose, and lives.

## A Note on Privacy and Purpose

The family stories and details shared in this book come from official records, such as birth and death certificates, as well as personal memories from myself and my relatives. Some names, identifying details, and events have been changed or adapted to protect privacy. Memory is subjective, and this work reflects my perspective at the time of writing.

I have shared explicit and provocative stories with purposeful vulnerability and compassion for all parties. My aim is not to assign blame or judgment but to illuminate the lessons learned through life's challenges and to inspire healing and understanding. I hope that by sharing my truth, others may find the courage to embrace theirs.

## Proverbs and Wisdom

Many of the proverbs shared in this book come from rich oral traditions worldwide. They reflect timeless wisdom passed through generations and are included here to honor and highlight universal themes.

## About the Author

Dra. Alejandra Acuña is a mother, proud Chicana, speaker, therapist, and retired tenured professor of social work with a lifelong dedication to healing, resilience, and personal growth. Shaped by a story of both struggle and strength, she has spent her career empowering individuals, families, and communities to navigate adversity and reclaim their power.

Through her writing, workshops, and private practice, Dra. Acuña inspires others to move beyond fear and self-doubt, embrace their full potential, and build lives rooted in purpose, connection, and joy. Her debut book, *Stones, Flowers, and Lessons Learned*, invites readers on a transformative journey of self-discovery, weaving personal storytelling, ancestral wisdom, and practical tools to light the way forward.

Based in Mount Washington, a cool Los Angeles neighborhood, Dra. Acuña continues to support individuals and organizations in fostering well-being, leadership, and transformation. When she's not writing, she's traveling across Mexico, savoring naps and nonfiction books, practicing hot yoga, Pilates, or dance, and learning the art of cooking.

www.ingramcontent.com/pod-product-compliance
Lightning Source LLC
Chambersburg PA
CBHW021212130626
46554CB00004B/1184